THE MISSOURI SESQUICENTENNIAL EDITION

WILLIAM E. PARRISH

GENERAL EDITOR

A HISTORY

UNIVERSITY C

OF MISSOURI

VOLUME I 1673 TO 1820

WILLIAM E. FOLEY

IISSOURI PRESS

Title page illustration drawn from *Louisiana and the Fair,* Volume 3, James
William Buel, editor, World's Progress Publishing Company (St. Louis, 1904).
Copyright © 1971 by The Curators of the University of Missouri.
University of Missouri Press, Columbia, Missouri 65201
Printed and bound in the United States of America
Library of Congress Catalog Number 76–155844
ISBN 0–8262–0108–3
Second Printing, 1986

PREFACE

For most Missourians the territorial period remains a remote and unfamiliar chapter in Missouri's history. At first glance, the present state bears little resemblance to the sparsely populated frontier territory of 1821. Yet, despite the dramatic transformation the state has undergone in the 150 years since it entered the Union, the foundation for Missouri's future development already had been established in the years preceding statehood. From the blending of cultures that occurred between the arrival of the first Europeans in the seventeenth century and the final triumph of statehood in 1821, Missouri's diverse social and cultural heritage had begun to take shape. The present study represents an attempt to trace the broad outlines of Missouri's development during those formative years.

Portions of this manuscript originated as a doctoral dissertation at the University of Missouri–Columbia, but they have since been substantially revised and expanded. Many individuals and organizations facilitated the research and writing of this study, and I wish to acknowledge the University of Missouri Press, the American Association for State and Local History, the University of Missouri Graduate School, and the Floyd Calvin Shoemaker Fund for financial assistance at various stages in its preparation. I am most appreciative of the help provided by the directors and staffs of the various libraries and historical societies I have visited, and my special thanks go to Dr. Richard Brownlee, Director of the State Historical Society of Missouri, and to Mrs. Francis Stadler, Archivist of the Missouri Historical Society. Mr. Albert U. Blair of the National Archives also provided assistance in securing pertinent materials.

To Professor Lewis Atherton, who gave freely of his valuable time and advice, I owe a special debt that I cannot adequately acknowledge. Likewise, my colleague Perry McCandless, who originally interested me in the study of early Missouri, provided encouragement and assistance during every phase of the project. William E. Parrish, the general editor of the series, read the manuscript and made numerous helpful suggestions, as did Dean W. Francis English who read an early draft. Beverly Jeffries, my research assistant, contributed substantially in the preparation of the sections concerning religion and education. Finally, my wife, Martha, deserves a very special note of appreciation for her assistance at every stage of the project. It is impossible to measure adequately the extent of her contribution.

The Missouri Historical Society has granted permission to reprint portions of my article, "James A. Wilkinson: Territorial Governor," which originally appeared in the October, 1968 issue of *The Bulletin.*

The author alone is responsible for any errors of fact or interpretation.

W. E. F.
Warrensburg, Missouri
November, 1970

CONTENTS

INTRODUCTION

During the 150 years since its tumultuous entry into the Union of States, Missouri has played a major role in both regional and national development. Situated at the confluence of two great rivers in the heart of America, it early earned the apt sobriquet "Mother of the West" for the role its citizens played in the opening of that area. All trails west had their origins here, and Missouri became the channel whereby large migrations of people and resources journeyed to the various Western frontiers. In return, the great wealth of that region, especially furs from the Rocky Mountains, Spanish gold over the Santa Fe Trail, and cattle from the Great Plains, flowed into Missouri and thence on to the rest of the nation. From its pioneering role in the settlement of the West to the part it plays today as a major center for the development of those tools used in outer space exploration, Missouri has frequently been in the forefront of the significant drama of national growth with leadership and resources to meet the needs of the times.

It thus seemed altogether fitting, as Missouri marked the sesquicentennial of its statehood, to produce a multivolume history that would detail the state's development and the role it has played both regionally and nationally. The University of Missouri Press readily agreed to publish the series, and the University of Missouri has generously underwritten leaves and research assistance for the various authors to complete their work. Each author is a specialist in his field, and the volumes are based on extensive research in both primary and secondary sources. The format calls for a general survey of the broad political, social, intellectual, and economic trends, rather than a highly detailed study of each period. Hence footnotes have been limited to explanatory matters, with a more detailed bibliographic essay accompanying each volume to point the reader to materials used and offer suggestions for further study.

In this initial volume, Professor Foley presents the story of Missouri's settlement and growth before statehood. Here are outlined the developments of many of the traits and patterns that would mark the state and its people in later times. Consequently he offers important insights and understandings into why Missouri and its citizens later played the roles they did upon the national and regional stages. Subsequent volumes will trace Missouri's story from statehood to the Civil War, through the Civil War and Reconstruction periods, during the age of the Populists and the Progressives, and from World War I to the present.

William E. Parrish
Fulton, Missouri
January, 1971

CHAPTER I

THE FRENCH LEGACY

THE TWO birchbark canoes with their seven passengers glided down the Mississippi in June, 1673, unnoticed except perhaps by an occasional curious Indian peering from behind the cover of the thick lofty forests lining the riverbanks. This tiny expedition under the command of the young French trader and explorer, Louis Jolliet, and his copartner Jesuit Father Jacques Marquette marked the beginning of Missouri's recorded history. To be sure, they were not the first Europeans to reach the Mississippi, but they were the first known to have set foot on Missouri's soil.

Although the Spanish conquistadors had penetrated portions of North America's vast interior more than a century earlier, they had failed to find the inducements necessary to encourage further exploration and settlement there. Hernando de Soto's quest for wealth and riches had brought him to the lower Mississippi in 1541, but his party had not ventured farther northward than the present state of Arkansas. Likewise, the expedition led by Francisco Vasquez de Coronado had abandoned its search for the mythical Seven Cities of Cibola and had returned to Mexico after reaching an unprosperous Indian village in western Kansas. These dismal results confirmed the Spanish decision to concentrate their colonial efforts in those areas that could promise more immediate returns in the form of gold and silver mines and stable Indian populations to operate them. Mexico and Peru became the focal points of Spain's thriving colonial empire in the sixteenth century, while immense stretches of the North American continent, including Missouri, remained unoccupied by Europeans.

Not until the seventeenth century did any European power successfully challenge Spain's New World monopoly, but shortly after the turn of the century both England and France actively entered the race for overseas possessions and planted

I

permanent colonies in North America. The English established themselves in compact settlements along the Atlantic coast while the French gradually spread across the great North American expanses. The French focused their initial activity in the vicinity of the St. Lawrence. Samuel de Champlain, the great French pioneer, explored that river and in 1608 established a village at Quebec. Although France's Canadian settlements developed very slowly during the early years, French fur traders and missionaries probed the continent's vast unexplored interior regions. By mid-century those hardy explorers had established French outposts on the far reaches of the Great Lakes.

Indians visiting these remote stations brought recurring reports of a great river—the "Mesippi"—and French officials eagerly sought to learn more about the waterway and its source. Some speculated that it might empty into the Pacific, while others believed that it probably flowed into the Atlantic in the vicinity of the English settlements in Virginia. Consequently, Jean Talon, the French intendant in Canada, commissioned Louis Jolliet to explore this unknown river, and Canada's new governor, the Comte de Frontenac, who arrived in 1672, added his endorsement to the proposed venture.

Jolliet went to the French settlement at Mackinac where he and his partner Father Marquette spent the winter making plans for the upcoming voyage. The journey finally got underway in mid-May, 1673, and by mid-June their party had reached the Mississippi. As the adventurers made their way down the river, they observed many strange and unfamiliar sights including fish so large they threatened to tear apart their canoes, herds of grazing buffalo, and vivid Indian paintings of strange monsters that looked down upon them from the river bluffs a short distance above the mouth of the Missouri. When they reached Arkansas, it had become apparent that the Mississippi headed neither toward Virginia nor the Pacific but continued instead on to the Gulf of Mexico. Fearful of encroaching upon Spanish domains, they decided against continuing their trip and turned back on July 17.

Following their return to Mackinac in September, Father Marquette continued to work among the Indians. When the spring thaws finally permitted Jolliet to depart, he hurried off

2

to report their findings to French authorities in Quebec. Father Marquette chose to remain in the wilderness, but the rugged climate took its toll and the dedicated priest died less than two years later. Deprived of the recognition he believed he had earned, Jolliet held a number of minor governmental posts before he died in relative obscurity in 1700.

Interest in the Mississippi Valley remained high, but nine years elapsed before René Robert Cavelier, Sieur de la Salle, became the first Frenchman to explore the river to its mouth. On April 9, 1682, he took possession of the Mississippi and its tributaries in the name of Louis XIV, in whose honor he called the territory Louisiana. La Salle's subsequent plans for creating a French empire in Louisiana failed to materialize. After a brief visit in France, he had returned to the New World with a small fleet, but his party missed its intended destination of the mouth of the Mississippi. Instead, they disembarked in Texas, and, while traversing the wilderness, La Salle met an untimely death at the hands of one of his own men in 1687.

Nevertheless, La Salle's discoveries had strengthened France's claim to the Mississippi Valley and paved the way for its occupation of the region. Missionary zeal, the search for precious metals, interest in expanding the fur trade, and a desire to discover a passageway to the Pacific that would open trade with the Orient all combined to propel the French advance into Louisiana in the eighteenth century.

Among the earliest French emissaries to enter the region were the Jesuit missionaries, whose efforts to bring Christianity to the Indians took them to the outermost edges of the frontier. Often traveling in the company of French traders, these pioneer trailblazers, whom the Indians called "Black Robes," seemed undaunted by the dangers of the wilderness.

The first-known missionary activity in the area that would become Missouri occurred in 1700 when Father Gabriel Marest, a French Jesuit, accompanied a band of Kaskaskia Indians who settled on the west bank of the Mississippi at the mouth of the River Des Pères, just within the present southern limits of St. Louis. The Kaskaskia had abandoned their village on the Illinois River to escape increasing harassment from the Iroquois tribes who recently had expanded westward. Moreover, recurring ru-

3

mors that a large French force had landed on the Gulf coast gave rise to hopes among the Kaskaskia that in a new location they could expect to receive greater protection from the French than they had enjoyed at their previous settlement.

Father Marest and the Jesuit missionaries who joined him at the Des Pères village supervised the construction of several cabins, a chapel, and a fort. Frenchmen residing adjacent to the Tamaroa Indian village at Cahokia, along with several members of the Tamaroa tribe, soon crossed the Mississippi to take up residence at the rapidly growing Des Pères village. Missouri's earliest settlement, however, was short lived. In 1703 the Kaskaskia, dissatisfied with their new location, decided to return to the eastern side of the river where they established still another village. Afraid they might be attacked by hostile Indians after the departure of the Kaskaskia, the French settlers who had come to Des Pères also moved away and the settlement disappeared as quickly as it had appeared.

Despite the abandonment of the village at River Des Pères, the lure of the unknown lands on the western side of the Mississippi continued to attract French adventurers. Numerous unauthorized explorers ascended the Missouri River hoping to establish commercial ties with the Spanish in New Mexico, look for gold and silver mines, or seek to engage in the lucrative Indian trade, but the first one to leave a definite account of his sojourn up the Missouri was Étienne Véniard de Bourgmont.

Formerly a commandant at Detroit, De Bourgmont first had come into contact with members of the Missouri Indian tribe in 1712, when they assisted the French at Detroit in a battle against the Fox. De Bourgmont subsequently left Detroit, married a Missouri Indian maiden, and joined her people at their village located on the river bearing their name near the mouth of the Grand River in north central Missouri. A semi-sedentary people, they frequently ranged long distances on their hunting trips in search of buffalo, deer, and elk. The length of De Bourgmont's stay at the village remains unknown. During the year 1714 he kept a diary of his activities among the Missouri, but no further account of his actions can be found until 1719 when he participated in the defense of the French post at Pensacola.

Shortly thereafter, he returned to France relating tales of his experiences in the wilderness to eager French audiences.

The Missouri Indians remained in the same general area until the 1790's, when raiding Sac and Fox war parties inflicted heavy casualties upon them. The scourge of smallpox, coupled with invasions by unfriendly Indians, so depleted their ranks that they were forced to seek refuge among friendly neighboring tribes. Some joined the Osage, others went to the Kansa tribe, while the largest segment took up residence with the Oto, thus ending the Missouri's existence as a separate nation.

Missouri's other resident Indian tribe in the early eighteenth century, the Osage, played a much more important role in the subsequent history of the region. Hunting was the central feature of Osage life. For extended periods of time all but the oldest residents and a few young children left their permanent villages to participate in hunting expeditions. Although only the men engaged in actual hunting, the women and children kept busy attending to routine domestic chores on these lengthy trips. During the summer and fall they pursued buffalo and elk, but in the spring their attention turned to bear and beaver. Despite the tribal preoccupation with the chase, the women did cultivate corn, beans, squash, and pumpkins, and gathered wild fruits, roots, and nuts.

The Osage maintained their permanent villages along the Osage River and in north central Missouri along the Missouri River. Located on the high river bluffs, their villages overlooked the broad expanses of the surrounding countryside from strategic vantage points. The nearby rivers provided an abundant supply of water, and timber flourished along the banks. The Osage scattered their dwellings at random throughout the villages, but they reserved an open space near the center for ceremonies and councils. They constructed their rectangular lodges, which were sometimes as much as 100 feet in length, by bending young saplings over a ridgepost to form the roof arch. Woven mats covering the framework constituted the exterior.

On a normal day smoke could be seen rising from the holes near the center of the lodges, while the residents went about

5

their daily routine. Men gathered to discuss the results of their latest hunt and to make plans for the upcoming ones; while some of the women busied themselves preparing the new skins for clothing and bedding, another group of women wove rush mats. Near the lodges, meat and corn dried on high racks that elevated the food above the reach of dogs roaming through the villages.

Constantly forced to defend their hunting grounds against encroachment by whites and enemy Indian tribes alike, the Osage gained a reputation for being hostile and warlike. During the Spanish period, officials repeatedly complained of Osage depredations and occasionally invited other tribes from outside of the territory to make war on the Osage. This basic pattern continued into the American period until gradually the Osage were forced to surrender control of their historic tribal lands.[1]

Europeans introduced many changes into the Indian way of life. By the time the first French traders reached the Osage and Missouri villages, those tribes had already acquired horses. Through the medium of intertribal trade, horses and European manufactured goods were transferred into the North American interior long before tribes in those areas came into direct contact with Europeans. The Indians procured their first horses from the Spanish settlements in the southwest, while firearms had first come to them via French and English traders in Canada.

Just as the Indians readily adapted to the use of horses and guns, European-made awls, knives, axes, metal kettles, buttons, and trade cloth soon replaced articles of bone, stone, pottery, and skin which the Indians had made previously for themselves. Likewise, the traders sometimes plied the Indians with liquor, which consequently became a much-sought-after commodity among the tribesmen. As the Indians became increasingly eager to acquire the white man's goods, they quickly learned that the European trader would readily exchange those articles for peltries and furs. Unfortunately, the early traders often capitalized upon the Indians' ignorance of relative values of the merchandise

1. During the 1820's the last of the Osage moved from Missouri to Kansas and Oklahoma, and in 1825 they signed a treaty with the United States in which they surrendered all claims to any lands in Missouri.

6

they traded to reap tremendous profits at the expense of the unsuspecting savages.

Although *coureurs de bois* and *voyageurs*[2] ascended the Missouri to trade with the Indians, and an occasional expedition set out in search for treasure-laden mines, French interest in Louisiana waned. In 1710 the French government named the founder of Detroit, Antoine de La Mothe Cadillac, to be governor of Louisiana. Cadillac, a man of only moderate abilities, had served the French in the New World for many years. Unfortunately his rigid, pompous, and overbearing manner frequently embroiled him in disputes with his subordinates and lessened his effectiveness as an administrator. Following his appointment to the Louisiana post, he returned to France to promote the development of the sparsely settled region he had been assigned to govern. Cadillac's efforts generated renewed French interest in Louisiana, and he persuaded Antoine Crozat, a wealthy merchant with important connections at the French court, to underwrite the cost of French activity in the province. In return for his financial assistance Crozat received a charter granting him extensive trading and mining privileges in the region. The boundaries outlined in the charter were extremely vague, but Crozat's grant included Missouri along with what are today the states of Louisiana, Mississippi, Tennessee, Illinois, and Arkansas. Encouraged by Cadillac, Crozat expected the exploitation of the region's mineral resources and the opening of trade with the Spanish in Mexico to return a handsome profit on his investment.

Governor Cadillac returned to Louisiana in 1713 determined to make the venture succeed. Shortly after Cadillac reached his headquarters at Mobile, Capt. Charles Claude Dutisne arrived at that garrison with ore samples containing large amounts of silver supposedly obtained from mines near Kaskaskia. Convinced that the long-sought goal would soon be realized, Cadillac personally set out in February, 1715, to find the heretofore elusive mines, dreaming no doubt of discovering untold riches equal to those the Spanish conquistadors had found in Mexico

2. *Coureurs de bois* and *voyageurs* are French terms commonly used to denote French-Canadian traders, trappers, and boatmen.

and Peru. Keeping his intentions secret, the Governor departed without informing his immediate subordinate in Mobile of his intended destination. When Cadillac's party reached Kaskaskia, its hopes were dashed upon learning that Dutisne's minerals had actually come from Mexico and had been given to Dutisne as a joke.

Undaunted, Cadillac refused to abandon his search and pushed ahead with his plans to visit the site of the Indian mines on the west bank of the Mississippi. Joined by recruits from Kaskaskia and a party of friendly Indians, the group crossed the river and traveled to the mouth of Saline Creek, located on the Missouri side approximately ten miles below present-day Ste. Genevieve, and from there they followed the clearly-marked Indian trails leading to the site of the diggings. After reaching the mines, Cadillac ordered his men to dig a trench, but when they reached a depth of seven to nine feet a rock ledge halted further progress. The Governor collected samples from the ore near the surface and returned to his headquarters on the Gulf.

Subsequent tests revealed an absence of silver in the ore. Cadillac's failure to find valuable metals was only one in a series of disappointments for Crozat's venture. Trade with the Spanish had failed to materialize because of opposition from the Viceroy of New Spain, and most other operations in Louisiana had proven equally unprofitable. Having already suffered heavy financial losses, with little prospect for recouping them, Crozat petitioned the King in 1717 for release from his obligations under the charter. The government granted his request, thereby relieving him of any further responsibility for operations in Louisiana.

Crozat's unhappy experience convinced French officials that the task of developing Louisiana was too great for any individual to undertake. Instead they decided to create a company that would be large enough to manage the job. In August the government formally chartered the Company of the West, granting that organization a complete monopoly of Louisiana's trade; ownership of all mines operated by the company; use of all forts, depots, and garrisons in the province; the right to import French goods into Louisiana duty free; reduced duties on goods shipped to France; control of Louisiana's commercial and Indian policies; and the right to name all officials in the province. In return the company agreed to send 6000 whites and 3000 blacks to the sparsely-populated territory within ten years.

The driving force behind the formation of the Company of the West was the colorful Scottish financier John Law, who, after amassing a considerable fortune at the gaming tables, had gained acceptance in the highest circles at the French court. In response to Law's intensive promotional activities, Frenchmen eagerly clamored to invest in the enterprise. In 1719 Law further expanded his operations when he supervised the creation of the Company of the Indies by consolidating the Company of the West with several other trading companies. Under his flamboyant direction this great speculative venture attracted large amounts of capital.

With sizable funds at its disposal the company had pressed ahead with its plans for Louisiana's development. In 1718 the directors appointed Pierre Duqué, Sieur de Boisbriant, to assume command of the Illinois country and Marc Antoine de la Loëre des Ursins to serve as intendant for the region. Both men were well-qualified for their respective positions. Boisbriant, a Canadian who had first come to Louisiana in 1700, was intimately acquainted with the Illinois Indians. Des Ursins had traveled from France to Louisiana with Cadillac in 1713 to serve as Crozat's chief agent at the mouth of the Mississippi. Full responsibility for overseeing the development of land on both sides of the Mississippi now fell to these two men. Shortly after his arrival Boisbriant ordered the construction of a fort about fifteen miles north of Kaskaskia, the largest settlement in the region. Completed in 1720, Fort Chartres served as the seat of government for Upper Louisiana and the Illinois country throughout the remainder of the French period.

Still hopeful of finding mines comparable to those Spain had discovered, company officials instructed Boisbriant and Des Ursins to initiate mining operations. In June, 1719, Des Ursins led an expedition across the Mississippi to the mines Cadillac had visited four years earlier. He supervised the digging of several shafts and reported finding pieces of ore, which he erroneously believed to be silver. Numerous expeditions on both sides of the river investigated various mining sites, but the mines on the west bank seemed to be the most promising. In response to the company's edict, primitive mining and smelting operations began to produce limited quantities of lead, but the search for more valuable minerals proved fruitless.

Meanwhile, the Company of the Indies named Philippe François Renault to oversee mining operations in Upper Louisiana and Illinois. Renault arrived in New Orleans in 1720, bringing with him a party of miners and Negro laborers along with an agreement that twenty-five additional blacks would be sent to his mines each subsequent year.[3] He quickly departed for the Illinois country to begin his duties.

After establishing a settlement near Fort Chartres to serve as his headquarters, Renault sent out many exploratory parties to select the most favorable site for mining operations. He ultimately chose a location on the opposite side of the Mississippi close to the Meramec River. Under Renault's direction, the Missouri mines began to produce lead on a regular basis. In 1723 Renault secured a grant from Boisbriant and Des Ursins for the lands on which his diggings were located, and only two years later production at his mines had increased to 1,500 pounds of lead a day. Although still in debt to the company for the slaves they had supplied him, Renault anticipated substantial profits in the near future and confidently predicted that the mines would soon provide all of the lead the company could use. Nevertheless, Renault continued to search in vain for the copper or silver mines that he believed would be even more lucrative. Renault operated the lead mines in Missouri until 1744 when he sold his holdings to the government and returned to France, but by that time lead mining had been fixed as an important part of the local economy.

While mineral resources had enticed Renault and his associates in Illinois to cross the Mississippi, the Indian trade beck-

3. The black slaves Renault brought to Upper Louisiana were not the first Negroes to arrive there. Des Ursins reported taking five blacks on his earlier mining expedition. Apparently based upon Henry Schoolcraft's account, Louis Houck stated that Renault brought 500 slaves with him. Existing records indicate that this number is much too large. Although Houck's figure was grossly inflated, blacks did play an important role in Missouri's development from the earliest days.

oned a growing number of French trappers up the Missouri. By 1720 many of these unauthorized adventurers traded with the tribes along the Missouri on a regular basis. The first officially-sanctioned visitor to reach those tribes was Charles Claude Dutisne. The son of a wealthy French family, Dutisne had come to Canada and had conducted extensive explorations, making him well-acquainted with the Indian tribes in the Upper Mississippi Valley. In 1713 he had led a party of Canadians across country to Mobile carrying the ore samples that precipitated Governor Cadillac's futile journey in search of silver mines. Subsequently Dutisne offered his services to the Company of the Indies and under its authority he completed the first authorized visit to the Osage in 1719, though undoubtedly numerous unofficial traders had preceded him. From the Osage villages he traveled on to the Pani villages in Oklahoma, despite the opposition of the Osage. He failed, however, in his attempts to reach the Padouca —later known as the Comanche—because of opposition from the neighboring tribes.

The growing restlessness of the tribes Dutisne visited underscored the need for closer supervision of Indian affairs by the company. Many of the unauthorized French traders in their ruthless attempts to exploit the savages had actually encouraged warfare between tribes in order to secure more Indian slaves in their trade. Moreover, recent Spanish incursions into the Missouri Valley greatly alarmed French officials. In response the directors of the Company of the Indies sought someone to take charge of troubled affairs in that region. They selected Étienne Véniard de Bourgmont. De Bourgmont had impressed company officials so with the information he had gained during his earlier unauthorized travels among the Missouri Indians that in 1720 they commissioned him captain of the Louisiana troops and commandant on the Missouri River.

Hoping to end all unauthorized trading along the Missouri and to discourage any possible Spanish plans to move into the area, they ordered De Bourgmont to construct a fort on the Missouri River. In addition the directors instructed him to negotiate a treaty with the Padouca securing a pledge to support the French in checking any further Spanish encroachment.

Finally the company authorized De Bourgmont to select some representative Indian chiefs to accompany him to France to acquaint them with France's great power.

De Bourgmont left France in 1722, but when he arrived in New Orleans he found that despite instructions from the company, officials there had neglected to make the necessary arrangements for his expedition. The reluctance of local authorities to assist De Bourgmont emanated from an unwillingness to deplete their limited supplies to equip an outpost which they considered ill-advised and unnecessary because of the remoteness of its proposed location. These obstacles failed to deter De Bourgmont, who pressed ahead with his plans.

In February, 1723, De Bourgmont and his poorly provisioned and undermanned force left New Orleans and headed up the Mississippi. With his group further weakened by desertions along the way, De Bourgmont had to seek reinforcements from among the troops stationed in the Illinois country before he could continue. Officials at Cahokia assigned Father Jean Baptiste Mercier of the Society of Foreign Missions, Ens. Louis St. Ange de Bellerive and six soldiers to accompany De Bourgmont's party up the Missouri River.

Additional assistance came from a band of Missouri Indians who had journeyed to the Mississippi to welcome their old friend De Bourgmont and to escort him to their village. Slowly the three barges and assorted canoes carrying the forty Frenchmen and their Indian helpers made their way up the broad Missouri. When they finally reached their destination in November, 1723, De Bourgmont ordered an immediate start on construction of the new outpost. Soon the sound of axes reverberated through the forests as the workers began to fell the tall trees to be used in building the new post. Numerous difficulties hampered progress on the fort, but one by one the buildings constructed of upright logs covered with thatched grass roofs began to rise in the wilds along the bank of the Missouri at a site located in present-day Carroll County.

By spring Fort Orleans had become a busy place. Indians from nearby villages freely mingled with Frenchmen amidst the crudely constructed log buildings, while missionaries attempted to convert as many of the Indians as possible. With the fort nearing completion, De Bourgmont turned his attention to planning for a trip to the Padouca. Both Governor Bienville in New Orleans and Commandant Boisbriant in Illinois had attempted to discourage the journey because they believed it would not be worth the expense and effort necessary for its completion. Neither managed to dissuade De Bourgmont, and he departed from Fort Orleans in July, 1724, on his way to the Padouca villages. Illness forced the commandant of the Missouri to return temporarily to the fort before accomplishing his mission, but he dispatched an employee of the Company of the Indies to the Padouca with presents. After his recovery, De Bourgmont again set out to visit the Padouca, stopping at the Kansa village to meet with representatives of various tribes, including the Missouri, Kansa, Oto, Iowa, Panimaha, and Padouca. From there he traveled to Padouca country to enter formal negotiations with that tribe. The Padouca proved agreeable to the Frenchman's proposals and he returned to Fort Orleans on October 5, 1724, with a treaty that aligned the Padouca with the French and contained their promise not to go to war against other tribes allied with the French. In celebration of the mission's positive results, the chant of the *Te Deum* rang out from the chapel at the fort.

Having successfully completed his first two assignments, De Bourgmont called a general Indian council to select certain chiefs to accompany him to France. The promise of many presents persuaded most of those designated to make the trip to accept, and they departed with the commandant for New Orleans. When the group reached France in 1725, they created an immediate sensation. The Frenchmen warmly welcomed their red brothers from the North American wilderness, and the Indians reciprocated by performing native dances at a Parisian opera house for their enthralled hosts; they also staged an exhibition of their hunting skills at a nearby estate. Moreover, the baptism at the Notre Dame Cathedral of the daughter of one of the Missouri chiefs, and her marriage to a Frenchman who had accompanied the group from the New World, had attracted considerable attention. The Indians subsequently returned to their homes to relate to their fellow tribesmen what they had seen, but De Bourgmont remained in France and never again visited the American shores.

The Company of the Indies continued to station a garrison at Fort Orleans until officials decided that the limited benefits derived from the fortification did not justify the heavy expenditures necessary to maintain it. Once the company abandoned the fort in about 1729, the French missionaries also found it necessary to withdraw from the area because of the growing danger from Indian attack. Gradually the wilderness reclaimed the once-thriving outpost on the Missouri.

The evacuation of Fort Orleans represented one more step in a general policy of retrenchment by the Company of the Indies. Since 1720 when the collapse of John Law's shaky financial empire had burst the entire "Mississippi bubble," interest in Louisiana had begun to decline. Although the stockholders, eager to recoup their losses, had continued to operate the Company of the Indies, most Frenchmen had grown reluctant to invest additional sums of money in the project. Like Crozat's earlier enterprise, the company had failed to earn a profit, and its anxious investors sought to reduce their expenditures in Louisiana in order to transfer their funds to other more lucrative opportunities elsewhere. Increasing Indian difficulties in the Illinois country finally prompted the company to petition the King in 1731 to take Louisiana back, and in that year the area again came under royal control.

The abandonment of Fort Orleans marked the second time the French had voluntarily withdrawn from a settlement on Missouri soil. The villages east of the Mississippi in the Illinois country remained the focal point of French activity. Traders, miners, and saltmakers frequently crossed the river, but they continued to maintain their permanent residences on the eastern bank. Not until the founding of Ste. Genevieve did the French establish a permanent settlement west of the Mississippi.

Unfortunately no account of the initial settlement of Ste. Genevieve remains, and the exact date of its founding is unknown. The best available evidence does suggest that the first residents probably took up occupancy there sometime prior to 1732.[4] For

4. Although 1735 has traditionally been given as the date for the founding of Ste. Genevieve, the first settlers probably came prior to that time. For a discussion of the limited data concerning the date of the es-

many years miners had worked the diggings in the area, and it seems likely that this activity may have attracted the first permanent settlers. It may well be that the village first served as a depot and shipping point for the lead sent down the Mississippi from Renault's mines. Saltworks also drew people to the Ste. Genevieve vicinity at an early date, with settlers who came there to make salt at the region's saline springs supplying inhabitants on both sides of the river with their product.

Situated on the Mississippi floodplain, Ste. Genevieve's original location proved to be less than satisfactory. Because of its frequently damp and muddy condition, Illinois residents generally referred to Ste. Genevieve as *Misère*—French for misery. The village grew slowly during its early years. Most of its initial settlers simply moved across the river from Illinois, bringing their slaves and other possessions with them. Although the proximity of the lead mines and saline springs may have induced many of the original settlers to make the move, most who came to Ste. Genevieve were farmers. These French habitants cultivated a variety of crops on the lands they cleared along the Mississippi including corn, wheat, oats, barley, vegetables, cotton, and tobacco. In addition, their hogs, cattle, horses, and other livestock grazed in the common pasture. For the most part, Ste. Genevieve's economic development merely represented an extension of French activity to the western bank of the river.

The tranquility of this small French village on the Mississippi belied the intense struggle that engaged France during much of the eighteenth century. A series of intermittent wars pitted France against England in a contest waged for control of colonial possessions throughout the world. In the course of these struggles involving many nations, alliances and loyalties frequently shifted, but France and England remained the great protagonists. The early encounters between these two countries proved inconclusive, and not until the Great War for the Empire was the question finally resolved in favor of the British.[5]

tablishment of Missouri's earliest permanent settlement, see Francis J. Yealy's *Sainte Genevieve: The Story of Missouri's Oldest Settlement*, 21–27.

5. I have chosen to use Professor Lawrence Henry Gipson's term the

In that decisive contest, for all practical purposes, the fall of Quebec to English forces in 1759 and the loss of Montreal in the following year sealed France's fate in North America. Hoping to reverse the course of the war, Spain joined France in the struggle against England in January, 1762, but the Spanish also went down to defeat at the hand of the superior English forces. With the outcome of the war a certainty, France pressed for a speedy end to the conflict on the best terms possible. To persuade the Spanish King to agree to sign the preliminaries of peace immediately, to compensate Spain for its losses, and to preserve friendly relations between the two nations, France offered to cede Louisiana to Spain. The Spanish accepted and the terms were incorporated in the secret Treaty of Fontainbleau signed in November, 1762. Although Louisiana had been a costly burden for the French to maintain, France based its decision to transfer the territory to Spain on political considerations rather than on the view that the colony was worthless.

With the stroke of a pen Louisiana passed from French to Spanish control. In addition, the French also surrendered all of Canada along with her territories east of the Mississippi to England, although she did manage to retain some key possessions in the Caribbean. As a consequence of France's humiliating defeat, the final terms of settlement of the Great War for the Empire, incorporated in the Treaty of Paris of 1763, forced her to withdraw completely from the North American continent.

Word of the agreement to transfer Louisiana from France to Spain did not reach the province for nearly two years, and in the interim the French had established a second settlement on the western bank of the Mississippi. The founding of St. Louis grew indirectly out of an official attempt to speed postwar economic recovery in Louisiana. Wartime financial policies had created serious inflation in the province, which in turn had adversely affected local business conditions. When Jean Jacques Blaise D'Abbadie assumed Louisiana's governorship in 1763, he sought to revive the lagging economy by granting a series of monopolies in various products for specified periods of time.

Great War for the Empire to designate the conflict otherwise known as the French and Indian War in America and the Seven Years War in Europe.

The grants made by D'Abbadie included one given to Gilbert Antoine Maxent, a well-known New Orleans merchant, bestowing on him the exclusive right to trade with the Indians on the Missouri River and the west bank of the Mississippi for a six-year period. Maxent then contracted with Pierre Liguest Laclede to establish and supervise a trading post in Upper Louisiana. Little is known of Laclede's early life except that he was the younger son of a well-established French family and had come to the New World to seek his fortune. Laclede was apparently well-educated, because he brought a 200-volume library with him when he moved to St. Louis.

In early August, 1763, Laclede and his thirteen-year-old clerk, Auguste Chouteau, left New Orleans with the supplies and equipment necessary to initiate trading activities and to establish the post. They reached Ste. Genevieve on November 3, but, unable to secure a large enough storage space to house their goods, they continued on to Kaskaskia. Having received permission to store their supplies at Fort Chartres, they established a winter headquarters at the village of St. Anne de Fort Chartres.

In December Laclede, accompanied by young Chouteau, crossed the Mississippi and selected a site on that river near the mouth of the Missouri for his new headquarters. They returned to Fort Chartres, but the following February Laclede dispatched Chouteau, then only fourteen years of age, along with a party of thirty workmen to begin construction of the trading post at the location he had previously chosen. Under Chouteau's direction, workers began to construct some temporary cabins to house men and supplies. In April Laclede paid a visit to the camp to inspect the progress of the post, which he named St. Louis in honor of the reigning King Louis XV, and to give Chouteau additional instructions for its completion. Along with the usual log buildings, Laclede ordered the construction of a stone dwelling to serve as company headquarters. This impressive building remained a St. Louis landmark for many years.[6]

As work on the new trading center progressed, the residents

6. For many years the building served as the Government House in St. Louis. After Laclede's death, Auguste Chouteau purchased the structure and, following a major renovation and enlargement, it was converted into the city's most elegant residence.

in the French settlements in Illinois had grown increasingly apprehensive about their future in view of the French cession of all territories east of the Mississippi to England. Laclede already knew of this transfer when he had come to Illinois, but official orders to evacuate the country first reached Capt. Neyon de Villiers, commandant of Illinois country, in April, 1764. De Villiers, who did not wait for his English replacement to arrive, departed in June for New Orleans along with most of his troops and about eighty French inhabitants who could not accept the prospect of living under the English flag. The departing commandant designated Capt. Louis St. Ange de Bellerive to command the small remaining French garrison at Fort Chartres and to await the arrival of British authorities to complete the formal transfer.

Meanwhile, Laclede actively recruited settlers for his new establishment from among the disheartened and dispirited French settlers in Illinois. Since word of the transfer of Louisiana to Spain still had not reached the area, many decided to cross the river and settle in St. Louis, which they assumed would continue under French control. By the time the residents in Upper Louisiana finally did learn of the cession of Louisiana to Spain, sometime in November or December of 1764, St. Louis was already a well-established village containing between forty and fifty families—a tribute to Laclede's promotional abilities.

Destined to become a great commercial center, St. Louis continued to attract new settlers, most of them Frenchmen who decided they preferred Spanish to English rule. Not all of the visitors who came to St. Louis were welcome, however. In October, 1764, a band of Missouri Indians arrived at the village with the intention of residing adjacent to Laclede's new trading headquarters. Although these Indians were not hostile, their presence alarmed the uneasy settlers and, after discussions and the granting of presents, Laclede persuaded them to return to their former villages.

Capt. Thomas Stirling, whom the British had assigned to occupy the Illinois country, did not reach Fort Chartres until October, 1765. At that time Captain St. Ange formally surrendered control to the English and withdrew across the Mississippi River to St. Louis, where he established his new headquarters in accordance with his instructions from New Orleans.

Following his arrival in St. Louis, St. Ange assumed command of the territories west of the Mississippi, exercising both civil and military control until the Spanish belatedly arrived to take charge of the area. Meanwhile, protests in New Orleans had caused French authorities to cancel all of the monopolies granted by Governor D'Abbadie, including the one given to Maxent, but Laclede had decided to remain in the village he had worked so hard to found. He purchased Maxent's interests in the company's St. Louis operations and became the settlement's most prominent citizen and its major trader.

Even in the waning days of French control, Missouri remained a primitive and largely unsettled wilderness. With only two small villages along the banks of the Mississippi, serious development of the region was yet to come in the Spanish period. Throughout the French era the settlements in Illinois east of the Mississippi had been the focal point of activity, with the western portions of Louisiana receiving only limited attention. Nevertheless, the French influence in Missouri cannot be measured in these terms, for it was the French who had established the foundation of the new society. During the ensuing forty years of Spanish control, Missouri remained thoroughly French in its appearance, language, customs, and outlook. France had left an indelible mark upon the Missouri heritage.

CHAPTER II

SPAIN ATTEMPTS TO BUILD
A BUFFER COLONY

SPAIN welcomed the acquisition of Louisiana from France as a means of more effectively safeguarding her valuable possessions in Mexico against the threat of foreign encroachment. During the nearly forty years that the Spanish flag flew over Louisiana, officials waged a relentless struggle to prevent English and subsequent American penetration west of the Mississippi. The creation of a strong viable colony that could serve as a protective barrier became the primary objective of Spanish policy in Louisiana. Although largely unsuccessful in their efforts, Spanish authorities demonstrated considerable flexibility in their attempts to adapt the cumbersome Spanish colonial system to meet the unique needs of the remote border colony.

France had ceded Louisiana to Spain in November, 1762, but the first Spanish official did not arrive in the province until March, 1766. Frequently, this lengthy delay has been interpreted as an indication of Spanish reluctance to assume control of the region. In reality Spain remained eager to occupy Louisiana, but a treasury depleted by heavy wartime expenditures, coupled with a serious shortage of troops, accounted for the lapse. Meanwhile, the French, unwilling to bear administrative costs for a colony that was no longer theirs, pressed the Spanish to take possession more speedily.

When Louisiana's first Spanish governor, Don Antonio de Ulloa, finally reached New Orleans in the spring of 1766, he received a cool reception from the disgruntled French residents because most still resented France's decision to cede the province to Spain. Since he had brought only a token force, Ulloa decided to delay the formal transfer until additional Spanish reinforcements arrived. In the meantime he worked through the acting French commandant at New Orleans, Capt. Charles Philippe Aubry.

Spain's delay in assuming control of Louisiana had created

numerous problems for the new governor. In Upper Louisiana the growing number of incursions by British traders already threatened to undermine Spanish authority in that area. Consequently, in 1767, Ulloa sent an expedition up the Mississippi under the command of Don Francisco Rui with orders to establish fortifications at the mouth of the Missouri River and to take command of the area north of that waterway. Ulloa's detailed instructions for Rui stressed the necessity for keeping the British out of Spanish territory and for maintaining cordial relations with the Indian tribes in the region. However, in assigning Rui to oversee those tasks, Governor Ulloa made no effort to supersede the authority of Captain St. Ange, the French commandant at St. Louis, who continued to act as the chief administrative official for that portion of the province south of the Missouri.

With orders to construct two forts along the banks of the Missouri near its junction with the Mississippi, Captain Rui proceeded to the location. When he discovered that high waters frequently flooded the site that Ulloa had selected for the principal fort on the north side of the river, Rui and his officers decided to locate the main structure on the south bank and to build only a small blockhouse on the opposite side. Unfortunately the entire mission suffered from Rui's incompetence, as the inept captain generated dissent wherever he went. Even before Fort Don Carlos had been completed, serious bickering and quarreling among the men threatened the project. At one point the workers refused to allow Captain Rui to enter the fortification. The situation grew even more serious when the storekeeper at the fort, accompanied by a party of twenty soldiers, deserted and headed down the Mississippi. Moreover, Rui's attempts to introduce new restrictions on the fur trade so aroused the leading St. Louis merchants that they issued a strong protest against his actions. They particularly disliked the Spanish official's attempts to restrict the trade to certain specifically designated places. In view of the constant turmoil, Governor Ulloa ordered the removal of Captain Rui and designated Capt. Don Pedro Piernas to replace him in August, 1768. Inclement weather impaired Piernas's voyage up the Mississippi, and the new commandant did not reach the fort on the Missouri until March, 1769.

Meanwhile, Ulloa faced serious problems of his own. His attempt to introduce Spanish mercantilist policy into Louisiana by limiting trade in the province to vessels owned and manned by the Spanish precipitated a revolt in New Orleans. On October 29, 1768, the Superior Council in that city ousted the Spanish governor of Louisiana, branding him a usurper. Without a sufficient force to resist the rebels, Ulloa prepared to evacuate the region. He sent new orders to Piernas, then on his way up the Mississippi to replace Rui, instructing him to withdraw from Upper Louisiana after he delivered Fort Don Carlos to Captain St. Ange. Piernas carried out his instructions and headed for New Orleans where he arrived in October, 1769.

By the time Piernas had completed his assignment and returned from Upper Louisiana, the Spanish had already successfully regained control of the province from the dissidents. Not long after Ulloa's forced departure, a Spanish fleet under the command of Louisiana's newly-appointed governor, Alexander O'Reilly, had appeared at the mouth of the Mississippi with instructions to restore Spanish authority. Charles III, who had selected O'Reilly to replace Ulloa, ordered the Governor to establish a new government and to punish the rebels who had defied his predecessor. In the face of this show of force, rebel opposition evaporated and O'Reilly re-established Spanish control without further resistance.

Once order had been restored, Governor O'Reilly carefully examined the situation in Upper Louisiana. Since the former French commandant, Captain St. Ange, still governed there, O'Reilly took steps to bring that area under full Spanish control. Because of its remote location, he decided to station a lieutenant governor in St. Louis with full authority to administer the region. O'Reilly named Don Pedro Piernas to fill the newly-created post. Piernas returned to St. Louis, and on May 20, 1770, St. Ange formally surrendered control of Upper Louisiana to the Spanish.

Shortly before his appointment as lieutenant governor, at Governor O'Reilly's request, Piernas had prepared a detailed report containing impressions of Upper Louisiana gathered during his recent visit there. Piernas found the climate in Spanish

Illinois to be healthy and pleasant.[1] Although the terrain varied appreciably, he reported that there were vast prairies and cleared level plains suitable for farming and for raising cattle. The fertile soil produced with only minimal cultivation a variety of crops including wheat, corn, cotton, and all types of vegetables. The abundance of wild game in the territory provided the inhabitants with both food and profits from the sale of skins. However, the new Lieutenant Governor suspected that the local preoccupation with hunting sometimes retarded the development of agriculture and industry in the area.

When the Spanish first occupied the region there were still only two settlements—Ste. Genevieve and St. Louis. Both had experienced substantial increases in population as a consequence of the French exodus from east of the Mississippi following the English occupation of that territory. By 1770, Ste. Genevieve, the older of the two, contained more than 600 persons; actually the town gave the appearance of being larger than it was because the houses were separated and scattered throughout the village. Flooding from the adjacent Mississippi had regularly created problems for the residents, but in 1785 the stream's rampaging waters completely inundated the village, forcing the inhabitants to abandon their homes for the safety of higher ground. After surveying the extensive damage produced by the high waters, most of the town's occupants decided against returning to their former dwellings. Instead they constructed a new village two miles back from the river.

At its new location, Ste. Genevieve quickly grew into one of the province's most prosperous settlements. Wheat was the dominant local crop, and some of the habitants cultivated extensive tracts of land with the help of large numbers of slaves. Lead mining and salt-making activities in nearby areas also contributed substantially to the settlement's growing affluence. By the end of the Spanish period, the village's more than 100 well-kept homes reflected the local wealth that made it more prosperous than most frontier towns.

St. Louis had a slightly smaller total population than Ste. Genevieve because fewer slaves lived there. Located on a ridge

1. Upper Louisiana was generally called Spanish Illinois.

high enough to spare it from the floods and dampness that plagued Ste. Genevieve, the village quickly developed into a thriving settlement. Because it served as the residence of the ranking governmental official in Upper Louisiana and because of its advantageous location, it quickly became the center of the growing fur trade. During the peak trading months of May and June, Indians from throughout the Missouri and Upper Mississippi valleys flocked to St. Louis to exchange their goods with the local merchants and to receive the presents annually distributed by the government.

Preoccupied with the lucrative fur trade, most St. Louis residents relegated agricultural activities to a secondary position. As a result, during the early years they sometimes had to import additional flour from Ste. Genevieve, and the village earned the nickname Paincourt—French for short of bread. Many have interpreted this to mean that the town was poverty-stricken, but on the contrary St. Louis prospered from the beginning.

In their attempt to win the allegiance and trade of the Indians, Spanish officials followed the practice of their French predecessors. They distributed among all of the major tribes large quantities of presents including such items as blankets, cloth, fancy garments, plumed hats, sewing needles, thimbles, ribbons, mirrors, combs, beads, vermilion, thread, awls, hoes, axes, knives, steels, wire, kettles, muskets, gunpowder, tobacco, and occasionally brandy even though its use in the trade was outlawed. The Indian chiefs particularly liked the elaborate medals and colorful decorations that the Spanish bestowed upon them. Besides the gifts officials annually presented to them, the Indians procured additional merchandise through the fur trade. Initially they brought their furs to St. Louis to trade, but gradually authorities approved the sending of regular traders to the nations along the Mississippi and lower Missouri. Seeking to maintain careful control over the Indian traffic, the government licensed all traders who in effect became ex officio Spanish agents to the tribes with whom they were authorized to trade.

In theory the trade was open to all Spanish subjects, but the requirement for a license issued by the lieutenant governor limited the number actually authorized to participate. The common practice of granting licenses to the highest bidder permitted a small number of influential traders to monopolize the most lucrative posts. Despite occasional attempts by some officials to liberalize Spanish trading policies, the closed system generally prevailed.

Spain's efforts to monopolize the fur trade in the Mississippi Valley did not go unchallenged. After the close of the Great War for the Empire, Great Britain waged a vigorous campaign to extend her influence beyond the Mississippi. In the intense international rivalry that developed, British agents regularly crossed the Mississippi to trade with the Indians and to incite them against the Spanish, while Spanish traders moved east of the river to woo the Indians there and to invite them to visit St. Louis to receive presents and to trade. Both nations protested the actions of their opponents, but neither managed to prevent the incursions.

Of the various tribes trading with the Spanish, the Osage proved particularly troublesome. In response to a series of depredations against the Spanish, Lieutenant Governor Piernas attempted to make the errant tribe come to terms by withholding goods and trade from them, but the Osage simply sought out British traders to replace the absent Spaniards. Consequently, during the winter of 1772, Canadian-born Jean Marie Ducharme and a party of traders secretly crossed the river from Illinois with two boatloads of trading goods. Having managed to slip past Fort Don Carlos unnoticed under the cover of night, the group traveled up the Missouri and traded with the Little Osage for nearly four months in violation of Spanish regulations.

Since the British traders' presence among the Osage negated the effect of Piernas's actions, the Lieutenant Governor took steps to end their illicit activities as soon as he learned of them. He organized a company of forty volunteers under the command of Pierre Laclede to seek out the interlopers. To reduce the cost of the venture for the government, Piernas reached an agreement with St. Louis traders Benito Vasquez and Joseph Motard, who promised to finance the expedition in return for a share of the confiscated furs. Laclede's force captured Ducharme's party and seized his goods, but the wily British trader escaped his captors and fled to Canada where he continued to trade. Laclede and his men brought the remaining members of

Ducharme's outfit to St. Louis where Lieutenant Governor Piernas questioned them. The volunteers also returned the captured goods. In accordance with his agreement the Lieutenant Governor gave Motard and Vasquez one half of the contraband and divided the remainder among the volunteers.

Continuing British intrusions into Spanish territory prompted Spain to intensify her efforts to strengthen her control in Upper Louisiana. As a part of this program, the Spanish government urged officials in the region to recruit additional settlers from among the French Canadians residing in Illinois. Although Don Francisco Cruzat, who had succeeded Piernas as lieutenant governor of Upper Louisiana in 1775, agreed with the plan, he indicated that most of the potential French settlers living in adjacent areas were too poor to make the move without some type of financial assistance. To overcome this obstacle the crown in 1778 authorized Spanish authorities to grant land to each family immigrating to Louisiana. As an added inducement it ordered funds to be taken from the royal treasury to provide each immigrant family with small quantities of grain, livestock, and essential farming implements during its first year in the province. Spain also extended the offer to French, Spanish, Italian, and German Catholics whom they invited to settle in Louisiana, but relatively few accepted the terms and the desired spurt in immigration failed to materialize.

The outbreak of the American Revolution created new problems for officials in Upper Louisiana. The contest threatened to destroy traditional Indian alliances as the uncertain tribesmen wavered in their loyalties. Don Fernando de Leyba, appointed lieutenant governor of Upper Louisiana in 1778, reported that large numbers of Indians had come to St. Louis seeking Spain's assistance. The unexpected influx soon exhausted the supplies provided for visiting Indians, and De Leyba had to exceed the amount he was authorized to spend for food to supply them. The war also interfered with the normal flow of merchandise into St. Louis, and when a shipment of trade goods from New Orleans failed to arrive, De Leyba had to purchase provisions from across the river.

Although the Spanish technically remained neutral until 1779, De Leyba established contact with George Rogers Clark long before that time, and, whenever possible, De Leyba rendered assistance to the Americans. Spain formally declared war on England on July 8, 1779, hoping to regain control of Gibraltar in Europe, to recover Florida in America, and to end all illicit foreign commerce with Spanish colonies. Following her entrance into the war, Spain instructed her colonies to attack British possessions, but the British did not wait for the Spanish to take the offensive. They seized upon Spain's entry into the war as an opportunity to gain control of the fur trade west of the Mississippi and possibly to capture New Orleans. In 1780 the British lieutenant governor of Michilimackinac, Patrick Sinclair, authorized trader Emanuel Hesse to recruit Indians for a proposed attack against Spanish positions along the Mississippi. The British also instituted patrols along the Mississippi and instructed their Indian allies to seize all non-British vessels attempting to ascend the river.

Word of the Spanish declaration of war reached De Leyba in February, 1780, and he immediately initiated preparations for both offensive and defensive military operations. The limited defenses of St. Louis created widespread apprehension among the local residents. Time had taken its toll on the wooden fortifications originally constructed by Captain Rui and his men at the mouth of the Missouri. Fort Don Carlos had so deteriorated in recent years that it was virtually worthless as a defensive establishment. In fact, when the soldiers stationed at that installation had been threatened by a possible Indian attack, they had retreated hastily to St. Louis, leaving the post unmanned. Concerned that the cannons at the abandoned fort might fall into British hands, De Leyba sent troops from St. Louis to rescue the weapons for use in defending the city.

In arranging for the defense of St. Louis, De Leyba was reluctant to spend monies from the royal treasury. Instead he adopted a program of procuring financial assistance through public subscription to provide the needed fortifications. In this manner he raised a substantial amount, including a sizable contribution from his own pocket. Following the fund drive, De Leyba announced plans for the construction of four stone towers to aid in the city's defense, and construction on the tower located on the west edge of the village began immediately. Although not fully completed at the time of the subsequent attack upon St. Louis, the tower known as Fort San Carlos housed the five cannons previously recovered by De Leyba, and it played an important role in repelling the enemy assault.

Insufficient funds forced the cancellation of work on the remaining towers. In a move necessitated by economy, De Leyba ordered the digging of two trenches to supplement the single tower; his insistence upon using local resources to finance defensive preparations worked a considerable hardship upon the local inhabitants. In addition to the monies they had subscribed, the St. Louis townspeople also contributed without compensation more than 400 workdays to construct the various fortifications and stand guard for the village.

On May 9, 1780, De Leyba received word that a sizable party of British and Indians had started down the Mississippi. To augment the meager force at the village he ordered the militia at Ste. Genevieve to come up the river. That force of sixty men, under the command of Lt. Don Silvio Francisco de Cartabona, arrived in Upper Louisiana's capital city four days later. Even with this welcome addition the total defensive force at St. Louis numbered only about 300 men. On May 23, a reconnaissance expedition dispatched by the Lieutenant Governor to scout British activity in the vicinity reported that the approaching enemy force had been spotted only twenty-six leagues from the city.

The actual attack upon St. Louis came three days later. On May 26, 1780, a combined force of British and Indians under the command of Emanuel Hesse swooped down upon the city. Estimates of the number of attackers varied greatly, but the entire force, composed mainly of Menominee and Winnebago Indians, did not exceed 950 and may have been considerably smaller. The volleys fired from the cannons located atop Fort San Carlos surprised the attacking forces, who had not expected to find the city fortified. Although it is doubtful that the cannon fire inflicted any serious casualties upon the attackers, it did frighten many of the undisciplined Indians who fled when they saw the town could not be taken easily. After the assault had been successfully repelled, the retreating forces took a heavy toll among the farmers and their slaves who had refused to take seriously the rumors of the impending attack and had remained

28

in the unprotected areas outside the city. The defensive preparations in St. Louis minimized the casualties, but the seventy-nine
persons listed in the official report as killed, wounded, or captured represented a heavy loss for a village of only 700.

Despite the successful defense of St. Louis engineered by De
Leyba, local residents strongly disliked him. They resented the
burdens imposed upon them by his requisitions for money and
labor. Their irritation against the Governor, who had become
seriously ill following the battle, increased when he refused to
approve the distribution of gifts among a party of Sac and Fox
Indians who had come to St. Louis to return six captives carried
away during the recent attack. In view of their exposed position,
the unhappy townspeople generally believed they could not
afford to alienate this sizable band of Indians who had shown
a willingness to make peace with the Spaniards.

Reports of a possible second attack upon St. Louis added to
the local sense of despair. Fearful that their settlement faced
certain destruction unless Spanish authorities took immediate
steps to improve their precarious situation, the residents of that
village sent a strongly-worded letter to the Governor General of
Louisiana denouncing De Leyba and demanding the construction of a fort and the stationing of at least 200 regular troops in
the area to protect them.

De Leyba's physical condition worsened and on June 23 Lieutenant Cartabona temporarily assumed the duties of the ailing
official. Five days later the unpopular Lieutenant Governor was
dead. The people of St. Louis now sought Acting Lieutenant
Governor Cartabona's assistance in requesting additional aid
from Spanish officials in New Orleans. They prepared a new
petition stressing the dangers they faced and assigned Auguste
Chouteau to deliver their request to authorities in the provincial
capital.

Meanwhile Cartabona attempted to meet the challenges confronting him with the limited resources at his disposal. He
divided the 150 members of the St. Louis militia into two companies and kept them on constant alert in case a second attack
should occur. Hoping to forestall further Indian unrest, he met
with representatives from various tribes and distributed the few
available goods among them. Despite these precautions local in-

habitants remained hesitant to leave the protection of the village. In view of the heavy casualties inflicted during the spring attack upon persons in the outlying areas, most farmers refused to venture into their fields on the outskirts of the village to harvest their crops. Consequently, Cartabona took the additional step of ordering a detachment of thirty men up the Mississippi to secure intelligence concerning British movements and to provide a warning for the workers in the fields in case of a renewed assault.

In response to the continuing pleas from Upper Louisiana, Gov. Gen. Bernardo de Gálvez offered all of the assistance he could muster. Although the current Spanish campaign against the British in Florida had seriously depleted his available resources, he did commission Francisco Cruzat to replace De Leyba. The popular Cruzat, who had previously held that post from 1775 to 1778, became the only man to serve two separate terms as lieutenant governor in Upper Louisiana. Gálvez immediately dispatched Cruzat to St. Louis with all of the supplies he could spare.

Cruzat took charge from Cartabona on September 24, 1780, after a record trip up the Mississippi from New Orleans.[2] He brought with him instructions to retain the friendship of the Indians, to defend Spanish possessions, and to remain on good terms with the Americans. Under Cruzat's direction the situation at St. Louis improved considerably in the ensuing months. In the fall of 1780 he successfully negotiated agreements with several Indian tribes. Combining skillful diplomacy with the use of gifts, he was able to persuade some members of the Iowa, Oto, and Potawatomi tribes to give up British medals and banners in return for promises of Spanish replacements, but he constantly complained that the scarcity of trade goods limited his effectiveness. Occasionally the Lieutenant Governor had to make purchases from St. Louis merchants, even though their prices were considerably higher than those at New Orleans. Over the years Spain expended large sums of money to win the allegiance of the Indian tribes, but it was never enough. After Spanish rule ended, Pierre Chouteau estimated that Spain's Indian ex-

2. It took Cruzat and his party only fifty-nine days to make the journey—remarkably good time for those days.

penditures in Upper Louisiana had averaged $13,500 per year. In certain critical times, however, they probably spent as much as $30,000 in a single year. Because of the problems that the use of liquor in the Indian trade created for officials attempting to control the Indian, Cruzat sought with only limited success to enforce the absolute ban on its use in the trade.

Continuing rumors of a new spring offensive against St. Louis prompted Cruzat to order the construction of a line of fortifications surrounding the city. Unlike his predecessor De Leyba, Cruzat did not hesitate to draw upon the royal treasury to provide essential supplies and equipment. Workers hurriedly constructed the wooden stockade on all sides of the village except for those sections along the river that were naturally fortified. Although the original specifications called for the structure to be eighteen feet tall and six inches thick, it was actually about nine feet in height when completed.

Acting entirely under his own initiative, Cruzat dispatched an expedition up the Illinois River. Under the command of Eugene Pourré, captain of the second militia company of St. Louis, the force departed on January 2, 1781. Recruits from St. Louis and Cahokia joined friendly Indian tribes in the surprise attack which destroyed the British fort at St. Joseph, Michigan on February 12, 1781. Urged to take the action by a delegation of Milwaukee chiefs, Cruzat had feared that failure to move decisively might cause wavering Indian tribes to revert to the British. As a secondary factor, he believed the mission might forestall another attack upon St. Louis in the spring. Certainly this highly successful operation provided a tremendous boost in morale to the beleaguered residents of St. Louis, who undoubtedly turned out in force to welcome the returning party when it reached the city on March 6.

Although Cruzat's military preparations successfully staved off further attacks against Upper Louisiana, they failed to check British influence among the tribes in the Upper Mississippi Valley. Spain did not have the money, men, or supplies necessary to capture control of the trade in that area. Cruzat constantly lacked the merchandise he needed for negotiations with the Indians. Many St. Louis traders enlisted in the militia to help defend the province and were unable to make their regular visits to the Indian tribes. Moreover, British harassment of navigation on the lower Mississippi impeded the flow of supplies from New Orleans and created a serious shortage of goods among the local merchants who normally supplied the traders.

Unable to provide enough merchandise for the Indian trade and unwilling to permit foreigners to provide it for them, the Spanish in effect forced many Indian tribes to turn to the well-supplied British traders. In short, Spain's position in the Upper Mississippi Valley declined drastically during the American Revolution. When the conflict finally ended, Great Britain had a virtual monopoly of the trade in the upper valley on both sides of the river, and she did not relinquish it after the war, as evidenced by her refusal to withdraw from her northwest posts in accordance with the terms of the Treaty of Paris of 1783. Because of the British inroads with the tribes along the Mississippi, Upper Louisiana's traders had to depend increasingly on the tribes on the Missouri for their trade.

Moreover, a growing number of Spanish traders secured merchandise for their trade from foreign sources. When Manuel Perez succeeded Cruzat as lieutenant governor in 1787, many traders from St. Louis and Ste. Genevieve maintained regular contacts with British traders in Canada. Not only did the Canadians provide superior trade goods, but they also paid higher prices for peltries, since England had become Europe's leading furrier. The northern trade route had one additional advantage: the cooler temperatures made it easier to preserve the quality of the finer furs. Thus, Upper Louisiana's traders regularly shipped their best pelts to Canada, while they sent mostly deerskins and buffalo hides to New Orleans, but, because the Canadian trade benefited Upper Louisiana and because Spain could not adequately supply its own traders, Lieutenant Governor Perez and his successor Zenon Trudeau generally overlooked the violations of Spanish regulations and permitted the illicit trade to flourish.

Although the British domination of the fur trade continued to concern Spanish authorities, they faced a new and potentially more dangerous threat following the close of the American Revolution. The conclusion of that contest had triggered a sizable migration of American settlers across the Alleghenies. As the

32

steady stream of these hardy frontiersmen poured into the regions adjacent to its territories, Spain began a lengthy campaign to block American expansion.

In 1784 the Spanish announced the closing of the Mississippi to American commerce. In taking this step, they hoped to destroy the western American settlements by shutting off their only commercial outlet. Spain also dispatched Don Diego de Gardoqui to Philadelphia to negotiate a settlement of Spanish-American differences. The new policy failed dismally. Opposition from the Southern states in the Continental Congress blocked Spanish attempts to swap a commercial treaty with the United States for an American agreement to accept the closure of the Mississippi for thirty years. Moreover, the Spanish proposals so antagonized the American frontiersmen that they threatened to use force to open the river if necessary.

The sudden realization that the American Congress could not make a treaty with Spain and that it might not be able to prevent its citizens from attacking Spanish possessions in America prompted Spain to modify its policies in 1787. Hoping to conciliate the irate westerners, Spain adopted a twofold approach to the problem by suggesting a willingness to allow Americans to send their produce down the Mississippi after the payment of a duty, and by inviting Americans to settle in their territory. These solutions had been recommended to the Spanish by Pierre Wouves d'Arges, a roving Frenchman who had lived in Kentucky for several years. Spain subsequently appointed D'Arges as a special agent to help implement the new policies.

The Spanish had always assumed that an increase in Louisiana's population would provide the most effective and the least expensive defense for that province. In the 1770's they had departed from their rigid policy of permitting only selected Spanish Catholics to immigrate to their colonies by inviting alien Catholics to settle in Louisiana, but a lack of funds had doomed the project from the start. Forced to deviate even further from standard policy in their quest to populate Louisiana, the Spanish agreed in 1787 to accept American Protestants who wanted to take up residence there. Believing that many of the inhabitants of the western territories of the United States were not strongly attached to their government, they hoped to transform them into loyal Spanish subjects. Even before they became the King's faithful servants, the Spanish reasoned that their presence would strengthen Louisiana, while their loss would weaken the American settlements from which they had migrated. To attract them, Spain promised to all immigrants who took a loyalty oath and became bona fide residents of His Majesty's domains, free lands, equal commercial privileges with all Spanish subjects, and religious toleration.

At about the same time that the Spanish announced their new policies, James A. Wilkinson floated down the Mississippi with a cargo of goods from Kentucky and a plan of his own for Spanish authorities to consider. The well-educated son of a wealthy merchant planter, Wilkinson had held the brevet rank of brigadier general in the American Revolutionary Army at the age of twenty. After his resignation from the service Wilkinson moved to the Kentucky frontier in pursuit of greater opportunity. There he formulated a scheme, not too different from that of D'Arges, which he now sought to present to officials in New Orleans.

Actually Wilkinson offered two proposals for their consideration, both of which were designed to advance Wilkinson's interests along with those of Spain. The first suggested that Spanish authorities use their control over navigation on the Mississippi and commercial privileges to create a faction in Kentucky loyal to Spain, which could then lead a move to separate that province from the United States. Wilkinson's alternative recommendation called for a liberalization of Spanish immigration policy to attract American settlers to Louisiana and thereby to depopulate Kentucky. Although Wilkinson preferred the first approach, he expected to act as the principal agent under whichever plan officials selected. Wilkinson's recommendations received an enthusiastic reception from Gov. Esteban Miró, an active advocate of American immigration for Louisiana. In fact, Wilkinson's second proposal so closely paralleled Miró's views that the Governor may have been instrumental in its formulation. Miró strongly endorsed Wilkinson's suggestions and forwarded them to officials in Spain for approval.

The Spanish court, already in the process of revising its policies

in Louisiana, carefully considered Wilkinson's proposals while
closely watching developments in the United States. After they
learned of the failure of D'Arges's mission and of Gardoqui's
continuing lack of progress in negotiations with the Confederation government, the Spanish Council of Ministers decided to
reject Wilkinson's proposal for encouraging a revolution in
Kentucky on the grounds that it was too dangerous. The Spanish indicated they would continue to follow the situation there
with interest, but until Kentucky became independent Spanish
officials refused to risk taking any direct action. They did adopt
Wilkinson's recommendation on immigration and named him
to replace D'Arges as Spanish agent in Kentucky. For his services
in promoting immigration to Louisiana, they granted the new
agent an annual salary of $2,000.

Meanwhile, from his post in Philadelphia, the Spanish minister to the United States, Don Diego de Gardoqui, had also
initiated plans to encourage American settlement in Louisiana.
Among those whom Gardoqui interested in the project was
Col. George Morgan. Variously a trader, public official, revolutionary soldier, Indian agent, and land speculator, Morgan had
been recently disappointed by a congressional refusal to approve
a land scheme in which he was involved. Consequently the
prospect of a Spanish land grant on the west bank of the Mississippi appealed to the ambitious American entrepreneur. After
having received encouragement from the Spanish minister, Morgan prepared a detailed plan for the establishment of a colony
in Louisiana along the bank of the Mississippi near the mouth
of the Ohio.

Seeking permission to establish a semiautonomous colony,
Morgan requested the right to name all local officials and to
make land grants in full title. Moreover, he recommended that
the colonists should be permitted to pass their own laws through
a representative assembly with the understanding that all such
statutes would be subject to a royal veto. Under Morgan's plan,
the colony would have complete religious freedom and immigrants would be permitted to bring all of their possessions into
the territory duty free. For himself Morgan requested that he
be given a commission in the Spanish army at the same rank

that he had held in the American Army, but without pay unless in actual service. In addition he sought grants of land for himself and his family along with a regular salary for his services.

Gardoqui wholeheartedly supported Morgan's project and approved the grant subject to final authorization from the Spanish Crown. On the strength of the minister's tentative approbation, Morgan prepared to make a trip to select a site and to survey the lands for his colony. He circulated handbills describing his proposed project and inviting interested persons to join him on the exploratory mission. From the large number who volunteered, Morgan selected seventy men to accompany him to Spanish Louisiana. The delegation departed from Fort Pitt on January 3, 1789, and reached the Mississippi on February 14.

Most of the members of his expedition remained at a Delaware Indian camp across from the mouth of the Ohio, while Morgan and a select group went to St. Louis to confer with Lt. Gov. Manuel Perez. Perez extended a cordial welcome to Morgan and supplied the party with horses, guides, and provisions for their venture. Having procured this assistance, Morgan rejoined his followers who had already moved further southward. Under Morgan's direction they selected a site for the settlement, which they named New Madrid, and began to survey the lands for it. During the spring of 1789 New Madrid was the scene of intense activity. The prospective residents cleared a large field, planted crops, built storehouses, and generally busied themselves in preparation for the expected rush of settlers.

With the necessary arrangements well under way, Morgan departed for New Orleans to discuss his plans with Governor Miró. Miró, however, had serious reservations about Morgan's activities from the outset. He had already concluded that the Spanish government should reject Morgan's proposals because his plans would allow the settlement to remain entirely American, and only one that would gradually transform the Americans into loyal Spanish subjects would be acceptable. In adopting this negative stance, Miró had been strongly influenced by the arguments of James Wilkinson, who looked upon Morgan's scheme as a threat to his own plans.

After his discussions with Morgan, Miró concluded that the American promoter had not intended to violate the King's will.

In the Governor's estimation, excessive zeal rather than improper motives accounted for Morgan's hasty actions. Consequently, he informed Morgan that although the terms of his proposed settlement were unacceptable, he could bring families to New Madrid under the regulations previously set down by the Spanish government in 1787. Governor Miró further agreed to confirm the grants that Morgan had already made to settlers, and promised him a grant of 1,000 acres of land with an equal amount for each of his sons. Finally he named Morgan vice commandant of New Madrid.

Following his departure from New Orleans Morgan returned to Philadelphia where he reported his conversations with Miró to Gardoqui. Morgan continued to believe that his original plan was preferable, but he indicated a willingness to continue to promote immigration under the terms Miró had outlined. However, within a short time Morgan lost all interest in the project, and he never returned to New Madrid.[3] Most of the men who had accompanied him to the settlement in 1789 decided against remaining there and returned to the United States, but others did come to New Madrid, particularly Frenchmen from Vincennes and the Illinois settlements.

On the whole Spanish efforts to encourage American immigration had failed to attract the large numbers of settlers that proponents of the plan had envisioned. Wilkinson's activities in Kentucky floundered, and he lost interest in the project after the Spanish decision in 1789 to reopen the Mississippi to American commerce subject to the payment of duties. Wilkinson had opposed that move strongly because he insisted the Americans would pay the duties rather than go to the trouble and expense of moving to Spanish territory. For this reason he considered it futile to continue campaigning to recruit American immigrants.

Governor Miró's successor in Louisiana, the Baron de Carondelet, de-emphasized plans for American immigration after he

3. Many factors account for Morgan's loss of interest. His dissatisfaction with the changes Miro had insisted upon undoubtedly cooled his ardor for the project. Moreover, following the death of his brother, Morgan inherited a sizable estate, including a large amount of land. Finally, with the change in governments as a result of the adoption of the Constitution, Morgan again hoped to revive his earlier land schemes in the United States.

took office in 1792, and in its place he attempted to introduce a more aggressive policy for defending Spain's New World possessions. He negotiated alliances with southern Indian tribes, whom he encouraged to resist further American expansion westward. He also contemplated resurrecting plans to promote a separatist movement in the western territories of the United States. Carondelet's efforts to shift Spanish policy came in the aftermath of the French Revolution when Spain found itself being drawn into war against its long-time ally—France.

When Citizen Edmond Genet came to the United States as the representative of the French government, he sought to convert the nation into a base for operations against England and Spain. Shortly after his arrival in 1793, Genet dispatched representatives to the western provinces of the United States to recruit Americans for an attack against the Spanish possessions in Louisiana and Florida. George Rogers Clark, the hero of the American Revolution in the West, accepted a commission from Genet, and in January, 1794, he issued a call for volunteers to open the Mississippi to duty-free navigation. In return for their services he promised all recruits large land grants.

Although the Washington Administration had successfully squelched the proposed invasion, along with Genet's other activities, the attempted filibuster had prompted Carondelet to take action to strengthen defenses throughout Louisiana. The Governor especially was concerned by an increase in the number of Osage depredations in 1792 and 1793 in Upper Louisiana. For many years the Spanish unsuccessfully had attempted to control this troublesome tribe, considered to be the most dangerous and warlike Indian nation west of the Mississippi. Efforts to force the Osage to come to terms by withholding all trade from them had been largely ineffectual. In 1787 authorities in Upper Louisiana had urged the Shawnee and Delaware tribes to take up residence in Missouri so they could act as a buffer between the hostile Osage and the Spanish settlements. During the early 1790's the Spanish invited these tribes and others in adjoining regions to make war against the Osage in an effort to destroy them. The resultant Sac and Fox raids into the territory did manage to eliminate an Osage ally—the Missouri tribe—but the Osage remained defiant.

The threatened invasion of Louisiana by the Franco-American force intensified the seriousness of the Osage problem, but the Spanish hesitated to pour large additional sums of money into the defense of the already costly colony. Consequently Governor Carondelet did not hesitate to accept Auguste Chouteau's offer to build, arm, and equip a fort at the principal Osage village located on the Osage River in what is now Vernon County. Chouteau also promised to maintain a garrison of twenty men at the post under the direction of his brother Pierre. In return he asked the Spanish to provide $2,000 a year to cover the salaries of the men stationed at the fort and to grant him a six-year monopoly of the rich Osage trade. The terms were incorporated in an agreement signed in 1794. Chouteau subsequently built the promised fortification, which he named Fort Carondelet in honor of the Governor. The newly-established post enabled the Chouteaus to supervise more effectively the activities of the Osage, but errant tribesmen continued to commit occasional depredations against Upper Louisiana's inhabitants.

The assistance the Osage received from the British traders had made it easier for them to sustain their independent course of action against the Spanish through the years. Therefore, Carondelet and his newly-designated assistant in St. Louis, Lt. Gov. Zenon Trudeau, embarked upon a more energetic program to protect Spanish territory in Upper Louisiana against British incursions. In 1792 Carondelet announced plans to liberalize Spanish trading policies as a part of this effort.

In October, 1793, Lieutenant Governor Trudeau summoned all of Upper Louisiana's traders to meet in St. Louis to consider a detailed set of proposed regulations designed to improve the efficiency of Spanish trading operations and to eliminate the most serious inequities within the system. The assembled traders listened carefully to Governor Carondelet's proposals and suggested a number of modifications including a recommendation that, whenever traders could not secure the merchandise they needed for the trade locally, they should be permitted to seek additional goods from British and American sources. Both Lieutenant Governors Perez and Trudeau had allowed this practice.

With an eye toward opening new areas for trade, some of the merchants also recommended that a company be organized with the exclusive right to control trade along the Upper Missouri—a region heretofore largely untapped by the Spanish. All of their recommendations were forwarded to New Orleans for the Governor's consideration, and he issued his final directives shortly thereafter. In accordance with those revised regulations the merchants reassembled in St. Louis in the spring of 1794 to arrange for an equitable distribution of the trade among themselves. They determined that there were nine posts that should be divided by lot among the twenty-nine recognized traders.

Their profits had been steadily declining in recent years. Whereas previously they could expect to receive a 300 to 400 per cent return on their investment, the current rate had dropped to only 25 per cent. Since growing competition for the limited trade accounted for much of the decline, some of the traders again pressed their request for permission to organize a company to open new areas for Spanish traders on the Upper Missouri. At a special meeting called by Jacques Clamorgan, merchants interested in the venture drew up a series of recommendations for the creation of the company. By pooling their resources the traders hoped to accumulate enough capital to finance the costly undertaking.

Not all merchants in Upper Louisiana desired to participate in the venture. Some considered it too expensive and too risky; others preferred to concentrate on the trade rights they had already been assigned along the lower Missouri; still others refused to join because of personal rivalries and jealousies. Nine traders did seek permission to go ahead with the project. Lieutenant Governor Trudeau, a prime mover behind the company, gave it his unqualified support. Not only did he believe that it would give a boost to the lagging Indian trade, but he also looked upon the Company of Explorers of the Upper Missouri as a perfect way to secure additional information about the remote region and to check the growing British presence along the Upper Missouri.

The organizers pressed ahead with their plans and elected Jacques Clamorgan to direct the new company. A slave dealer, fur trader, merchant, financier, and land speculator, Clamorgan typified the merchant capitalist so common to the frontier. Since his arrival in Upper Louisiana in late 1783 or early 1784, the new director had cultivated the friendship of influential individuals throughout the Mississippi Valley. Even before Spanish officials had given their final approval for the Missouri Company, Clamorgan dispatched a trading party from St. Louis with instructions to open commerce with the Mandan villages on the Upper Missouri. To direct the expedition, Clamorgan selected Jean Baptiste Trudeau, St. Louis's part-time schoolmaster who apparently expected the fur trade to be more lucrative than teaching. Following its departure in June, 1794, Trudeau's party managed to advance only as far as the Arikara country, where hostile Indian tribes in the region prevented the traders from reaching their intended destination. Although Trudeau remained in the Indian country until 1796, his efforts failed to produce the desired results. Meanwhile, in the spring of 1795, the company had sent out a second party with additional merchandise and instructions to join Trudeau, whom they supposed to be trading with the Mandan, but the second group did not get even as far as the first. After losing its supplies in an encounter with the Padouca, the party returned to St. Louis empty-handed.

In view of the poor showing of the first two outings, the Missouri Company hired James Mackay, a Canadian fur trader who had recently become a Spanish subject, to replace Trudeau as principal explorer and director of the company's operations in the Indian country. Mackay's party left St. Louis in August, 1795, and headed northward, hoping to reach the Pacific Ocean via the Missouri River. Although this expedition did manage to take one small Mandan post from the British, the mission was otherwise a complete failure.

Discouraged by the poor showing in these ventures, interest in pursuing operations on the Upper Missouri rapidly declined among most members of the company. Many lost confidence in Clamorgan, who gradually gained control of a large number of the company's original shares for himself. In an attempt to revive the lagging venture, Clamorgan sought additional concessions from the Spanish government and asked that the company's present monopoly over all trade on the Upper Missouri be extended to include that of the Upper Mississippi as well. Carondelet agreed to grant Clamorgan's request despite strong protests from the St. Louis merchants. Clamorgan reorganized the company's operations, but a series of unexpected reverses soon brought the promoter to the brink of financial ruin. Temporarily saved from a total collapse by the efforts of prominent St. Louis businessmen who feared the possible effects of his bankruptcy upon the business community, Clamorgan never fully recovered his losses. By the end of the century his competitors began to secure concessions to the trade rights he formerly had monopolized, but the British grip on the trade in those regions was now stronger than ever.

Governor Carondelet's continuing campaign to fortify Spanish possessions in the New World against British and American incursions encountered an unexpected obstacle. A sudden shift in Spanish policy caused the Governor's superiors to overrule his renewed attempts to promote the separation of the western provinces from the United States and to use Indians against American settlers. Manuel de Godoy, Spain's minister of foreign affairs and a special favorite of the Queen, initiated a drive to secure accommodation with the United States. Godoy had decided to seek an end to the current conflict with France, whose armies already had overrun northern Spain. In taking that step, Spain deserted its recent alliance with Great Britain, and the Spanish foreign minister feared that in retaliation the British might attempt to secure United States cooperation for a joint assault against Florida, Louisiana, and other Spanish possessions. Hoping to forestall any such Anglo-American *rapprochement*, the Spanish offered to settle all outstanding differences with the United States on the most generous terms possible. In the subsequent Treaty of San Lorenzo, negotiated in 1795, Spain granted the United States free navigation on the Mississippi and the right of deposit at New Orleans.[4] Moreover, she agreed to accept American demands for the thirty-first parallel as the southern boundary of the United States.

The provisions of the treaty dismayed Governor Carondelet, because they cancelled the effect of his arduous efforts to check American encroachment along the Mississippi. Believing his policies offered the best hope for safeguarding Spanish interests,

4. The Treaty of San Lorenzo is commonly referred to as Pinckney's treaty.

he considered the agreement a serious mistake. Nevertheless, in accordance with his instructions, he proceeded to implement the treaty as rapidly as possible.

As a result of the peace treaty with France and the Treaty of San Lorenzo with the United States, Spain found itself once again at war with Great Britain. The renewed danger of a British invasion from Canada caused Governor Carondelet to shift his attention to the defense of Upper Louisiana. Carondelet's apprehension had been increased by reports that during the recent visit to St. Louis by French Gen. Victor Collot, many of the residents had openly called for the return of Louisiana to France. The Governor believed that the combined threat of a British attack and a possible local uprising required a decisive Spanish response. Consequently he ordered a force of more than 100 Spanish regulars to accompany Lt. Col. Don Carlos Howard to St. Louis. Carondelet had selected Howard to assume personal control of all military operations in Upper Louisiana. Howard's instructions called for the deportation to New Orleans of any suspected French agitators, the destruction of any British establishments along the Missouri and Mississippi rivers, the organization of nine militia companies in Upper Louisiana, and the strengthening of the fortifications at St. Louis.

The arrival of Howard's sizable expeditionary force in St. Louis in 1796 must have awed the residents of that village. He soon concluded that the rumors of local insurrection had been greatly exaggerated and that the greatest danger to the settlement came from the British in Canada. To augment the dilapidated fortifications of St. Louis, Howard supervised the construction of four stone towers and a wooden blockhouse. During the summer of 1797, with the help of a band of Sac and Fox warriors, he also led an unsuccessful raid against the British establishment at Prairie du Chien.

In addition to the military preparations under Howard's direction, Governor Carondelet revived attempts to promote immigration from the United States because he believed the American settlers would aid in defending Louisiana against the British. In 1796 and 1797 the Spanish commandants in Upper Louisiana circulated handbills outlining the advantages of settling in Spanish territory and offering liberal land grants to those willing to make the move. Prior to this time the vast majority of immigrants who came into Upper Louisiana had been Frenchmen from Canada and the settlements east of the Mississippi, but after 1796 almost all of the newcomers were American.

A combination of factors produced the sudden American influx beginning in the fall of 1796, but the promise of free lands and no taxes at a time when many of the choicest lands in the United States had been occupied provided the most powerful inducement. The flow became so heavy that concerned Spanish authorities in Louisiana attempted to turn back the tide in 1799. Their efforts proved futile. By 1804, when the United States formally took control of Upper Louisiana, more than three-fifths of its inhabitants were Americans.

For some time officials had recognized that, despite all of their efforts, Spain's grip on Louisiana had weakened steadily. The original Spanish eagerness to secure Louisiana and transform it into a protective barrier for Spain's other New World possessions gradually had been dissipated by repeated failures and the growing expenses of maintaining the vast territory. Consequently, by 1795 the Spanish government had reached the conclusion that further attempts to develop Louisiana into a buffer against Anglo-American penetration would be a waste of money and effort. For this reason Godoy had been willing to make the extensive concessions to the United States in the Treaty of San Lorenzo.

From that time on Spain sought to utilize Louisiana primarily as a tool in diplomatic negotiations. Although the French had shown little interest in their former province during the quarter century immediately following its cession to Spain, the French Revolution had rekindled interest in expanding France's overseas territories, and a growing number of Frenchmen began to call for the return of Louisiana to France. During the 1790's the two nations discussed the possible retrocession of the territory on numerous occasions, but no final agreement had been reached. The Spanish were prepared to surrender the colony, but they were determined to await the most opportune moment to unload it to ensure receiving a good price for it.

The right time did not arrive until after Napoleon had come to power in France. Following his defeat at the hands of the

British in Egypt in 1798, Napoleon turned his attention to the creation of a French Empire in the New World. With this in mind he instructed Foreign Minister Talleyrand to attempt to secure the return of Louisiana. Aware of the Spanish royal family's concern because the Duke of Parma, the husband of a Spanish princess, had no position, the French offered to expand the Italian province of Tuscany into the Kingdom of Etruria and give it to the Duke and his wife in return for the retrocession of Louisiana. The Spanish refused to include Florida in the transfer, but otherwise they accepted the terms outlined by the French. They incorporated the preliminary agreement into the Treaty of San Ildefonso signed on October 1, 1800.

The treaty pleased both nations. With Louisiana now in his possession, Napoleon could proceed with his plans to build an empire in the New World. On the other hand, Spain believed she had rid herself of an increasingly costly burden and at the same time remedied an embarrassing situation within the royal family. Spain did not formally surrender the province for nearly four years. During that time the unexpected course of events drastically altered the situation in Louisiana, but after 1800 the end of Spanish rule in Louisiana was clearly in sight.

CHAPTER III

A FRENCH COLONY
UNDER SPANISH RULE

ALTHOUGH the Spanish ruled for almost four decades, they did little to shape life in Upper Louisiana. Of the small number of Spaniards who ever resided in the territory, most came to occupy key civil and military posts, and they normally departed following the expiration of their term in office; the few who settled in the province were quickly absorbed by the predominant French elements. Consequently, Upper Louisiana remained thoroughly French until its transfer to the United States in 1804.

When the Spanish assumed control of the region in 1770, scarcely more than 1,000 inhabitants lived in the entire area, and many of them had only recently arrived. Almost all of the white residents were Frenchmen who had come from settlements in Illinois, Indiana, Lower Louisiana, and Canada. The majority had crossed the Mississippi to escape English rule after the transfer of the territory east of the river to Great Britain at the close of the Great War for the Empire.

During the ensuing Spanish years the province experienced a gradual increase in population. Frenchmen from adjacent areas continued to make up the bulk of the newcomers until the late 1790's, when a substantial number of Americans began to enter the territory. In contrast to their French counterparts who preferred to reside in villages, the Americans usually located on isolated farms. Therefore, even though they constituted a majority of the population near the end of the Spanish period, the widely-dispersed Americans exerted relatively little influence over provincial affairs.

Upper Louisiana also had a significant number of Negroes in its population. Because of the shortage of labor many early French residents had imported Negro slaves into the territory. Renault brought black workers with him in 1720 to help operate his mines. After they assumed control, Spanish authorities had authorized the importation of additional Negroes into the territory in an attempt to promote the cultivation of certain needed crops. Moreover, following the passage of the Northwest Ordinance of 1787 by the United States Congress, some American slaveowners moved to Upper Louisiana in order to avoid the prohibition against servitude in the Northwest Territory. Blacks cultivated crops in the fields, labored in the lead mines, acted as domestic servants, and performed numerous other chores for their white masters in Upper Louisiana.

Both French and Spanish authorities enacted black codes to regulate the conduct of slaves. These codes contained provisions making it illegal for slaves to leave their owner's property without passes, to carry arms, to riot, to assemble unlawfully, to strike their masters, to plot conspiracy, to resist arrest, to engage in trade, or to own property. The type of regulations contained in the codes offers abundant testimony that blacks did not tacitly accept their inferior status, and that even these rigid regulations failed to completely subdue the Negro slave. In 1781, Lt. Gov. Francisco Cruzat expressed concern about the unruly conduct of the slaves in St. Louis, and he called for the strict enforcement of all statutes designed to control their actions.

Not all blacks in Upper Louisiana, however, were slaves. The sketchy records indicate that there was always a small number of free Negroes in Upper Louisiana during the colonial period. Many of these people had been freed by their masters as a reward for loyal service, but some managed to accumulate enough money to purchase freedom for themselves. Others were mulatto children whose white parent could not bear to see his or her own offspring enslaved. Little is known about the activities of the free blacks in this early period, except that some did receive land grants that they were then allowed to sell. Even free Negroes, however, were restricted in their movements, especially in their contacts with slaves because officials feared their presence might encourage defiance among those still enslaved.

In addition to their Negro slaves, the inhabitants of Upper Louisiana also utilized Indian slaves. Like their black counterparts, Indian slaves performed a variety of services for their masters, but most apparently served as domestics. Often the enslaved Indians had been captured during intertribal wars and then sold by their enemies to the white traders for liquor and other merchandise. Occasionally the demand for Indian slaves caused the traders to encourage warfare among the tribes in order to increase the supply. Both French and Spanish officials struggled to eliminate Indian enslavement because of the serious problems it created for them in maintaining harmonious relations with the Indians. But, despite Spanish orders that all Indian slaves be freed, Indian servitude did not completely disappear until near the end of the Spanish period.

Upper Louisiana's growing population spawned a series of new settlements, most of which sprang up along the banks of the Mississippi. Initially each consisted of only a handful of hardy souls attempting to carve a foothold in the surrounding wilderness. Some never advanced beyond that stage, but others joined St. Louis and Ste. Genevieve as thriving frontier villages and eventually became important commercial and political centers in early Missouri. For the purpose of administering these widely-scattered settlements, the Spanish divided the region into five districts—St. Louis, St. Charles, Ste. Genevieve, Cape Girardeau, and New Madrid. Each district soon embraced a growing number of settled areas.

Several small settlements grew up in the district of St. Louis in addition to the district's principal village, which also served as Upper Louisiana's capital. Two of the most important were Carondelet, established by Clement Delor de Treget near the mouth of the River des Pères in 1767, and Florissant or St. Ferdinand, located north of St. Louis and founded in about 1787. By the time the United States acquired Louisiana the latter village had become the second largest town in the district with more than sixty houses. These villages were French, but, by the end of the eighteenth century, many Americans had settled in the outlying areas of the district. This basic pattern of settlement prevailed in the other Spanish districts as well.

In the adjoining district of St. Charles, Louis Blanchette, a Canadian trader, moved up the Missouri in 1769 and established the settlement of St. Charles, originally known as Les Petites Cotes—the little hills. The village, comprised mostly of hunters and traders, remained the westernmost settlement of any significance for many years. Concerned by reports of American plans to establish a post across from the mouth of the Missouri, Lt. Gov.

Zenon Trudeau encouraged François Saucier to found a settlement in 1799 in the nearby region between the Missouri and the
Mississippi rivers at Portage des Sioux. The village drew most of
its inhabitants from the French establishments on the east side
of the Mississippi and became the St. Charles district's second
most important settlement.

In the oldest and most populous of the districts, Ste. Genevieve,
the village of Ste. Genevieve continued to be the dominant
settlement after its relocation in 1785, although other smaller
settlements also had developed in that mining district. Two of
the most important were Mine à Breton and New Bourbon.
Mine à Breton grew up adjacent to the rich lead mine of that
name that had been discovered in about 1775, while, in 1793,
settlers occupied the area two and one half miles below Ste.
Genevieve known as New Bourbon.

Two Canadian traders, François and Joseph Le Sieur, dispatched by Gabriel Cerré, a prominent St. Louis merchant, established a trading post on the bend in the Mississippi near the
mouth of the Ohio in 1783, marking the beginning of settlement
in the district of New Madrid. Known as L'Anse à la Graisse,
or the cove of grease, the area took its name from the abundance
of buffalo and bear meat available in the region. This was the
site Col. George Morgan subsequently selected for the seat of
his proposed settlement of New Madrid. Although his plans
failed to materialize, many settlers did take up occupancy there
in subsequent years and the name chosen by Morgan remained
as a reminder of his efforts.

Cape Girardeau's origins were slightly different. Louis Lori-
mier had arrived in the territory with a party of Shawnee and
Delaware Indians whom the Spanish had invited to take up
residence on the western bank in 1778. A French trader who
had supported the British during the American Revolution,
Lorimier had been driven from his trading post in Ohio by the
Americans. After coming to the territory, Lorimier and the
Indians had temporarily taken up residence in the vicinity of
New Madrid. In 1793, Governor Carondelet authorized him
to establish a permanent settlement in any of the vacant lands
along the western bank of the Mississippi from which he could
supervise the activities of the Shawnee and Delaware. He se-

lected Cape Girardeau for his headquarters and, in 1795, Spanish officials approved a grant of land for Lorimier at that location.

At about the same time, a steady stream of Americans began to pour into the adjacent area. Andrew Ramsay, who came to Cape Girardeau from Kentucky in 1795, persuaded some of his fellow countrymen to join him there, and a group of Germans also settled in the district. Few Frenchmen located in Cape Girardeau, and it consequently became the most Americanized of the original Spanish districts. Because of the American practice of occupying widely-separated areas, only scattered small settlements existed in the district and no sizable town or village developed until after the United States took control of the territory. At that time Lorimier donated land and money for the construction of a suitable seat for the district government at Cape Girardeau.

Upper Louisiana's population increased tenfold during the Spanish years, but the territory remained a remote, sparsely-populated frontier region. In 1804 when Spain transferred control to the United States, the entire province had an estimated population of only 10,350, 15 per cent of which was slave. Most of the inhabitants were clustered along the banks of the Mississippi, and except for Indian traders only a small number had ventured more than a few miles into the interior.

Aside from a few poorly marked trails requiring an experienced frontier traveler to follow them, roads were virtually nonexistent in Upper Louisiana during the Spanish period. Because of the hardships of overland excursions, residents traveled by water whenever possible, with the Mississippi River providing the most direct access to Upper Louisiana's remote villages. Despite their isolated locations and difficulties of frontier travel, these tiny communities maintained regular contact with one another and with the outside world. The boats that routinely arrived and departed from the principal settlements brought the latest news along with their usual cargoes.

River transportation, although it was the most desirable means to travel, was not without its hazards. Swollen streams, rampaging waters, floating debris, and underwater obstructions often interrupted a voyage, and boats occasionally capsized or sank, causing heavy property losses and an occasional loss of life.

During the winter, frozen streams and ice jams temporarily closed the waterways to traffic.

Upper Louisiana's residents employed boats of various kinds and descriptions. The pirogue, made from a hollowed out log and shaped like a canoe, was commonly used to carry smaller loads. Larger cargoes had to be transported in the bateau, a flat-bottomed boat with an enclosed area covered by a roof in the rear section. The trip downstream with one of these vessels was relatively easy, but the task of rowing a loaded bateau upstream against the current was arduous. It took Governor de Leyba ninety-three days to make the trip from New Orleans to St. Louis in one of these boats in 1778.

The keelboat gradually replaced the bateau as the vessel most commonly used to transport large cargoes up the rivers. This covered freight boat with a keel could be propelled upstream in a variety of fashions. Sometimes it was poled along the shallow waters close to the shore, but when deep waters or soft bottoms made this impossible, the boat was literally pulled up the river by men walking along the bank tugging at the cordelle, a piece of rope attached to the mast. If neither of these methods proved feasible, then the boat had to be rowed. Only occasionally did favorable winds make it possible to hoist the square-rigged sail located on the center mast to relieve temporarily the struggling boatmen. In this backbreaking fashion the rugged boatmen painfully moved the sturdy keelboats laden with merchandise upstream to their destination at a rate of between ten and fifteen miles a day. The trip downstream took considerably less time, with a voyage from St. Louis to New Orleans requiring between twenty-five and thirty days.

In addition to the keelboats that regularly made the trip, Upper Louisianians often constructed flatboats to carry their heavy cargoes down the Mississippi. When they reached their destination, they dismantled the boats and sold the lumber.

For the most part life in Upper Louisiana tended to be easy-going and uncomplicated. The inhabitants carried out their activities at a leisurely pace, which seemed particularly suited to the sleepy French villages where most of them resided. The activity and restless energy so characteristic of the American frontier were conspicuously absent from this tranquil setting.

The French village differed markedly from the American town in many ways. In lieu of shops, stores, and inns built along carefully planned streets, the French constructed their residences, which also doubled as places of business, along narrow dusty lanes that turned to mud whenever it rained. The dwellings did not adjoin one another; instead, each was surrounded by gardens, orchards, barns, stables, and other outbuildings, all enclosed by a stockade fence made of cedar pickets or in the case of a more lavish residence by a high stone wall.

Although there were likely to be a few stone houses scattered throughout the village, the great majority of residences were built of logs. In contrast with the American practice of placing logs horizontally in construction, the French erected their logs in an upright position, plastered over the cracks with mortar, and whitewashed the exterior. The two most distinctive characteristics of the French buildings were their steep hip roofs and their porches or galleries. Originally designed to shed water from thatched roofs, the distinctive roof style was retained by the French long after the use of shingles had canceled the need for the sharp angle of incline. Except for the simplest dwelling, the residences generally had a porch on one, two, three, or all sides depending upon the affluence of the owner. These galleries performed dual functions: they kept the rain off the plaster, preventing dampness, and they shaded the structure in the summer, keeping it considerably cooler. Glass was generally used in the casement windows, which swung in and out on hinges in contrast with the vertical sliding windows preferred by Americans. One or two chimneys built of "cat and clay," a paste made of mud mixed with cut straw, serviced the fireplaces that provided the heating and cooking facilities.

The houses varied considerably in size and in elegance. The less prosperous habitants and *voyageurs* lived in one-room dwellings with dirt floors, while some of the wealthier merchants resided in multiroom mansions with highly polished walnut floors. In most houses the interior walls were plastered and whitewashed. The size of the smaller dwellings limited the interior furnishings to a few items probably produced locally, including a bedstead, bedding, a table, chairs, a cupboard for utensils, and a chest for clothing. In contrast, some of the more elaborate homes contained handsome mahogany and cherry armoires and cabinets, mirrors imported from France, lavishly carved tables often set with costly china and sterling silver, and a variety of other fine pieces of furniture.

As he passed by these dwellings, a person traveling along the village streets frequently had to sidestep an abandoned plow or cart that its owner had carelessly left along the narrow passageway. Likewise, cattle, horses, sheep, and other livestock wandered aimlessly through the village generally unnoticed by the local residents. An occasional band of Indians seeking to confer with officials, or a party of returning traders, might create a temporary stir of excitement, but the normal calm quickly returned.

On the outskirts of the village the habitants worked sporadically in the common fields maintained for their use, with each resident receiving a strip to cultivate.[1] Those wealthy enough to afford slaves secured larger tracts, which they worked with the assistance of their bondsmen. The townspeople usually made some attempt to construct a fence around the common field to ward off stray animals and other possible marauders. The village also maintained woodlands and grazing areas for common use.

The inhabitants of these placid villages were a pleasant, cheerful, and hospitable people. Since there were no regular accommodations for visitors, residents graciously opened their doors to strangers. Class lines were only loosely drawn; while the wealthier, more prominent citizens played a dominant role in directing local affairs, they mingled freely with the poorer members of the village to whom they were related closely by ties of affinity and consanguinity. Fun-loving and congenial, the French enjoyed numerous types of amusement and recreation. The men often passed their time with a game of cards or billiards, or took in a horse race. Fond of gambling, Frenchmen often wagered sizable sums of money on the races as well as other favorite games of chance. The women engaged in the usual small talk and looked forward to the dances normally held on Sunday afternoons following mass. Sunday was a day for worship and

1. Although residents of Upper Louisiana could secure separate land grants from officials, most Frenchmen preferred to cultivate tracts in the communal fields.

gaiety, with holidays and special days on the church calendar providing additional opportunities for celebrations and festivities that featured music and dancing. Everyone from old to young, rich and poor, attended the elegant balls frequently held in most villages.

For the French in Upper Louisiana, religion and social life were closely connected. From the time of the first settlements the Catholic Church had been an important force in the life of the community. During the early years the Jesuits directed most of the missionary and religious activity in the area, but, shortly before France ceded the province to Spain, French authorities, fearful of the growing power and wealth of the order, expelled members of the Society of Jesus from Louisiana and confiscated their property. Inasmuch as the Spanish crown also took steps to remove the Jesuits from their possessions, the Capuchins with their brown habits soon replaced the "Black Robes" as the dominant religious order in Upper Louisiana.

The transfer of the territory from French to Spanish control also brought about a change in ecclesiastical jurisdiction. Responsibility for directing the spiritual affairs of the Upper Mississippi Valley passed from the Bishopric of Quebec to the Bishopric of Cuba. The changeover imposed some temporary hardships upon residents in the area when Spanish clerical authorities prohibited some French priests under Canadian control from conducting services in Spanish territory. Because of the chronic shortage of priests in the remote province during the early years, even the largest settlements in the province often lacked a resident clergyman and had to rely on the services of the ecclesiastics residing in nearby Illinois settlements, who periodically crossed the Mississippi to perform baptisms and marriages, to conduct funerals, and to visit the sick.

In the absence of a regular priest, laymen sometimes presided at prayer meetings, weddings, and funerals, but since only a priest could celebrate a mass, the use of lay personnel provided only a partial solution to the problem. Spanish authorities sought to improve the situation by importing Irish priests, educated in Spanish seminaries, to serve in Upper Louisiana. With Ireland ruled by Protestant England, many young Irishmen went to Spain to secure a Catholic education. Because they spoke English, Spanish officials believed they would be effective in dealing with the growing number of Americans in the territory.

Both the French and the Spanish governments established the Catholic faith as the official state religion and granted financial assistance for its maintenence. The Spanish crown furnished land for churches and cemeteries, provided funds to construct the necessary parish buildings, and paid the salaries of the clerics. In addition to his salary from the Spanish treasury, the priest normally received a contribution of one twenty-sixth of the people's produce, along with the usual fees and gifts for interment, baptisms, and marriages. However, when Father François Hilaire attempted to collect a full tithe from his Ste. Genevieve parishioners in 1774, they lodged strong protests with Spanish officials who promptly ordered the curate to stop the practice.

Originally the Spanish permitted only Roman Catholics to settle in Upper Louisiana, but in an effort to attract more settlers they agreed in 1787 to admit American Protestants and to grant them limited religious toleration. In taking this step, the Spanish government did so with the expectation that these new immigrants would be transformed into loyal Spanish subjects and converted to the King's faith within a generation. Consequently all non-Catholic services were prohibited, and only Catholic clergymen could conduct marriages and baptisms, but, in actual practice, the Spanish seldom enforced these restrictions rigidly. Officials in Upper Louisiana interpreted the laws so broadly that any Christian could be declared a Catholic for legal purposes, and commandants married non-Catholics in civil ceremonies. Moreover, itinerant Protestant ministers occasionally conducted religious services for Americans in Spanish Louisiana, and, as long as they were private, local authorities usually made no attempt to interfere. Most individual residents of the territory probably adopted a philosophy of live and let live as far as religious beliefs were concerned. Even in the French villages, all of which remained predominantly Catholic, there was a tendency to leave religious matters to the priest.

The libraries of some of the wealthy citizens contained volumes by the French philosophes and other freethinkers whose works had been condemned by the Church. Moreover, priests and Spanish officials complained of the lax moral standards of the inhabitants of Upper Louisiana. Nevertheless, the province contained many devout Catholics who regularly attended mass whenever it was celebrated, participated in the religious processionals the clergy conducted on special occasions, and prominently displayed crucifixes over the gateways to their residences as a symbol of their faith; but even these individuals did not display the kind of intolerant zeal that produced religious conflict and strife in other communities.

Limited educational opportunities in Upper Louisiana during the Spanish period placed even the most rudimentary education beyond the reach of the average child in the province. Although an occasional priest conducted classes for parish children, the few schools that existed were private. Jean Baptiste Trudeau, an active participant in the fur trade, operated a small school in St. Louis intermittently between 1774 and 1827. With encouragement from Governor Carondelet, Madame Maria Josepha Pinconneau *dit* Rigauche opened a school for girls in the same village in 1797. While Madame Rigauche failed to receive the monthly stipend promised her by the governor, she did secure a land grant in 1800.

Ste. Genevieve also had a primary school during most of the Spanish period. The prominent Peyroux family maintained an active interest in education in that community. One member, Madame Marguerite Peyroux de la Coudreniere, willed her home to the district in 1791 to be used as an orphanage and school, and in 1795 her son bequeathed land and books to the school. Augustine Charles Fremon de Lauriere, a royalist who left France after the revolution, opened a unique school in Ste. Genevieve in 1796. Stressing practical education, the school promised to offer courses designed to prepare students to earn a living and to teach them proper conduct. Even though the venture lasted only two years, Fremon's approach to education placed him many years ahead of his American contemporaries in both teaching techniques and curriculum.

In New Madrid, Col. George Morgan had included a proposal for the operation of English schools supported jointly by local families and the government in his master plan for the colony, but nothing came of it following Morgan's abandonment of the colonization project. In 1796 a local New Madrid priest asked the government to build and help support a school in the district, but there is no evidence that the authorities ever acted on the proposal. There were, however, private schools operating in New Madrid in 1793 and in 1802. The first-known English school in the territory opened in about 1799 at the Ramsay settlement near Cape Girardeau. Known as the Mount Tabor school, it offered instruction to only a small percentage of the growing number of Americans who had moved into that district.

Because of the limited educational opportunities in Upper Louisiana, many of the more prominent families sent their children outside of the territory to obtain suitable schooling. Wealthy St. Louis merchant Auguste Chouteau sent his son to Canada, as did his fellow townsman Bernard Pratte; two of Charles Gratiot's sons attended a Catholic college in Bardstown, Kentucky. The expense of sending children away for an education, however, confined this practice to only the wealthiest families. Although the lack of local educational facilities greatly concerned men like Chouteau, the average resident probably remained too preoccupied with the more immediate needs of frontier living to give much attention to the problem.

Even with Upper Louisiana's failure to develop a comprehensive educational system, the territory could scarcely be considered a wasteland of intellectual activity. A number of well-educated individuals in most of the larger communities kept abreast of the latest international literary, scientific, and philosophical currents. Their extensive private libraries provided the most eloquent testimony to the breadth of their wide-ranging interests. A few residents in Ste. Genevieve, New Bourbon, and New Madrid had substantial collections of books, but those in St. Louis had the largest holdings. By the time of the transfer of the province to the United States in 1804, the private libraries in that village contained between 2,000 and 3,000 different titles on a wide variety of topics including political theory, history, philosophy, theology, science, literature, drama, economics, law, travel, and geography.

There were numerous well-read individuals in the territory, but conditions there did not encourage any serious local literary activity. Aside from a satiric poem criticizing Spanish officials after the attack on St. Louis in 1780, which tradition attributed to the local schoolmaster Jean Baptiste Trudeau, a few commercial and historical journals comprised Upper Louisiana's entire literary output during the Spanish period. However, without local printing facilities, many years elapsed before even those meager efforts appeared in print.

Since only the surface of the region's tremendous potential resources had been tapped, economic conditions in the territory remained primitive. Sparsity of population, distance from markets, and a crude agriculture all contributed to the low state of development. Most of Upper Louisiana's settlers were habitants or farmers. The French labored in the common fields while the growing number of Americans cultivated their outlying acreage.

In the spring the inhabitants went into the fields with their hand tools, horse-drawn carts, and wooden plows hitched to a team of oxen to break ground and plant their crops. Those wealthy enough to afford slaves took them along to perform the backbreaking work. Once the crops were in, the French only occasionally attempted to cultivate or plow their fields, preferring instead to let nature take its course until harvest time. Even with such haphazard methods, the yields were surprisingly large. In contrast, the American newcomers generally tried to keep their fields free of weeds and to pay more attention to regular cultivation. As a result the American harvests yielded appreciably more than those of the French.

A wide variety of crops grew well in Upper Louisiana. Wheat, corn, cotton, flax, hemp, and tobacco were the most important staples, and residents cultivated oats, barley, beans, melons, pumpkins, and other vegetables for their own consumption. Their orchards and vineyards produced apples, peaches, plums, and grapes from which they made cider, brandy, and wine. Although they distilled whiskey from some of their grains, liquor remained a major import item. Because livestock could be maintained with a minimum of expense and effort by allowing the larger animals to graze in nearby woodlands and meadows where they fed upon grasses, nuts, roots, and berries, most farmers raised cattle, hogs, and sheep.

Agricultural production in Upper Louisiana increased steadily during the Spanish period despite the continued prevalence of primitive farming techniques. Most of the commodities went to supply the local population, but barges destined for New Orleans began to carry larger amounts of flour, grains, salted meats, and dairy products from the settlements along the Mississippi.[2]

Second only to agriculture in its over-all importance, the fur trade played a key role in the settlement and development of Upper Louisiana. St. Louis, after its founding in 1764, had become a center of the growing trade in the Missouri and Mississippi valleys. Operating within the framework of Spain's monopolistic system, a small number of influential traders grew rich from the exclusive rights they garnered for themselves. St. Louis's leading merchants engaged in the profitable business of outfitting the expeditions that regularly set out to trade with the Indians. Despite the decreasing profits caused by the growing competition for the trade—especially from British traders—large quantities of furs from tribes along the lower Missouri annually poured into St. Louis warehouses. Although St. Louis merchants dominated the trade in Upper Louisiana, residents in other villages often exchanged goods with local Indians in return for furs and peltries. One estimate placed the average annual value of furs and peltries in Upper Louisiana during the last fifteen years of Spanish rule at $203,750.

Lead mining, also vital to the economy in Upper Louisiana, changed little until near the end of the Spanish period. Workers continued to dig the lead in shallow pits, seldom more than ten feet deep, and the crude smelting process they employed derived only about 35 per cent of the lead from the ore. Since the mines remained open only three to four months each year, the miners maintained their permanent residences in Ste. Genevieve and New Bourbon, rather than at the actual diggings. Operations continued at the sites along the Meramec worked by Renault and other French mining pioneers, but the accidental discovery of rich deposits northwest of Ste. Genevieve at Mine à Breton in 1773 shifted some of the activity to that region. Other smaller diggings were located in adjacent areas.

Shortly before Spain relinquished control of the province, Moses Austin arrived in Upper Louisiana from the United States to engage in the lead business. Austin, who previously had op-

2. Population growth, rather than improved techniques, accounted for most of the increased agricultural output.

erated lead mines in Virginia, came to the territory in 1797 to inspect its mineral deposits. Impressed by the quality of the ores there, he secured a grant from the Spanish authorities to an extensive tract of land at Mine à Breton. Within a short time Austin had revolutionized mining operations in the province. He sank the first mining shaft in the district and introduced a new type of furnace capable of removing 65 per cent of the lead from the raw ore; other miners soon began to bring their ores to his furnace for smelting. As a result of Austin's innovations, the output of lead in Upper Louisiana increased substantially. When the United States acquired Louisiana, Austin estimated that the annual value of the territory's lead exports exceeded $40,000.

A small number of residents engaged in saltmaking—the one other important contributor to the local economy. Most of the activity was concentrated along the Saline River below Ste. Genevieve. By boiling the waters from that stream in large kettles, they produced enough salt to supply the settlements on both sides of the Mississippi, along with a growing number of Kentucky's inhabitants. Although the district of Ste. Genevieve produced the major portion of Upper Louisiana's supply, a saltworks north of the Missouri located on the Salt River manufactured some additional salt until Indian hostilities forced its abandonment.

A few French merchants residing in the principal villages dominated economic activity in Upper Louisiana. They traded, bought, and sold any commodity they believed would earn them a profit. Consequently, these resourceful traders often dabbled in one or more of the major local enterprises—fur trading, farming, lead mining, or saltmaking. They maintained regular contacts in Canada, the United States, and New Orleans as well as with all of the settlements of the province. From these varied sources they imported all types of merchandise which they then offered for sale to local residents from their places of business located in their homes. The risks in these frontier ventures were often great, but so were the potential profits.

The shortage of specie, a common situation in undeveloped areas, frequently made economic transactions difficult, but it did not dissuade Upper Louisiana's energetic merchant-traders. Barter became a common form of exchange, and they routinely accepted payment in any of the commodities produced locally. Moreover, in an attempt to facilitate trade, Spanish authorities had approved the use of peltries as legal tender unless otherwise expressly stated in a contract or agreement.

In line with Upper Louisiana's elementary economic system, its government under the Spanish was equally uncomplicated. The simple political structure, which combined civil and military authority, adequately met the needs of the sparsely-settled region. The territory's highest resident official, the Lieutenant Governor, lived in St. Louis where he presided over important civil and criminal proceedings, supervised Indian affairs, licensed traders, directed public works, issued land concessions, authorized surveys, and commanded military operations. His immediate superior, the Governor General of Louisiana, established policy for the entire province at his headquarters in New Orleans, subject to instructions from the captain general in Havana.

In each of the larger villages Spanish officials appointed a commandant to oversee local matters. He served as judge in civil matters involving small amounts, commanded the district militia, issued permits to travel in the province, sought to maintain friendly relations with local Indians, recommended individuals for land grants, encouraged the development of the area under his jurisdiction, and kept his superiors informed on all local happenings. In the smaller and more remote settlements a syndic performed similar duties. Decisions made by these officials could be appealed to the Lieutenant Governor or to the Governor General, but they seldom were. The administration of justice was simple and direct; the right of trial by jury did not exist. There were no elections; all officials were appointed. However, despite its authoritarian framework, in actual practice the Spanish system functioned in a mildly liberal manner, and the vast majority of inhabitants showed no signs of dissatisfaction.

Unlike the United States, Spain offered free lands to attract bona fide settlers into Upper Louisiana, but, under Spanish law, the process for acquiring a completed title was so complicated that few residents went through the proper channels to establish a final title. To secure a concession, the settler submitted a petition to the local commandant asking for a grant of land. When the settler desired a particular tract, he described it in his petition; if he had not decided where to settle, as was often the case, he asked for a certain amount of land that he could locate subsequently in any vacant area. If the commandant approved the request, he endorsed the petition and sent it to the Lieutenant Governor, who issued a concession. Special concessions described the lands to be granted, while the general or floating concessions merely specified the amount of land conceded. After the delivery of the concession, the Lieutenant Governor then ordered a survey of the actual lands selected, although frequently these surveys were never completed. In fact, the Spanish government had not made any regular provision for surveying lands in Upper Louisiana until 1795 when it named Antoine Soulard as Surveyor General for the region. If and when the survey was made, the approved petition and order of survey, along with the completed report of the surveyor, had to be presented to the proper office at New Orleans for final confirmation of title. The distance from New Orleans, compounded by the hardships and expenses of frontier travel, made this final step prohibitive for the vast majority of Upper Louisiana's residents.

Because of the abundance of land and the smallness of the population, Spanish officials routinely granted concessions to those who requested them, and, during the waning days of the Spanish regime, they became increasingly generous in disposing of the lands. Before he left office in 1799, Lt. Gov. Zenon Trudeau reportedly signed a series of blank concessions that were distributed after his departure and filled in illegally by those who secured them. Trudeau's successor, Carlos Dehault Delassus, supposedly granted extensive concessions to members of his family and to his friends.

Moreover, officials made no effort to encourage settlers to secure full titles. Local commandants accepted the incompleted concessions as authorization to hold the lands and raised no questions when they were sold or inherited. The unexpected sale of Louisiana to the United States in 1803 drastically altered the situation, and the confused state of the land titles created a tremendous headache for American officials. In fact, the American acquisition of the territory brought many changes for the residents of the tranquil French settlements in Upper Louisiana.

CHAPTER IV

UPPER LOUISIANA COMES
UNDER AMERICAN CONTROL

THE FIRST unconfirmed reports of the secret transfer of Louisiana from Spain to France reached Washington in 1801. Surprised American officials realized that if the rumors were correct, the unexpected shift would create serious problems for the United States. A warning to the French minister of the grave possible consequences to Franco-American relations should France occupy New Orleans produced only a vague response. To obtain more precise information on the subject, President Jefferson dispatched Robert Livingston to France in the fall of 1801. The President instructed the new American minister to France to attempt to prevent the retrocession if at all possible. If it were too late for that, he directed Livingston to secure the cession of West Florida to the United States. When the French repeatedly evaded his persistent inquiries, the American minister decided the transfer probably had been concluded, and he communicated his suspicions to the Jefferson Administration.

Believing the French might soon take control of Louisiana, the United States intensified its behind-the-scenes diplomatic maneuvering early in 1802. The Americans quietly urged France to recognize America's rights to navigate the Mississippi and to deposit goods at New Orleans. Furthermore, Jefferson made it clear that if the French refused to acknowledge American rights, the United States might have to seek an alliance with Great Britain.

Interest in reviving the French Empire in the Western Hemisphere had prompted Napoleon Bonaparte to seek the retrocession of Louisiana. As a part of his master plan for the New World, the French leader sent a large force under the command of his brother-in-law, Gen. Victor Emmanuel Leclerc, to reestablish French authority and restore slavery in Saint Domingue in February, 1802. A bloody slave rebellion there in the 1790's had placed a former slave, Touissant L'Ouverture, in control of the island. Since pressing problems in Europe had prevented the French from attempting to depose the black leader immediately, they had commissioned him captain general of the island in an attempt to give an appearance of continuing French control. When Napoleon did dispatch troops to Saint Domingue in 1802, he set into operation the first step of his plan to return France to the New World—restoration of full French control on the island. Initially General Leclerc's forces appeared to gain the upper hand and Touissant voluntarily surrendered to the French general, only to be sent in chains to France where he died in prison the following year. Toussaint's imprisonment and death failed to end the rebellion. Yellow fever and the continued resistance of the former slaves slowly turned the tide against the French forces on the island.

While Napoleon's troops were sustaining heavy losses in the Caribbean, Spanish authorities made a dramatic move in Louisiana, which, despite the Treaty of San Ildefonso, they still controlled. In October the Spanish intendant at New Orleans announced the closing of the port of New Orleans to all foreigners. This action greatly aroused the western American frontiersmen who had been apprehensive since first learning of the retrocession. They demanded that immediate steps be taken by the United States to reopen the right of deposit on the banks of that vital artery. Although Spain had the right to close the port of New Orleans, she violated the Treaty of San Lorenzo by refusing to grant the United States an alternate site to unload American goods. Orders to close the port came from Spain, but Spanish authorities led American officials to believe that the intendant at New Orleans was solely responsible for the action. The exact reasons for Spain's decision to close the port remain in doubt, but her unhappiness with Americans who used the right of deposit as a means to smuggle goods into Spanish territory illegally may have been a major factor.

Having concluded that the action had been initiated by Spanish officials in New Orleans, the United States moved to resolve the problem through diplomatic channels. The President decided to send James Monroe as a minister plenipotentiary to negotiate with France and if necessary with Spain to find a solution to the situation. Monroe departed in March with instructions to attempt to purchase the island of New Orleans along with as much of the Floridas as possible. Despite Federalist attempts to capitalize politically on the difficult situation by urging the use of force to gain an outlet on the Gulf, the great majority of westerners, most of whom were staunch Republicans, supported Jefferson's approach to the problem.

Events soon vindicated the President's decision. On the day before Monroe arrived in Paris to join Livingston, France's Foreign Minister Talleyrand asked Livingston if the United States would be interested in purchasing all of Louisiana. Leclerc's death in Saint Domingue and France's futile attempts to regain control of that island had caused Napoleon to lose interest in colonial activity in the New World and turn his attention to other more promising spheres. The need for additional funds to help finance plans for the expected renewal of the contest with Great Britain must have been a factor in the First Consul's sudden decision to offer to sell the province to the United States. In taking the step, however, the astute French leader also realized that it would forestall the growing possibility of an Anglo-American *rapprochement*. Napoleon considered retaining America's friendship vital to France's national interest.

Although they had not been authorized to negotiate for the purchase of the entire province, Livingston and Monroe worked out an agreement to that effect with the French Minister of Finance, Francois Barbe-Marbois. Since they believed that if they failed to act quickly, the offer might be withdrawn, the American ministers had decided to go ahead without waiting for final authorization from their superiors in Washington. The terms of the agreement drawn up by the representatives of the two nations were incorporated in a treaty of cession, and the United States agreed to pay fifteen million dollars for the territory. The treaty also stipulated that for a period of fifteen years duties charged French and Spanish vessels in all ports of the ceded province would not exceed those paid by American ships. Finally Article III of the proposed treaty specified that Louisiana's residents were to enjoy all rights and privileges given to American citizens and were to be speedily incorporated within the United States. On May 2, 1803, officials observed the signing of the Treaty of Cession in formal ceremonies in Paris.

Word that Livingston and Monroe had arranged to purchase all of Louisiana first reached the United States in July, 1803. Most Americans enthusiastically received the unexpected news, but some hard-core Federalists objected to the purchase from the outset. Fearing that the addition of this vast territory to the United States would destroy the balance of the Union, New England's opponents of the Administration ominously predicted the dire consequences they believed would follow the transaction and openly challenged its legality.

Hoping to allay Federalist fears and to remove objections concerning the constitutionality of the purchase, Jefferson framed a lengthy and involved constitutional amendment designed to facilitate the acquisition of the new territory. The President already had expressed doubts concerning the constitutional legality of the recently completed transaction to his closest advisers. To overcome any possible legal obstacle Jefferson's suggested amendment opened with the simple and direct statement: "The Province of Louisiana is incorporated with the U. S. and made a part thereof."

In the remainder of the proposed amendment the President attempted to deal with the more practical problems arising from the acquisition of Louisiana. Following a provision intended to safeguard the rights of the region's Indian inhabitants, the President's proposal outlined a detailed plan for administering the newly-acquired territory. It called for the division of Louisiana along the thirty-first parallel, north latitude. For the more populous portion of Louisiana south of that line, later named the Territory of Orleans, Congress was authorized to erect promptly a territorial government that would guarantee for its inhabitants all rights possessed by other territorial citizens of the United States. Because Jefferson agreed that it would be preferable to postpone any immediate large-scale expansion of the Union, his amendment would have closed Upper Louisiana to further settlement by whites for the foreseeable future. To ensure this, Congress could not have disposed of any of the lands north of the thirty-first parallel until authorized to do so by a new constitutional amendment.

In order to open additional lands east of the Mississippi River to white settlement, a further provision would have permitted the exchange of the remaining Indian lands there for tracts in the closed portion of the Louisiana Territory. In addition, Congress was to be empowered to promote the relocation of Upper Louisiana's white inhabitants on the east side of the Mississippi by offering to exchange their lands on the west bank for comparable tracts in other parts of the United States.

By closing Upper Louisiana to any further immediate settlement, Jefferson hoped to ensure a more orderly and controlled settlement process. The relocation of the Indians living east of the Mississippi in lands situated on the western bank provided an opportunity to fill up the eastern side and to prevent a possible drain on the population already located in those areas. Only after those regions of the United States already opened to settlement had been fully occupied would it be necessary to consider expansion into the trans-Mississippi west. When that seemingly distant time arrived, Jefferson believed the government could then "lay off a range of states on the Western bank from the head to the mouth & so, range after range advanc[e] compactly as we multiply." To the President, a pre-eminent representative of the American Enlightenment, such a scheme seemed to be more practical and more efficient than the helter-skelter rush he feared would otherwise occur. Such views stood in stark contrast to those of the frontiersman with his eyes focused on the "Great Spec," and Jefferson's ordered plan encountered rugged opposition on the Louisiana frontier.

Jefferson's proposals actually failed to generate much enthusiasm from any quarter. His advisers gave them only a lukewarm reception; the Federalist opposition, sensing a potential political issue, was openly critical. When the President submitted his proposed amendment to the members of his Cabinet for their opinions, Secretary of the Treasury Albert Gallatin indicated that he considered it unnecessary. While he agreed with the ideas in the amendment, Robert Smith, Secretary of the Navy, warned the President against adding such detailed restrictions to the Constitution. Both he and Secretary of State Madison suggested briefer versions to Jefferson. Senator John Breckinridge of Kentucky, who also expressed sympathy for the plan, cautioned Jefferson that if the existing bona fide land grants in Upper Louisiana were extensive it would be virtually impossible to keep additional Americans from settling in the region. Even more skeptical was Massachusetts Federalist Senator Rufus King who advised a friend that despite the President's avowed intentions to keep the area closed, "Nothing but a cordon of troops will restrain our people from going over the River and settling themselves down upon the western bank."

Failure to secure general support for his proposed amendment, coupled with a growing fear that Napoleon might retract his offer to sell, forced Jefferson to revise his plans. While he remained uncertain concerning the constitutional authority for incorporating the territory into the Union, he conceded as a matter of practical necessity the need to proceed with the ratification of the transaction, confident that the people subsequently would approve the action. The President even wrote to some of his friends suggesting they not openly discuss the constitutional problems in order to avoid any possible adverse effects on the final success of the treaty. By the time the special session of Congress called by the President to consider the Louisiana question opened on October 17, 1803, Jefferson had abandoned the idea of pressing for his constitutional amendment. Instead he had determined to let members of Congress resolve the matter in whatever fashion they deemed best.

Fear that France might withdraw the offer to sell prompted the large Republican majority in the Senate to confirm the treaty speedily. Nevertheless, extended debate on the measures to implement the treaty followed in both houses, with New England furnishing the strongest opposition to the Administration's handling of the acquisition of Louisiana. Convinced that the potential states in the newly-acquired territory would further reduce their influence, the President's Federalist adversaries questioned his authority to make the commitment contained in Article III which provided that:

> The inhabitants of the ceded territory shall be incorporated in the Union of the United States, and admitted as soon as possible, according to the principles of the Federal constitution, to the enjoyment of all the rights, advantages, and immunities of citizens of the United States; and in the mean time they shall be maintained and protected in the free enjoyment of their liberty, property, and religion which they profess.

Although they conceded the right of the United States to acquire new territory, either by purchase or conquest, and to govern it as a dependent province, the Federalist critics contended that neither the President nor Congress could incorporate the inhabitants into the Union of the United States.

In seeking to combat all such allegations, Republican spokesmen contended that Article III did not make statehood mandatory. According to Virginia's Senator John Taylor, the congressional act incorporating the inhabitants into the Union as a territory would fulfill the requirements of the treaty. Although it may have served its purpose in countering the opposition in Congress, this interpretation did not correspond with the point of view held by many of Louisiana's most prominent citizens who never tired of quoting Article III in defense of their rights. Numerous petitions from the inhabitants of the territory, addressed to Congress in subsequent years, based their demands for increased rights upon the provisions of the Treaty of Cession.

While political consideration determined most of the debate, some members did genuinely fear the possible effects of the sudden addition of such a large area to the United States. Critics branded as impractical Jefferson's suggestion that the area be turned over to the Indians for the present. In claiming that the distance separating Louisiana from the national capital made its gradual alienation from the United States certain, Senator Samuel White of Delaware viewed the expected and inevitable flood of Americans into the province as a great curse. He predicted that Louisianians might even persuade certain parts of the United States on the east side of the Mississippi to join them in separation. Since they argued that Louisiana would not be settled for years to come, Administration supporters rejected such dire predictions. They preferred to stress the positive benefits to be gained from the purchase of Louisiana. Representative John Randolph of Virginia avowed that Louisiana provided the means to eliminate future Indian wars by permitting the removal of the Indians east of the Mississippi.

Although the debate over Louisiana continued, Congress lost no time in passing a bill authorizing the President to take possession of the new territory. The controversial measure empowered the Chief Executive to designate whatever officials he considered necessary to govern the territory and to protect the fundamental rights of territorial inhabitants. Many congressmen objected to granting the President such extensive authority over the territory, but they reluctantly had agreed to support the measure, amended to provide that it would remain in effect only until the end of the present term of Congress.

With the passage of this temporary presidential authorization, the Administration took immediate steps to complete the transfer of Louisiana to the United States and to establish a temporary government for the territory. President Jefferson appointed Mississippi's territorial governor, William C. C. Claiborne, and the commanding general of the United States, James A. Wilkinson, to supervise the formal transfer for the United States and to take charge of the new territory. In designating Wilkinson for the important post, the President knew nothing of the General's earlier intrigues with Spanish authorities in Louisiana.

As officials prepared to occupy the newly-acquired territory, an unexpected crisis developed. Despite the Treaty of San Ildefonso, Spain had never transferred Louisiana to French officials, and perhaps because of their unhappiness with France's sale of the province to the United States the Spanish hesitated to relinquish control of the province. Much to the relief of worried American officials Spain belatedly retroceded Louisiana to French representatives on November 30, 1803, and at ceremonies held in New Orleans on the following December 20, the territory officially came under American control.

Even though the exchange at New Orleans included the transfer of Upper Louisiana as well, the Administration planned a separate ceremony for St. Louis to mark the transaction in that region. The task of directing the activities in Upper Louisiana and governing it during the interim period went to Capt. Amos Stoddard. As acting commandant of Upper Louisiana, Stoddard received his instructions from General Wilkinson and Governor Claiborne. The new commandant, a captain of artillery in the United States Army at the time of his appointment, came to the new job with a varied background. A veteran of the American Revolution, he had practiced law for a number of years in Maine before returning to military service.

Stoddard arrived in St. Louis on February 24, 1804, at which time Spanish Lt. Gov. Carlos Dehault Delassus and a number of citizens of the territory greeted him. He immediately initiated preparations to assume control, but the tardiness in the arrival of his men caused by ice on the river and the unexpected illness of Delassus delayed the official ceremonies of transfer until March 9 and 10, 1804. At the ceremonies Stoddard represented both France and the United States; in order to eliminate the expense of sending a representative to the distant post, Pierre Clement de Laussat, French commissioner for the transfer of Louisiana, had designated Stoddard to act as agent for the French government. He authorized him to receive Upper Louisiana from the Spanish and instructed him to deliver the territory to the United States.

The formal termination of Spanish authority in Upper Louisiana came on March 9, 1804. In the presence of the small crowd gathered to observe the proceedings Delassus and Amos Stoddard, acting as France's agent, signed the formal documents at the Government House, followed by an exchange of flags and a volley of cannon fire. Capt. Meriwether Lewis, in St. Louis to complete arrangements for his upcoming expedition to the Pacific coast, witnessed the exchange for the United States. On the next day Stoddard assumed control of the government in the name of the United States and the Stars and Stripes officially flew over the territory for the first time. In the only other formal observance of the transfer in Upper Louisiana, Capt. Daniel Bissell took charge of the small Spanish post at New Madrid for the United States on March 18, 1804.

Louisiana's transfer to the United States raised many questions for the inhabitants of that territory. Undoubtedly most of the French and many of the Americans would have preferred to remain under the Spanish system with its simple and direct government and its immunity from taxation, but despite their misgivings the residents of Upper Louisiana displayed no outward signs of hostility toward the new government. ". . . I have not been able to discover any aversion to the new order of things; on the contrary a cordial acquiescence seems to prevail among all ranks of people," Amos Stoddard reported to the Secretary of War on the day of the transfer. Since they could do little to alter the situation immediately, most of the territory's occupants adopted a wait-and-see attitude.

The United States government took all possible precautions to prevent any unfavorable reaction to American control. Officials instructed Stoddard to treat the inhabitants with politeness and cordiality and to see that their religious and property rights were protected. On the day he assumed control for the United States, Stoddard issued an address designed to reassure the local residents. Reminding them that the Treaty of Cession had pledged that they were to be incorporated into the Union and admitted as soon as possible to full rights and privileges of United States citizenship, the new commandant promised that they could expect fair and equitable treatment from their new government. On the subject of the greatest immediate interest to most inhabitants of the territory—the confirmation of land claims—Stoddard indicated that the American government would confirm their titles speedily.

Most of St. Louis's leading citizens did turn out for the lavish celebrations organized to mark the transfer of the territory to the United States. In accordance with the local custom, Delassus entertained the newly-arrived Stoddard and his party with a dinner and a ball. The American commandant felt obliged to repay the generous hospitality extended to him by the people of St. Louis by hosting a gala affair at his residence. Sparing no expense to ensure a successful evening, the commandant reported that the elaborate event had cost him $622.75.

Undoubtedly Meriwether Lewis and William Clark managed to take time out from their last-minute preparations to attend the local celebrations. President Jefferson had selected these two young men to explore and to gather as much information as possible about the vast unoccupied area stretching from the Mississippi to the Pacific. Although the President's original plans for the project predated the acquisition of the Louisiana Territory, the unexpected transfer of that region to the United States had enhanced the mission's importance. Since December, 1803, the two leaders had been assembling the necessary men and equipment at their camp located on the Wood River, a small stream opposite the mouth of the Missouri. During this period they visited St. Louis from time to time, and both quickly gained acceptance in that city's highest social circles.

When the final supplies had been loaded on the boats, the group broke camp on May 14, 1804, and under Clark's guidance they headed up the Missouri. After reaching St. Charles the expedition stopped to await the arrival of Lewis, who had remained in St. Louis to complete the final arrangements for the trip. Lewis arrived on May 20, along with Amos Stoddard, Auguste Chouteau, and various other prominent residents of the territory who had accompanied him on the trip from St. Louis. On the following day the crew of forty-five, including Clark's black slave York, began their historic journey amidst the rousing cheers of the well-wishers who had gathered along the bank to see them off.

Following their departure, Captain Stoddard returned to St. Louis to continue his administrative duties. The President had installed him as commandant of Upper Louisiana until Congress provided a permanent government for the newly-acquired province. In the meantime the basic structure of the Spanish governmental system was temporarily retained. The new American commandant assumed all functions, both civil and military, previously exercised by Spanish officials; but, in contrast with former Spanish practice, American officials directed him to keep civil and military functions carefully separated.

The United States government went to great lengths to maintain this division. Gov. William C. C. Claiborne issued Stoddard's instructions on civil matters, while Gen. James Wilkinson provided assistance on questions pertaining to military affairs.

When Captain Stoddard's military superior, Maj. James Bruff, arrived in St. Louis some time in the summer of 1804, Stoddard retained authority in civil matters, and Bruff assumed control of military activities. This arrangement continued in effect until October 1, 1804, when the territory came under the jurisdiction of the officials of the Indiana Territory.

Except for the strict admonition to keep civil and military functions apart, Stoddard enjoyed wide discretion in governing the territory. In most instances he reappointed the former commandants of the Spanish government to direct civil affairs in their particular districts. Governor Claiborne agreed with the wisdom of this practice, but warned Stoddard to watch the commandants' conduct to prevent any abuse of authority on their part. Although Stoddard retained the commandants to help smooth the transition, he complained to Claiborne that in reality these officers rendered him little actual assistance. Most cases still came to him for final decision on appeal from local officials. Stoddard's attempts to unravel the practices and procedures utilized by his predecessors proved to be an exasperating experience for the commandant. Because of the difficulty in determining proper jurisdiction in judicial proceedings, Governor Claiborne advised him to refer all doubtful cases to the courts soon to be established in Upper Louisiana by the new government Congress had authorized to become operative in October, 1804.

Spanish land claims posed by far the most serious problem for the interim administration; the cession of Louisiana had produced a wave of speculative activity within the territory. Confident that a new flood of immigrants would send land values in Upper Louisiana soaring, speculators had begun to accumulate as many private land claims as possible even before the United States had taken formal control of the region. They knew that in line with the experience of other American territories, the settlement of private claims would more than likely delay the sale of public lands for many years. Consequently land jobbers recognized the importance of the existing private claims, most of which they assumed the United States would quickly confirm.

Private claims in Upper Louisiana were extensive, blanketing the lands along the Mississippi from New Madrid to 150 miles above the mouth of the Missouri and stretching inland between 60 and 120 miles. Since private claims encompassed virtually all of the most desirable areas for settlement, newcomers found it necessary to purchase a concession or a permit to settle before they could take up residence in the territory.

Americans like Rufus Easton and John Rice Jones, who had come from the United States following the announcement of the cession, joined local residents including Jacques St. Vrain, Louis Labeaume, Charles Gratiot, Auguste and Pierre Chouteau, Jacques Clamorgan, and James Mackay in the race to acquire titles. The competition for the claims sent prices upward as the value of real property in Upper Louisiana appreciated rapidly.

The quest for lands also encouraged fraud. Taking advantage of the incomplete state of most land titles in Upper Louisiana, some individuals obtained, through influence or bribery, ante-dated petitions from Spanish officials confirming large land grants to them. The holders of these counterfeit titles believed the United States government would either be unable or unwilling to separate the bona fide from the fraudulent grants because neither had been registered and recorded in New Orleans, and records in Upper Louisiana were incomplete and unreliable.

Shortly after his arrival in Upper Louisiana, Stoddard had reported to his superiors in Washington that he suspected widespread attempts were being made to defraud the United States of extensive tracts of land. As Stoddard became more familiar with the complexity of the problem, he developed a more favorable attitude toward the claimants and their problems. He repeatedly indicated that he believed all bona fide land grants would be confirmed by the United States, but local residents, particularly those with extensive claims, remained apprehensive. As one of his first official acts Stoddard had ordered the inhabitants of the territory to surrender all public records, especially those related to land claims, to the American authorities for safekeeping. He promised that each claimant would be provided with an attested copy of original documents. In issuing these instructions Stoddard sought to ascertain the nature of the various land titles and to provide a safe deposit for all original papers relative to such claims, but his action disturbed claimants who objected to giving up the original copies. Their concern over the commandant's order was quickly overshadowed by reports warning of a far more menacing threat. Rumors reached the territory that the United States had decided to validate only those titles issued in accordance with Spanish regulations prior to October 1, 1800—the date of the Treaty of San Ildefonso. Under pressure from his constituents, Stoddard informed the Administration in Washington of the multiple problems facing bona fide claimants in establishing their titles, but the uneasy residents, up in arms over the latest statements attributed to high-ranking government officials, began organizing to protect their vital interests.

Other problems were competing for Stoddard's attention, with Indian affairs requiring a disproportionate share. Shortly after the transfer of Louisiana to the United States, hundreds of Indians descended upon St. Louis expecting to receive gifts from their new leader. Since both the French and Spanish had regularly purchased their friendship with presents, the Indians naturally looked for the continuation of this practice, thereby creating an added problem for the hard-working commandant.

Stoddard also had to face the dilemma, common to territorial officers, caused by the conflict of interest between the Indian and the frontier settler. In April, 1804, he issued a proclamation ordering the execution or seizure of a party of vagabond Indians who had recently killed several settlers, yet, at the same time, the fair-minded commandant noted that the Indians often had just grounds for complaint. As an example he cited a recent incident in which a white man had killed an Indian, apparently for no justifiable reason, but the grand jury had refused to return a bill of indictment in the case.

Of the tribes in the area, the Sac and Fox proved particularly troublesome for Captain Stoddard to handle. In the spring of 1804 a band of Sac warriors went to war against their long-time rivals the Osage in a dispute over hunting grounds. One of their raiding parties attacked a group of Osage on their way to St. Louis in a boat owned by a local fur company, and killed and captured a number of enemy tribesmen. Stoddard condemned the raid, and in a council held with the Sac and their allies the Fox, he demanded the immediate return of the Osage prisoners. They responded to Stoddard with a protest against the white seizure of their hunting grounds in the Louisiana Territory. Envious of what they believed to be the preferred treatment which the United States accorded to the Osage, the Sac and Fox representatives requested the establishment of an American trading factory for their use. To underscore their demands they also let it be known to the commandant that the British, with whom they were on good terms, had invited them to a meeting in Canada.

Relations with the Sac further deteriorated when a small group of young braves attacked a white settlement on the Cuivre River a few miles north of St. Louis. Believing the

Americans had recently granted gifts to the Osage because they feared them, the Sac warriors staged an assault in which they killed three settlers, under the assumption that it would strengthen their bargaining position with the United States. Fearing that a general war was about to begin, some settlers abandoned their homes in the area while others began making preparations to defend themselves against further Indian depredations. They appealed to Major Bruff for protection, and some even proposed that they attack nearby Sac villages in retaliation for the raid, but Bruff managed to dissuade them. Nevertheless, feelings against the Indians remained high as the nervous settlers maintained constant vigilance against any renewed hostilities.

Because of the constant dangers facing Upper Louisiana's isolated settlements, Captain Stoddard had undertaken the organization of a territorial militia early in his administration. Although the American militia system differed little from the one previously employed by the Spanish, the commandant experienced difficulty in obtaining an accurate count of the actual number of male citizens in the territory capable of bearing arms. Despite the problems, they organized companies of varying size in each of the major settlements.

A dispute over slavery also required the commandant's attention shortly before he left office. A growing restlessness among the territory's nearly 2,000 slaves prompted a St. Louis committee to petition Stoddard to enforce the black code, which under French and Spanish regimes had kept the slave population under control. The slaveowners blamed the current unrest on rumors being circulated by certain whites that the slaves in the territory were about to be freed. Although New Englander Stoddard personally found the institution distasteful, he agreed to establish whatever regulations the local slaveholders considered necessary to maintain order.

Stoddard's willingness to cooperate with local residents made him extremely popular in the territory. Although his administration lasted less than seven months, it had been an unqualified success. During this time, Stoddard had presided over the orderly transfer of authority from Spain to France, and then to the United States; had established an acceptable interim government; had successfully minimized discord within the territory;

and had persuaded, at least temporarily, most of the territory's inhabitants that they stood to benefit from the American acquisition of Louisiana. In fact, not until they learned of the terms of the act creating a government to replace Stoddard's rule did the local residents openly display widespread dissatisfaction with the newly-established American regime.

CHAPTER V

THE CREATION OF A GOVERNMENT
FOR UPPER LOUISIANA

THE TRANSITION to American control in Upper Louisiana had been peaceful and orderly, but some of the inhabitants grew increasingly restive as reports of the congressional debates began to filter back to the territory. Persistent rumors of plans to close the area to further settlement, to relocate eastern Indians in the region, and to confirm only those land titles that had been fully completed under the provisions of Spanish law prior to October 1, 1800, greatly alarmed local residents.

The Stoddard administration had been created to serve only until Congress could devise a permanent government for the region, but the President decided to recommend its continuation with only minor revisions. Since he still wanted to prevent any additional settlement in Upper Louisiana and to resettle tribes of eastern Indians in the unoccupied portions of the territory, Jefferson favored retaining a more authoritarian administrative system in that trans-frontier area.

The President discussed the situation with Senator John Breckinridge who had been assigned the task of preparing a bill creating a government for the Louisiana territory. Having detected a reluctance on the part of Breckinridge to draw up the measure, Jefferson sent him the outline of a bill that provided for the division of Louisiana into two territories and the organization of a government for each section. The Kentucky senator apparently concurred with the President's ideas on the subject. On December 30, 1803, he introduced Jefferson's measure in Congress—or at least a close facsimilie—but in accordance with the President's request he did not reveal the identity of the bill's author.

Section 8 of the Breckinridge Bill, as the measure was called, dealt specifically with Upper Louisiana and basically continued the current form of government. The bill simply transferred the executive and judicial power from the territory's temporary administrators to a governor appointed by the President. Local affairs remained under the direction of commandants appointed to govern each of the districts. The bill also authorized the President to negotiate the exchange of Indian lands east of the Mississippi for comparable tracts on the west bank.

The lengthy congressional debate that followed the introduction of the Breckinridge Bill disclosed that many legislators had serious reservations about its provisions. Members of Jefferson's own party characterized the government created by Section 8 as a form of military despotism. While they personally doubted the readiness of the territory's inhabitants to govern themselves, many congressmen hesitated to suspend the provisions of self-government even temporarily and much of their discussion focused on the difficult problem of how to keep Upper Louisiana closed to any further settlement without infringing upon the rights of persons already residing there.

To remedy the general dissatisfaction with provisions of the Breckinridge Bill, Senator James Jackson of Georgia suggested that Section 8 be deleted and that Upper Louisiana be annexed to the Indiana Territory for administration. Most of Jackson's colleagues agreed that his proposal had merit, but they feared that it might necessitate a drastic revision in Upper Louisiana's existing territorial laws. In order to avoid this possibility, without sacrificing the benefits to be derived from Jackson's measure, they suggested that the Senator modify his resolution to provide for the extension of the government of the Indiana Territory to Upper Louisiana rather than for the actual consolidation of the two territories. In this way both territories would be governed by the same officials, but each would retain its own separate system of laws. This alteration also permitted Congress to avoid an immediate decision on the status of slavery in Upper Louisiana, which would have been required had the laws of Indiana been extended to that region.

Accordingly, Senator Jackson withdrew his original motion, and Virginia's Senator Wilson Cary Nicholas offered a substitute amendment authorizing the officers of the Indiana Territory to govern the District of Upper Louisiana. Striking out Section 8 of the original bill, the Senate quickly approved the provisions of this compromise measure, which, according to Senator William Plumer, had been agreed upon in a meeting of the Republican senatorial caucus. The President did not object to the change, although it differed from his original proposal.

Debate in the House of Representatives on the Louisiana bill centered upon a problem not considered by the Senate in its original deliberations. In response to reports of widespread fraud and speculation in Louisiana land titles, Representative John Rhea of Tennessee had introduced a resolution calling for the enactment of a law nullifying all grants of land made by Spanish officials subsequent to October 1, 1800—the date of the Treaty of San Ildefonso by which Spain had retroceded Louisiana to France.

When Rhea moved to attach the provisions of his resolution to the Louisiana bill, then under consideration in the lower chamber, some members objected that the resolution might nullify legitimate grants. They contended that the settlement of land claims in Louisiana was a judicial rather than a legislative matter. However, most congressmen believed that decisive action was necessary to check the fraudulent grants, and the House quickly approved the inclusion of the resolution in the Louisiana measure.

Differences between the House and Senate versions of the Louisiana bill had to be ironed out in a conference committee which reported a bill dividing Louisiana into two territories: the Territory of Orleans—the area south of the thirty-third parallel—and the District of Louisiana—the remainder of the region. The District of Louisiana was to be governed by officials of the Indiana Territory. Indiana's territorial government followed the specifications established by the Northwest Ordinance for first-class territories. A governor, a secretary, and three superior court judges, all appointed by the President, administered the territory, with the governor and judges authorized to adopt all statutes necessary for governing the territory. However, in extending the legislative authority of Indiana's governor and judges to the District of Louisiana, Congress eliminated the restriction imposed upon all previous first-class territorial legislatures by the Northwest Ordinance, which had confined them to the adoption of statutes already enacted by one of the original states. The bill also authorized the President to divide the District of Louisiana into several subdistricts and to appoint a commandant to direct each of these. Subject only to the superintendence of the governor of the Indiana Territory, the commandants were primarily responsible for local government. They exercised both civil and military powers, and the new law specifically granted them command over both the regular troops and the militia in their particular districts.

Existing laws of the District of Louisiana were to be continued in effect until altered or repealed by the governor and judges of the Indiana Territory. The law nullified all land grants in Louisiana made after October 1, 1800, and sanctioned the use of force, if necessary, to remove any unauthorized persons from settling on the public lands of the United States. In addition, Congress empowered the President to enter into agreements providing for the resettlement in Upper Louisiana of Indian tribes living on the east side of the Mississippi River. Both houses agreed to accept the provisions outlined in the committee's report, and President Jefferson signed the bill into law on March 26, 1804. When news of the congressional debates on the Louisiana bill finally reached the territory, the unhappy local residents lost little time in publicly expressing their displeasure with certain particularly unpalatable features of the bill, but their protests came too late to prevent its final passage.

Louisianians strongly objected to being governed by officers of the Indiana Territory. The distance from Vincennes, the capital of Indiana Territory, to Louisiana made rapid communication both difficult and impractical, and this promised to create serious problems for the residents of Upper Louisiana. Actually, the prospect of absentee officials alarmed many of the territory's inhabitants far more than the failure of the new government to provide for any elective officers. Being unaccustomed to democratic institutions, Upper Louisiana's most influential citizens did not appear unduly eager to secure a representative government.

The new law also intensified the prevailing uncertainty over the status of slavery in the District of Louisiana. Although slavery was permitted in the Territory of Orleans, the act of Congress that provided for the government of Louisiana had avoided any mention of the subject with regard to Upper Louisiana. This omission, coupled with the assignment of officers from a territory in which slavery was prohibited by the Northwest Ordinance, explained the uneasiness of local slaveholders.

In view of the recent Indian hostilities in Upper Louisiana, the section of the Louisiana government act providing for the relocation of eastern Indians in Upper Louisiana did not add to the measure's popularity locally. Residents recognized that the adoption of this plan would increase the danger to themselves and further complicate the already difficult problems of frontier defense.

The restrictions placed upon the confirmation of land claims proved to be by far the most explosive issue and the one that generated the greatest amount of local discontent. The prospect of having large numbers of Spanish land titles rejected spread alarm and apprehension throughout the territory. Indeed, it would be difficult to exaggerate the importance of the Spanish land claims question, because this issue more than any other dominated politics throughout Missouri's territorial period.

As soon as they learned of the proposed restrictions, a select group met in St. Louis on April 2, 1804, to discuss the provisions of the Louisiana bill, which they considered contrary to the welfare of the territory and more particularly to their own personal interests. Word of the bill's final passage had not yet reached Upper Louisiana, and so the members decided to create a committee of five to inform the American government of the strong local opposition to the measure. Auguste Chouteau, Bernard Pratte, Charles Gratiot, Peter Provenchere, and Louis Labeaume, chosen by those present to serve on this committee, were then authorized to make arrangements for a general meeting of citizens from throughout the district of St. Louis to secure a broader endorsement for their proposals. In a further attempt to stimulate action and arouse interest they empowered the committee to take steps to promote common action with other sections of the territory.

The committee of five summoned residents of the district of St. Louis to meet on April 15, 1804. Those who responded to the committee's call gathered at Auguste Chouteau's home on the appointed date and, as their first order of business, elected their host to preside over the meeting. Chouteau informed those present of the actions taken at the previous meeting. This second assembly did little more than ratify the measures previously adopted by the smaller group and enlarge the original committee from five to seven members.

Although its exertions had come too late to prevent the passage of the Louisiana bill, this group did not abandon its efforts. After receiving word that the distasteful bill had become law, the seven-member committee immediately began to press for changes in the new law. They prepared a circular calling for a convention of representatives from all parts of the District of Louisiana to meet in St. Louis on September 1, 1804, to chart a course of action for the territory. The authors of the circular suggested that the delegates could meet with Gov. William Henry Harrison of Indiana, who was expected to visit the territory sometime after October 1, 1804. In attempting to assemble delegates from all sections of the territory, the St. Louis committee stressed that the proposed general meeting would provide a forum to acquaint the new Governor with their views and to protest the recent violation of the rights guaranteed to the inhabitants of the territory by the Treaty of Cession. Clearly they felt that the recent congressional action had not served their best interests.

The committee recommended that each district send deputies with full powers to represent its citizens, and that representation be apportioned according to population, with one representative for each 700 inhabitants. A list attached to the circular indicating the number of representatives allocated to each district, in accordance with the census of 1800, ensured the St. Louis group control of the assembly.

Some citizens of the territory did not respond favorably to the invitation. Meeting on September 2, 1804, in Ste. Genevieve, a committee of Americans residing there and at New Bourbon prepared a series of resolutions questioning the motivation behind the actions taken at St. Louis. They suggested that the proposed convention represented a carefully concealed attempt by a small group of influential men to extend their control over the territory. Instead of joining the St. Louis-dominated assembly, this particular group decided to appoint their own representative to consult with Governor Harrison.

Nevertheless, in spite of these charges, the land-claimant group pushed ahead with their plans, and twelve of the seventeen delegates called for from the various districts of Upper Louisiana finally met in St. Louis on September 14, 1804. They elected Charles Gratiot, a deputy from St. Louis, as presiding officer. In one of its first actions the assembly decided to have Amos Stoddard, still acting as civil commandant of Upper Louisiana, administer an oath to the officers and delegates of the convention. The oath, which pledged loyalty to the United States and adherence to its Constitution and laws, represented an obvious attempt to court the favor of American officials.

Following the administration of the oath, Gratiot sought to place a positive interpretation on recent developments when he attributed the passage of the unpopular congressional legislation to a lack of accurate information on conditions in the District of Louisiana. He advocated a concerted effort to counter the erroneous reports that had pictured Louisiana's inhabitants as a group of land-hungry schemers seeking to secure vacant lands. To ensure the most favorable possible reception for their proposals, Gratiot cautioned the members of the assembly to set a good example by showing respect for all laws of the territory, including the ones they were seeking to have repealed. In addition, he encouraged the deputies to extend a cordial and respectful greeting to Governor Harrison and his party when they arrived in the territory.

Not all of the delegates accepted Gratiot's moderate evaluation of the situation, but the disgruntled members of the convention advocating a more radical course of action failed to carry the day. The forces favoring moderation managed to retain control of the proceedings, and the convention defeated a motion by one of the delegates calling for assistance from France and Spain in case the United States failed to adhere to the guarantees contained in the Treaty of Cession. The group did agree to petition Congress to repeal the unpopular recent legislation, but they rejected a proposal submitted by residents of the Territory of Orleans which called for the unification of all of Louisiana. The citizens of Upper Louisiana preferred to remain separate from the Territory of Orleans.

Upon the advice of Amos Stoddard, the delegates decided against requesting a military government, though they most probably would have preferred one. Following a conversation with Pierre Chouteau, Albert Gallatin reported to Jefferson ". . . as to the Government of Upper Louisiana, he is decidedly in favour of a military one & appears much afraid of civil law and lawyers. . . ."

Even the petition to Congress asking for repeal of the law providing for the government of Louisiana had to be revised before the deputies would accept it. Moderate members, led by Auguste Chouteau, felt that the unusually strong language contained in the original draft of the petition might defeat its purpose, so they consulted with Stoddard, who suggested some revisions in the wording of the petition.

Nevertheless, even after the changes proposed by Stoddard had been made, the petition clearly evidenced the obvious discontent of its signers. It read in part:

> While we were indulging these fond expectations unmixed with distrust or fear, the act of the last session of your honorable Houses, entitled 'An act erecting Louisiana into two Territories, and providing for the temporary government thereof,' came to our knowledge, and snatched from our eager grasp the anticipated good. The dictates of a foreign government! and incalculable accession of savage hords [sic] to be vomited on our borders! an entire privation of some of the dearest rights enjoyed by freemen! These are the leading features of that political system which you have devised for us . . . .

Basing much of their appeal on the provisions of Article III of the Treaty of Cession, which had promised their speedy incorporation into full rights and privileges of citizenship, the petitioners called upon Congress to repeal the recent act creating a government for Louisiana; to take steps to provide for the permanent division of Louisiana; to grant Upper Louisiana its own governor and judges along with an elected legislative council; to provide the district with a delegate to Congress; to acknowledge the right to hold slaves and to import them into the territory; and to recognize all contracts engaged in, conformable to the laws of Spain, during the time that Spain ruled Louisiana. The latter provision sought to protect all Spanish land titles, including those granted after October 1, 1800. Members of the convention signed the final petition in St. Louis on September 29,

1804, and on the following day unanimously elected Eligius Fromentin and Auguste Chouteau to present the petition to Congress, in behalf of the inhabitants of Louisiana, and to represent their interests in the national capital.

At first glance one might be tempted to find in these early meetings the beginnings of representative government in the territory. In fact, shortly after arriving in Louisiana, William C. Carr, an early territorial lawyer and public official, offered this democratic interpretation to Senator Breckinridge. A closer evaluation of the proceedings, however, indicates that such was not the case. Rather than laboratories of frontier democracy, the meetings in St. Louis appear to have been agencies used by a small group of well-established citizens holding a substantial number of unconfirmed land titles, who sought to continue to exert influence upon the territory and to retain the favored position with territorial officials that they had enjoyed under previous administrations. Most important, they hoped to secure confirmation of all their land claims from the American government. The signers of the petition sent to Washington were almost entirely French or long-time American residents possessing extensive Spanish land claims in the territory.

Equally significant, these meetings revealed the existence of a deepening distrust between the old-time French and the newly-arrived American elements in the territory. The resolutions of the American-dominated committee of Ste. Genevieve and New Bourbon emphasized the need to take steps to eliminate the jealousy dividing the two groups. Unfortunately, this division increased in intensity under the succeeding Wilkinson administration, and only after the removal of Wilkinson as governor did the two groups reach an understanding that permitted a *rapprochement* between them.

Even while preparations were underway to secure changes in Upper Louisiana's new government, the Jefferson Administration took steps to put the recently-enacted law into effect. Only five days after signing the measure into law, Jefferson wrote to Governor Harrison of the Indiana Territory, informing him of the provisions of the new act and outlining for him the additional duties he would assume beginning October 1, 1804. Harrison, who had anticipated that he might be designated to govern

Upper Louisiana, already had begun to secure information concerning the territory.[1]

In his preparations Harrison may have been somewhat overzealous, because his instructions repeatedly cautioned him against initiating any unnecessary or abrupt changes in the District of Louisiana after the new government went into effect. Secretary of State Madison advised that the new law did not envision the adoption of an entirely new code of laws for Upper Louisiana as Harrison had proposed. Instead, Madison suggested that the Governor and judges should confine their initial lawmaking activities to statutes for organizing the courts, the militia, and laying the territory out into districts. At about the same time, the Department of War counseled Harrison not to make any agreements for the relocation of Indians in Upper Louisiana until more information could be obtained concerning existing land claims in the territory. Keenly aware by then of the discontent in the territory, the Administration proposed, insofar as possible, to follow policies that would allay rather than aggravate the unrest.

The appointment of commandants, as provided by the new law, also received the President's personal attention. Since they would direct both civil and military affairs of their respective districts, Jefferson sought individuals whom he believed could be depended upon to exercise prudence in the combination of these powers. Nevertheless, many Republicans so opposed the consolidation of civil and military authority that they refused to be mollified by the President's careful examination of the prospective candidates. Secretary of the Treasury Albert Gallatin refused even to discuss the appointments with the President.

Despite the reservations of Gallatin and others, Jefferson selected competent men to occupy these positions. He commissioned four commandants: Samuel Hammond for St. Louis, Return J. Meigs, Jr., for St. Charles, Richard Kennon for Cape Girardeau, and Seth Hunt for Ste. Genevieve. All except Hunt, who was given the rank of major, received commissions as

1. As early as August, 1803, Harrison had written to Lieutenant Governor Delassus requesting information concerning Upper Louisiana's current government, because he believed that the area might be annexed to the Indiana Territory.

colonels. Following their appointment, Secretary of War Dearborn addressed lengthy instructions to these men; although he
directed them to exercise civil rather than military authority
whenever possible, in actual practice the commandants' duties
turned out to be largely military after the creation of a separate
set of local civil officials by Governor Harrison and the judges.

In view of the numerous reports of settlements on public
lands, Dearborn particularly stressed the importance of the commandants' duties to remove all intruders. Likewise his concern
about the precarious defenses of Upper Louisiana prompted him
to instruct these officials to take immediate steps to reorganize
the militia in each district. Possibly anticipating problems, the
Secretary urged the commandants to maintain friendly relations
with high-ranking officers in the Regular Army who were stationed in their district and under their command. Nevertheless,
the regular soldiers never accepted the commandants, and jealousy and suspicion separated the two groups as long as the commandants remained in control.

The inauguration of Upper Louisiana's new government occurred on October 1, 1804, without fanfare. Since the Governor
and judges remained in the Indiana Territory, they met in
Vincennes on that date and passed fifteen laws to govern the
District of Louisiana. With the exception of a single statute
regulating marriages that passed in April, 1805, no further addition had to be made to the district's territorial laws during the
period that Indiana's officials governed it.

Although Congress failed to restrict Louisiana's administrators
to the adoption of laws previously enacted by one of the original
states, Harrison and the judges did not introduce any significant
innovations in their legislation. They enacted laws providing for
the punishment of crimes, the appointment and regulation of
local officials, the establishment of a system of territorial courts,
the organization of the militia, the levying of local taxes, the
regulation of boatmen, and the control of slavery. With the exception of the act regulating boatmen, all of Louisiana's initial
statutes were based upon provisions contained in the laws of the
Northwest and Indiana territories. The legislators did not
demonstrate any particular ingenuity or originality in creating
Louisiana's new laws, and instead preferred to rely upon estab-

lished practices and customs. Consequently Upper Louisiana's first statutes closely approximated those of most other early nineteenth-century territories.

In the creation of administrative districts for the territory, the President had recommended to Harrison that the existing divisions be retained, and the Governor responded with a proclamation recognizing the districts of St. Charles, St. Louis, Ste. Genevieve, Cape Girardeau, and New Madrid. Under the laws enacted for the District of Louisiana each of the territory's five districts or counties had a court of common pleas, a court of general quarter sessions of peace, a probate court, and individual justices of the peace. The justices of the peace, who were appointed by the Governor, heard petty civil and criminal cases.

Four times a year the justices of the peace in each district combined to form the court of general quarter sessions of peace. This court had jurisdiction in all criminal cases that did not involve capital offenses. In addition to its judicial functions, the court of quarter sessions served as the principal administrative agency in each district, handling such matters as levying local taxes, approving district expenditures, and authorizing contracts for the construction of roads, bridges, jails, courthouses, and other public buildings and works. Other district officials who assisted in local administration included the sheriff, coroner, assessor, recorder, and constable.

The court of common pleas, which was organized similarly to the court of general quarter sessions of peace, had jurisdiction in civil cases involving less than $100. In actual practice the same men served on both courts concurrently. The superior court of the territory, composed of the three territorial judges appointed by the President, met biannually to hear all civil cases involving more than $100 and all capital cases. As the territory's highest judicial body it also had appellate jurisdiction in cases from the lower territorial courts.

While still in Vincennes, Governor Harrison had filled many of the newly-created territorial offices. Harrison's list of appointments contained the names of virtually all of Upper Louisiana's established leaders. The Governor's good judgment in selecting local men undoubtedly made the new government more acceptable to Louisiana's unhappy residents and averted, at least temporarily, additional local unrest.

After having taken the necessary steps to put the new government into effect, Indiana officials set out to visit their new jurisdiction. Accompanied by an escort of mounted regulars, Governor Harrison and a party that included the three judges of the superior court received a cordial welcome upon their arrival in St. Louis on October 12, 1804. Auguste Chouteau lavishly entertained Harrison at his stately mansion and even went so far as to suggest that the Governor join him in a business partnership, an offer Harrison discreetly declined. Harrison was not a total stranger to the residents of Upper Louisiana. Prior to the American acquisition of the territory he had carried on a cordial correspondence with Lieutenant Governor Delassus, and after a relatively short time in St. Louis it was clear that he had made a favorable impression on the leading residents of that community.

Moreover, the Governor's popularity in St. Louis did not suffer from his decision to waive the fees usually charged for the issuance of licenses to trade. Just as Spain had waged a determined campaign to reduce British influence in the Upper Mississippi Valley, the United States government continued this policy. Accordingly, Harrison refused to grant any trade permits to British citizens or British sympathizers.

When Governor Harrison reached Upper Louisiana the Indian situation was still ominous. Residents of the scattered settlements north of St. Louis lived in constant fear of a renewed attack by Sac and Fox warriors, whose recent hostilities had brought death and destruction to the area. Although the tribal leaders acknowledged that four of their members had committed the murders, they still had not turned the guilty individuals over to American authorities as they had been instructed to do. However, shortly after Harrison's arrival, a delegation from the two tribes surrendered one of the guilty warriors to the Governor. Harrison agreed to pardon the other three guilty braves if they would testify against the prisoner in custody, and even considered releasing the fourth warrior on a legal technicality, but the strong protests of Major Bruff, commander of the regular troops in the district, dissuaded him. Instead he appealed to the President to grant the imprisoned Indian a pardon. In the meantime the Sac brave remained confined in the St. Louis guardhouse.

Harrison's conciliatory approach to the Sac and Fox representatives grew out of his desire to negotiate a cession of lands from the tribes. Secretary of War Dearborn previously had instructed the Governor to conclude a treaty with those nations. Prior to entering negotiations, Harrison arranged with Auguste and Pierre Chouteau to distribute more than $2,000 worth of goods among the tribal chiefs who had come to St. Louis to return the prisoner. When he proposed that they discuss the possible relinquishment of some of their lands, Harrison found the Indians to be in a receptive mood. Eager to secure American protection against the Osage, whom they considered protégés of the United States, the visiting Sac and Fox delegates gladly turned to negotiations as a means to end further discussion of the Cuivre River killings.

With the assistance of the Chouteaus, Governor Harrison worked out an agreement with the representatives of the two tribes, extending American protection to the Sac and Fox and promising an annual annuity of $1,000. The United States also pledged to establish government trading factories for their use. In return the two tribes relinquished all claims to their lands east of the Mississippi River as well as to a sizable portion of their hunting grounds on the western bank of the river, but the Indians were to be permitted to live and hunt on the ceded lands until the United States disposed of them.[2] The agreement also contained an article calling for a cessation of all hostilities between the Sac and Fox and the Osage. At the insistence of the Chouteaus, who had extensive claims to lands in the ceded area, a further proviso in the treaty stipulated that the cession would in no way invalidate land grants in the region made by the Spanish.

2. The land east of the Mississippi River surrendered by the Indians included a portion of southern Wisconsin and the area in Illinois north and west of the Illinois River. The land on the west bank included all of the present Missouri counties of Ralls, Pike, Lincoln, St. Charles, and Warren, along with parts of Marion, Shelby, Monroe, Audrain, and Montgomery counties.

Although members of the delegation who negotiated the treaty had been authorized to make payments for the recent murders, they had not been empowered to make the vast concessions embodied in the final agreement that they signed. Consequently many members of the two Indian nations resented the treaty terms their representatives had approved, and the resulting bitterness and resentment poisoned American relations with the Sac and Fox for nearly thirty years. Moreover, Harrison's attempts to resolve the Indian problem provoked a serious rift between civil and military authorities in Upper Louisiana. Major Bruff strongly disapproved of the leniency shown by Governor Harrison in handling the Indians. As a result of these differences, jurisdictional disputes arose between the two men. Bruff especially objected to the Governor's claim to have supreme control over the military in Louisiana, and on this issue Secretary of War Dearborn agreed with Bruff that Harrison had over-extended his authority.

Even though Louisiana's new government just had gone into effect when the second session of the Eighth Congress convened, word of the widespread territorial dissatisfaction with the provisions of the Louisiana act already had reached Washington. Nevertheless, Jefferson made no mention of the measure's unpopularity in his annual message to Congress, nor did he suggest that any revisions be made in Louisiana's territorial government. Despite the President's failure to propose any changes, Congress again turned its attention to Louisiana's problems when confronted with strongly-worded petitions seeking the repeal of legislation passed at the previous session. Eligius Fromentin presented the petition from the inhabitants of the District of Louisiana, drafted in St. Louis the preceding September, to Jefferson's son-in-law, Virginia Representative John W. Eppes, and he submitted it to the House of Representatives on January 4, 1805. The St. Louis convention had designated both Fromentin and Auguste Chouteau to deliver the petition and to represent the territory in the capital, but a case of the gout forced Chouteau to return to St. Louis after traveling only a short distance.

The petitioners in Upper Louisiana received an added boost from their new Governor, who lent his complete support to

their efforts. In a letter written to accompany the St. Louis petition, Harrison stressed the strong attachment of the Louisianians
to the United States, and he attributed the harsh language contained in their petition to an understandable resentment produced by the insulting misrepresentations that had been made
about them. Harrison informed Auguste Chouteau of his exertions in behalf of their petition, relating that he had sought to
destroy the distorted belief that Frenchmen were disdainful
toward the American government.

Although Congress treated Fromentin courteously, the petition from Upper Louisiana did encounter delays as a result of
letters from the territory disparaging the recent proceedings at
St. Louis. Undoubtedly much of the difficulty stemmed from
a letter written by Rufus Easton to the President, in which he
argued that while the residents ostensibly objected to the law
because it attached the District of Louisiana to the Indiana Territory, this was merely a means to disguise their real opposition
to the clause on land titles. Easton, who had come to the territory
only a short time earlier, contended that the petition did not
represent the wishes of the people of the District of Louisiana,
but only those of a small group of men seeking confirmation of
questionable land claims.

As a result of such accusations, Congress proceeded with caution in making changes in Louisiana. Furthermore, many members had been disturbed by the language of the petition itself,
especially the charges that the congressional law had violated
provisions of the Treaty of Cession. They suggested that the
Louisianians would have made a much stronger case for their
requests had they based their petition upon an appeal to the
rights guaranteed by the general principles underlying the
American system of government, rather than on the provisions
of the treaty with France. Nevertheless, they did approve two
important new pieces of legislation for Upper Louisiana.

In accordance with the request contained in the petition
adopted in St. Louis, Congress granted Upper Louisiana its own
territorial government. In creating a separate government for
the area Congress considered advancing the territory directly
to the second stage of government outlined in the Northwest
Ordinance. The original Senate bill, which passed through com-

mittee without alteration, provided for a popularly-elected general assembly to be composed of ten members. Although a subsequent amendment completely altered the character of the bill before its final passage, the original version of the measure had anticipated eliminating the first stage of government from the territorial process, a policy later adopted for other territories.

The measure finally approved by Congress removed the District of Louisiana from the control of the officers of the Indiana Territory and renamed the province the Territory of Louisiana. Closely adhering to the first grade of territorial government outlined in the Northwest Ordinance, the act vested executive authority in a governor, appointed by the President for a three-year term. The governor also served as commander in chief of the territorial militia and as superintendent of Indian affairs for the territory. A secretary, appointed for four years, had to record and preserve the papers and proceedings of the territorial government and transmit official reports to the national government. Three judges, serving four-year terms, comprised the highest judicial tribunal in the territory.

The bill authorized the territorial legislature, composed of the governor and the three superior court judges, to establish inferior courts and prescribe their jurisdiction, and to make all laws deemed conducive to the good government of the territory, as long as those laws did not conflict with either the provisions of the Constitution or the laws of the United States. Congress continued to exempt Louisiana's legislature from the restriction imposed on all other first-class territories that limited them to the adoption of statutes already enacted by one of the original states. This act, approved on March 3, 1805, provided for the new government of the territory to go into effect on July 4, 1805.

While willing to grant the inhabitants of Upper Louisiana a separate territorial government, most congressmen remained determined to check speculation and fraud in land titles. An act for ascertaining and adjusting land titles, approved on March 2, 1805, sought to establish regular procedures for the confirmation of land claims in Louisiana. Although it repealed the unpopular law of March 26, 1804, the new law retained extremely rigid guidelines for approving titles by creating a board of land commissioners for Upper Louisiana to validate land titles. Composed of a recorder of land titles and two additional members, the board was empowered to consider and rule upon grants presented for confirmation, in accordance with the provisions spelled out in this act and subject to the approval of Congress.

In outlining the conditions for confirmation Congress sought to ensure the approval of all legitimate claims made by bona fide settlers on small tracts of land. The act, however, did not provide for the wholesale confirmation of all land grants sought by local residents. Consequently, these measures failed to eliminate discord in Upper Louisiana. The large claimants redoubled their efforts to secure approval for their grants, and under the leadership of the new governor, James Wilkinson, the territory entered a period of factionalism and bitterness seldom seen even in unstable frontier communities.

CHAPTER VI

POLITICAL FACTIONALISM
ON THE FRONTIER

FOLLOWING the transfer of Louisiana to the United States, Americans flocked to the territory in growing numbers as lawyers, businessmen, and land speculators joined the migration begun by pioneer farmers in the late eighteenth century. Like their American predecessors in Upper Louisiana, these newcomers expected to profit from the region's untapped resources, but unlike previous American settlers they intended to participate actively in shaping the future of the newly-acquired territory. Already concerned about the American government's hesitancy to confirm their land titles, the threat of a new political force made long-time residents increasingly apprehensive about the rapidly changing situation.

President Jefferson chose Gen. James A. Wilkinson to serve as governor of this troubled territory. Of Jefferson's appointments in Louisiana, the selection of Wilkinson proved to be the most controversial. Throughout his varied career Wilkinson remained above all else an opportunist who employed whatever methods he deemed most likely to advance his own interests. From secret agent for the Spanish government to commanding general of the United States, the peripatetic Wilkinson's search for fame and fortune often led him down strange and conflicting paths. A political chameleon who successfully made the transition from Federalist to Republican in 1800, General Wilkinson epitomized the driving personal ambition and materialistic standards common to the American frontier.

Despite his notorious reputation, the enigmatic Wilkinson retained a substantial number of influential friends, including Vice President Aaron Burr and a number of important senators. Jefferson's reasons for naming Wilkinson to the top post in the territory remain a matter of conjecture. Although he maintained that he had selected Wilkinson because his military background equipped him to handle Upper Louisiana's distinctive problems, some have speculated that the President may have nominated the controversial general to please Aaron Burr, whose favor he was then courting in preparation for the upcoming impeachment trial of Justice Samuel Chase over which Burr was to preside.

Whatever the President's motive may have been, Wilkinson turned out to be a most unfortunate choice, for in his attempt to bring order to the unsettled frontier the new Governor had soon alienated most of his fellow officials and a large segment of the territory's population. While in Louisiana, Wilkinson did not alter his already well-established habits, and Jefferson's decision to name him governor in 1805 only intensified his personal ambition. The appointment must have come as welcome news to the hard-pressed general, who for some time had sought an additional office to help alleviate his chronic financial difficulties. The $2,000 annual salary paid to territorial governors handsomely augmented the $225 monthly sum that Wilkinson received as a brigadier general in the Army, and the new position dangled the prospect of even greater rewards before the self-seeking general.

Jefferson named Joseph Browne to the office of territorial secretary largely upon the recommendation of Browne's brother-in-law, Aaron Burr. John B. C. Lucas, Rufus Easton, and Return J. Meigs, Jr., received appointments from the President as judges of the superior court and ex officio members of the territorial legislature. Lucas, a native of France who had immigrated to the United States in 1784, had quickly ascended the political ladder in western Pennsylvania. Recommended for the judicial post in Louisiana by his close personal friend Albert Gallatin, Lucas was a member of the United States House of Representatives at the time of his nomination. Undoubtedly the endless opportunities in the newly-created territory played a major role in his decision to move to the edge of the frontier. Moreover, Lucas viewed the appointment as a means to end the lengthy absences from his family necessitated by his frequent trips to Washington, and he was eager for his family to reside again among French-speaking people.

Rufus Easton, a lawyer originally from New York, had come to the territory shortly after the American acquisition hoping to take advantage of the rapidly unfolding opportunities, particularly land speculation. After Easton arrived in Louisiana he solicited a territorial office in order to advance his political and economic fortunes. Because of his important political connections in New York and Washington, he was able to secure appointment as St. Louis's first postmaster, in addition to his judgeship.

Return J. Meigs, Jr., already had been commissioned commandant of the district of St. Charles by Jefferson. Meigs had previously served as a territorial judge in the Northwest Territory and as chief justice of the Ohio Supreme Court, and so brought valuable experience to the new government. Unlike Lucas and Easton, however, he remained in Louisiana for only a short period of time.[1]

General Wilkinson reached St. Louis on July 1, 1805, three days before he assumed the duties of governor. The new executive received a warm welcome from local leaders, who lost no time in initiating attempts to gain his favor. On the day of his arrival Wilkinson dined with Auguste Chouteau, the village's wealthiest resident, and other prominent members of the community. Well-known for his elaborate entertaining, Chouteau undoubtedly provided the Governor with a lavish demonstration of the hospitality that made Upper Louisiana's French residents famous. Wilkinson's acceptance of Chouteau's invitation to dinner on his first day in the territory offended Maj. James Bruff. Undoubtedly influenced by Governor Harrison, whose relations with Bruff had been strained, Wilkinson had postponed meeting with the territory's ranking military officer until the conclusion of the festivities honoring his arrival.

The people of St. Louis observed the inauguration of the new government with a Fourth of July celebration, and many attended the dinner and gala ball given to honor the occasion. Such amenities, coupled with Governor Harrison's personal recommendation to Wilkinson that he align himself with the leading French inhabitants, soon won the new Governor over to the cause of the long-time residents. Throughout his administration Wilkinson showed a marked tendency to favor their interests.

1. Returning to Ohio in 1806, Meigs later served as a governor, United States senator, and Postmaster General of the United States.

Despite the gaiety of the festivities in St. Louis, Governor Wilkinson soon sensed an underlying factionalism and discord within the territory that seemed to increase daily. Much of the strife stemmed from the continuing disagreement about the validity of unconfirmed Spanish land titles. Competition to win the favor of the newly-appointed territorial officers further intensified budding personal rivalries and widened the breach between the territory's established French residents and the growing number of American newcomers. Shortly after he became governor, Wilkinson wrote the Secretary of War avowing his intention to remain aloof from factional squabbles and indicating that he expected his proposed course of action to produce a general lessening of tensions throughout the territory. Unfortunately, subsequent developments failed to justify the Governor's optimistic predictions. Instead of avoiding involvement in the territorial contests, as he had proposed to do, Wilkinson found himself deeply and personally caught up in them. As a result, he eliminated any chance to use his office to resolve the problems and to restore the tranquility of an earlier era.

Even the most skillful of politicians would, as governor, have encountered difficulty in reconciling the conflicting interests and in maintaining any degree of harmony among men who had accepted positions in the territorial government in hopes of advancing their prestige and fortunes, but Wilkinson demonstrated neither skill nor political sagacity in handling his fellow officials. The Governor's determination to exercise complete control over the territory, strengthened no doubt by Jefferson's occasional references to the establishment of a military government in Louisiana; his attempts to develop a group of officials personally loyal to him, while eliminating all who expressed opposition; his predisposition to favor the territory's influential French inhabitants; and his jealous refusal to cooperate fully with the judges in legislating for the territory—all greatly intensified Louisiana's existing instability.

The most serious unrest in the territory occurred in the district of Ste. Genevieve. As the center of the territory's lead-mining operations and the location of some of the largest Spanish land claims, that district had been particularly attractive to the speculators, fortune hunters, and adventurers pouring into the territory. Disputed claims to the richest mines kept the region in constant turmoil and, as in later American mining frontiers, occasional outbursts of violence accentuated the lawless local conditions temporarily prevailing.

One of the most notorious characters in the district was John Smith T, who had come to Louisiana from Tennessee hoping to take advantage of the unsettled situation. Smith, who had added to his name the letter T, for Tennessee, to distinguish himself from the other John Smiths, had purchased a large floating claim shortly after his arrival. His attempt to locate that claim on lands already occupied by Moses Austin triggered a long-standing dispute between the two men. Not only did Smith T seek to claim Austin's Mine à Breton tract, but he also initiated an intensive campaign to secure Austin's removal as chief justice of the Ste. Genevieve court of common pleas.

Governor Wilkinson became involved in the volatile situation in Ste. Genevieve as a result of the attempts by the district com-mandant, Maj. Seth Hunt, to prevent unauthorized persons from continuing to mine on the public domain. Acting under orders from Wilkinson, Hunt moved to prevent persons without bona fide claims from working the mines. His actions created a furor among the miners, who contended that by custom the Spanish had permitted them to dig on His Majesty's domains. Because of the intensity of the outburst the commandant agreed to allow them to continue mining for twenty additional days in order to give him time to secure the reinforcements necessary to implement his directive.

No doubt with encouragement from Moses Austin, Hunt had included John Smith T among those whom he had ordered to vacate the mines. According to the commandant, Smith T had made an unlawful and unauthorized settlement on the basis of a floating and probably antedated claim. Smith T, in appealing to the Governor to overrule Hunt's decision, stated that he had purchased the 500-acre floating claim in question from Major Hunt himself, and that Hunt had tried to block his attempts to locate the claim because of the interference of Moses Austin, who had personal designs on the land. Wilkinson proved amenable to Smith T's plea, and he instructed Hunt to allow Smith T to remain and not to interfere any further with his mining operations. Furthermore, the Governor reprimanded the Ste. Gene-vieve commandant for having speculated in Spanish land claims.

The reasons for Wilkinson's decision to reverse his original instructions and to support Smith T in the fracas are not entirely clear, but possibly Wilkinson believed that Smith T, who had two brothers in the Army and a brother-in-law in Congress, might prove to be a valuable ally in his future operations. The French inhabitants of the district probably feared the com-bined authority of the Americans, Hunt and Austin, and they may have interceded against the commandant as well. Whatever the reasons, a heated exchange ensued between Ste. Genevieve's commandant and the Governor. Hunt accused the Governor of failing to adhere to the principles he had initially laid down re-garding the exclusion of unauthorized persons from the public lands; Wilkinson responded by denouncing Hunt for speculat-ing in land titles, for writing insulting letters to his superior, for having publicly questioned the wisdom of Wilkinson's appoint-ment as governor, and for general insubordination. As a conse-quence of their differences, Wilkinson removed Hunt as com-mandant and ordered that the Major be placed under arrest and brought before a tribunal for investigation.

In attempting to remedy this touchy situation, Secretary of War Henry Dearborn informed Wilkinson that although Hunt's conduct had disappointed him, he was unwilling to believe Hunt guilty of intentional wrongdoing. Dearborn did ask for Hunt's resignation, but he instructed the Governor to provide a board of investigation if Hunt should request it. Hunt, who had already announced his intention to resign his post, decided not to ask for the board of investigation, but he later went to Washington to attempt to clear his name and also to use his influence against Governor Wilkinson. As a result of the events at Ste. Genevieve, Seth Hunt had emerged as one of the earliest leaders of the opposition to the Governor.

While the Hunt-Wilkinson controversy still raged, Aaron Burr arrived in St. Louis in September, 1805, for talks with Governor Wilkinson. The discussions held in Louisiana between these two men remain shrouded in mystery. Because of the ab-sence of any authoritative records of their conversations, any conclusions about Burr's visit must be based largely upon conjecture. It does seem certain, however, that these two old friends, who had met the preceding June for four days at Fort Massac,[2] discussed the need for cultivating persons in Louisiana who could be counted upon for support in any future undertakings they might initiate, including a possible invasion of Mexico to be launched from St. Louis.

Insofar as the local situation was concerned, the Burr-Wilkinson intrigues introduced further complications into Louisiana's already confused political climate. Rufus Easton, a territorial judge and key figure in the subsequent controversy that erupted between the Governor and the judges, believed that his estrangement from Wilkinson had resulted from the unfavorable response he had given to Burr's overtures. Indeed, it is probable that the lack of interest shown by several territorial inhabitants may have turned the Governor against them.

By October, 1805, two clear-cut factions began to emerge from Louisiana's muddled political environment. With James Wilkinson as the catalyst, the territory divided into pro-Wilkinson and anti-Wilkinson groups. The party supporting the Governor embraced not only most of the territory's French inhabitants, who greatly feared the growing American influence in the province and looked to Wilkinson for assistance, but also the largest Spanish land claimants in Louisiana, who believed the Governor favored the confirmation of their grants, and a motley collection of Burrites and miscellaneous adventurers personally attracted by James Wilkinson. The membership of the pro-Wilkinson faction included such well-known Louisianians as Charles Gratiot, Auguste Chouteau, Jacques Clamorgan, John Mullanphy, Bernard Pratte, Peter Provenchere, Joseph Browne, John Smith T, and James Donaldson.

The opposing group, composed almost entirely of Americans who had arrived in the territory since the United States had taken control, brought together many persons who disliked Governor Wilkinson for one reason or another. A group of young and energetic American lawyers formed an important segment of this faction. These aspiring attorneys, who sought advancement through land speculation as well as politics, played an important

2. Fort Massac was located on the Ohio River at the mouth of the Tennessee River in the Illinois Territory.

role in the introduction of American law and government in Louisiana, and as a result they soon became a very powerful force in territorial politics. As such, they threatened Wilkinson's position and influence, and were consequently natural targets for the jealous Governor's wrath. Rufus Easton, William C. Carr, and Edward Hempstead—three of the most important early members of this group—led much of the attack against the Governor. Along with other potential land speculators interested in blocking confirmation of the huge tracts of Spanish land claims in order to enhance their own chances for speculation, they rallied many persons to the anti-Wilkinson party. Joining them were individuals who had clashed with the Governor on different occasions, including James Bruff, Seth Hunt, Moses Austin, John B. C. Lucas, and Samuel Hammond.

Louisiana's political upheaval seriously jeopardized normal governmental operations within the territory. Strained relations between the Governor and the judges of the superior court delayed the opening of the territorial legislature for several months while they debated whether or not the Governor possessed an absolute veto. On October 12, 1805, Judges John B. C. Lucas and Rufus Easton urged Wilkinson to convene the territorial legislature to deal with pressing matters of public concern, but while always avowing his readiness to cooperate with the judges for purposes of legislation, Wilkinson continually postponed the date on which the legislature was scheduled to meet.

The dispute between the Governor and the territorial judges spilled over into the October term of the general court. Angered by the Governor's failure to meet with them to enact legislation, the judges declined on the opening day of the general court to recognize Wilkinson's appointment of James Donaldson as public prosecutor. They rejected Donaldson on the technicality that his commission designated him as district attorney, while the current law provided for an attorney general. Following their refusal to approve Donaldson under the authority of the Governor's commission, the judges asked him to serve as a court-appointed prosecuting attorney so that essential judicial business could be completed, but Donaldson, a loyal supporter of Wilkinson, refused on grounds that acceptance of the judicial appointment would represent a formal renunciation of the Governor's right to designate the nominee. The court then named William C. Carr to occupy the post temporarily.

Unwilling to bow to the general court's decision, Governor Wilkinson sent Donaldson back to the courtroom on the following day with a commission naming him to the post of attorney general. The justices again declined to recognize Donaldson's commission, this time on the grounds that under the act of Congress the Governor possessed only power to appoint district officials, and the attorney general was not a district official. They concluded that only a new law passed by the territorial legislature could authorize Wilkinson to name an attorney general for the territory. By their narrow and admittedly questionable construction of the law, the judges hoped to force the Governor to come to terms with them.

Infuriated by this open challenge to his authority, the Governor decided to alter his plan of attack in the struggle with the judicial officers and turned his attention to the selection of the grand jury for the October term of the general court. Governor Wilkinson instructed Sheriff Josiah McLanahan, who summoned the members of the grand jury, to call every judge and justice of the peace in the district of St. Louis for service on the jury about to be empaneled. This ensured that the grand jury would be strongly pro-Wilkinson in its composition, inasmuch as the district officers whom the Governor had designated for selection to serve on the jury were mostly long-time French residents whom he had continued in office.

The indictments subsequently returned by the grand jury revealed its partisan character. Labeling the actions of the general court indecorous and insulting, the members of the jury criticized the court for restricting their power to call witnesses and for forcing them to meet in unsatisfactory quarters. They also remonstrated against the judges for having failed to recognize Donaldson's appointment as attorney general. Moreover, the grand jury indicted Judge Rufus Easton on a charge of having obtained a deed for 600 acres of land through fraudulent practices. The jurymen, predominantly French and for the most part holders of substantial Spanish land claims, had taken this opportunity to even the score with Easton, whose letter to Jefferson in January, 1805, had seriously hampered the efforts of their agent,

Eligius Fromentin, who had gone to Washington to present a petition on behalf of the St. Louis group.

A minority of the grand jury, however, issued a protest against the actions of the majority. The dissenting opinion came from the few American members of the jury, who denied that the charges against Easton had been substantiated by the testimony given before them. The indictment, they said, "was made more to gratify personal hatred and cruel Revenge." Furthermore, they rejected the charge that the grand jury had been treated improperly by the members of the general court. Instead the four dissenting members of the jury charged that the present-ment had been drawn up in secrecy at a special night session to which only part of the jurors had been summoned. This action they considered to be an unwarranted violation of their rights and duties as members of the grand jury.

Elaborating on these allegations, William C. Carr reported that on the night before the grand jury returned its indictments a large number of jurymen, chiefly French, had been seen at the Governor's residence until late at night. Although Wilkinson later denied holding any conversations with the members of the jury, there can be little doubt that the jury's actions reflected, at least indirectly, the Governor's influence. A regular jury subse-quently acquitted Easton of the charges contained in the grand jury's indictment, but the proceedings had damaged his reputa-tion in national circles. Even the judicial processes had been suborned by the territory's political squabbles.

Following the adjournment of the general court, the major participants in the dispute directed their attention to Washing-ton in a search for a possible cure for the territory's political ills. Since all officials of the Louisiana Territory who had taken office on July 4, 1805, had received recess appointments, their names now had to be submitted to the Senate for confirmation if they were to remain in office; both sides hoped to prevent the confir-mation of members of the opposing faction. As a result of the controversy that had developed around Rufus Easton, the Presi-dent decided not to reappoint him, but otherwise he made no alterations in his original choices for the top Louisiana posts.

Upon receiving word that his judgeship had been terminated, Easton went to Washington armed with letters of endorsement in order to vindicate himself of the charges lodged against him. While in Washington, Easton wrote directly to Jefferson, avowing the correctness of his conduct and demanding that the President reveal the nature of the charges that had caused him not to grant a reappointment. Jefferson issued a tart reply to Easton's communication, but did agree to meet with him. Their conference, however, failed to change the President's mind.

With Easton's removal now unalterable, local residents sought to influence the outcome of the Senate's vote to confirm Wilkinson and John B. C. Lucas. Opponents of the Governor described him variously as power-hungry, unable to distinguish between civil and military authority, and as the principal source of the territory's political woes. By emphasizing the unfortunate consequences of the combination of civil and military powers, the anti-Wilkinson forces hoped to benefit from the strong Republican aversion to the consolidation of the two offices. To counter the possible adverse effects of such arguments, Wilkinson's supporters circulated petitions and wrote letters avowing his popularity with the vast majority of the territory's citizenry. Lucas's rigid stand against the confirmation of Spanish land claims aroused opposition to his appointment from the pro-Wilkinson group.

The Senate confirmed the nominations of both Wilkinson and Lucas by very narrow margins and only after lengthy discussion. Although neither faction had been able to secure a total victory, the decision to retain Wilkinson in office represented a triumph for the pro-Wilkinson group. It should be noted, however, that Wilkinson had to receive solid support from Federalist members of the Senate to secure approval, while Lucas, although by a narrower margin, had been able to win confirmation despite unanimous Federalist opposition.

When word of Wilkinson's confirmation as governor reached St. Louis in March, 1806, his friends and supporters announced the good news to their fellow villagers with the ringing of bells and the firing of cannons. They capped their spontaneous celebration by building a large bonfire and, to the accompaniment of a hastily organized band, the merrymakers danced and drank toasts to the health of the Governor long into the night. The boisterous enthusiasm of his followers failed to remove Governor

Wilkinson's growing uneasiness about his future in Louisiana. The echoes of the noisy gathering scarcely had died away when renewed rumors predicting the Governor's removal again began to circulate through the village.

While pleased with Judge Easton's ouster and the confirmation of Wilkinson, the Governor's supporters still had not been able to gain their most cherished objective: the confirmation of all Spanish land titles. The board of commissioners, created by Congress to review land claims in the Louisiana Territory, had held its first session on December 1, 1805, in St. Louis. Meeting at a time when the territory's political strife had entered one of its most vitriolic phases, the commissioners found themselves caught up in the animosities engendered by the larger struggle.

Under normal circumstances the tasks confronting the board would have been formidable. Nearly two years had elapsed since American control had been formally established in Upper Louisiana, and American authorities still had not been able to determine to their satisfaction how Spanish officials had gauged the legitimacy of land titles. Moreover, many officials in Washington had grown even more hesitant to act as the result of the widely held belief that numerous antedated and forged claims threatened to defraud the United States of large quantities of land. When combined with the turbulent conditions in the territory, the obstacles blocking a satisfactory solution to the land-claims problem must have seemed insurmountable.

Political considerations played a major role in the selection of the first three members of the board of commissioners—James Lowry Donaldson, Clement Biddle Penrose, and John B. C. Lucas. Donaldson, an Irish-born lawyer, had been active in Maryland politics; Penrose was a member of the prominent Biddle family of Philadelphia and a nephew of Governor Wilkinson; and Lucas, a member of Louisiana's superior court, had earlier served as Albert Gallatin's successor in Congress from the western Pennsylvania district.

Almost from the beginning of its deliberations, the board found itself badly split. Penrose and Donaldson, both close associates of the Governor, staunchly supported his policies. Consequently the initial decisions handed down by the Penrose-

Donaldson majority evidenced an obvious predisposition to favor the large land claimants.

Lucas, the dissenting member of the board, strongly disagreed with his colleagues' views. As a territorial judge and a caustic critic of Governor Wilkinson, Lucas launched a full-scale campaign to counter the Governor's efforts in behalf of the holders of large land grants. In the end Judge Lucas's persistent efforts to block the wholesale confirmation of Spanish land titles in Missouri earned for him almost universal contempt among Louisiana's land claimants. Rigid and somewhat doctrinaire, Lucas contemptuously rejected cries for leniency. Several factors influenced his unbending position: as a result of an encounter with land speculators in Pennsylvania, the irascible Lucas had developed a strong suspicion of all who engaged in that activity on a large scale. Moreover, the available evidence convinced him that a large majority of the territory's biggest claims had been secured through fraudulent practices. Finally, Lucas must have realized that his substantial personal landholdings in the vicinity of St. Louis would appreciate in value more rapidly if the number of Spanish claims validated was limited.

The extent of fraud in Spanish land claims can never be fully determined. If all land claims that had failed to fulfill every requirement of the Spanish law to the letter had been judged fraudulent, then the number of valid claims would have been small. The key to the problem depended upon the extent of deviation to be allowed from the provisions of the Spanish law. Congress wrestled with this question long after Missouri's territorial period, and even then complete agreement proved impossible.

Under the Spanish system officials in Upper Louisiana routinely gave grants to those who applied and generally ignored the restrictions imposed on such grants by Spanish law. As a result, the low value of lands and their ready availability combined to make the question of titles a rather moot point before 1803. Unconcerned with the need to establish complete titles to their land, most settlers had given little thought to the problem, but the American acquisition of Louisiana, accompanied by a rapid appreciation in land prices and a great increase in population, completely reversed this situation. The sudden change unleashed a flurry of belated activity by bona fide settlers seeking to secure completed titles to their land, but it also led to numerous attempts to secure additional lands to which the claimants had no legitimate right. Although Lucas's stand probably embodied too narrow an interpretation, in view of the situation the judge did have solid justification for opposing the indiscriminate confirmation of titles that many residents of the territory desired, especially in cases involving extremely large claims.

William C. Carr, territorial land agent, joined Lucas in opposing the liberal interpretation favored by Penrose and Donaldson. Charged by the Secretary of the Treasury with investigating cases of suspected fraud and representing the United States in questions involving public lands, Carr frequently corroborated the reports of Judge Lucas.

Both Lucas and Carr expressed their disapproval of Governor Wilkinson's attempts to meddle in the land-claims controversy. In an obvious effort to enhance his own popularity, Wilkinson had advised the uneasy residents of the territory not to sell their claims in panic because he intended to use his influence to secure confirmation of their grants. The situation had been further aggravated by Wilkinson's continuation of Antoine Soulard as surveyor general of the territory—a post he had held under the last two Spanish governors. Soulard, whose close association with the St. Louis land junto could not be denied, retained complete control over territorial surveys. In February, 1806, Congress remedied the situation by extending the authority of the Surveyor General of the United States to the Territory of Louisiana. Efforts by Governors Harrison and Wilkinson to retain Soulard and his assistants failed, and Surveyor General Jared Mansfield secured the appointment of Silas Bent as principal deputy surveyor of Louisiana. Following his arrival in the territory in the fall of 1806, Bent reported finding numerous erasures, inaccuracies, and apparent alterations in Soulard's surveys. Undeterred, the former surveyor general continued to appear before the board of commissioners to vindicate his surveys.

Concerned by the Governor's attempts to interfere in the land-claims problem, Secretary Gallatin wrote to Jefferson suggesting that "General Wilkinson be advised that he has nothing to do with the land business." Shortly thereafter, Gallatin again warned the President that Wilkinson should be watched closely, pointing out that he had allied himself with every large Spanish land claimant in Louisiana, including Charles Gratiot, the Chouteaus, and Antoine Soulard.

Unfavorable reports on the activities of the board of commissioners further increased the Administration's apprehension. A clue to the board's inclination came when the commissioners announced the appointment of Charles Gratiot as clerk and Philip Marie Leduc as translator, since both men were intimate associates of the Spanish land claimants and had sizable interests themselves. Furthermore, when Attorney General John Breckinridge upheld the charges made by the territorial land agent that the extreme liberality of the decisions of the commissioners had injured the interests of the American government, Secretary of the Treasury Gallatin recommended to Jefferson that the commissioners be removed. The President submitted the whole matter to the members of his Cabinet for their consideration, and, although they unanimously agreed that the decisions handed down by the commissioners had been illegal, only Gallatin and Secretary of War Dearborn felt that removal would be justified. Relying upon the opinions of Madison and Breckinridge, Jefferson decided that despite the commissioners' incorrect interpretation of the land laws, their errors had not emanated from improper motives.

According to the President's wishes, Secretary Gallatin prepared a set of instructions for the land commissioners, informing them of the Attorney General's opinion so that they could revise their decisions to conform with his rulings. Gallatin also admonished the commissioners to adhere strictly to the letter of the law in the future and to leave to Congress any attempts to liberalize policies of confirmation.

The commissioners slightly modified their positions as a result of Gallatin's instructions, but relations between Lucas and the other members remained strained. Donaldson and Penrose often met to transact official business at irregular times and places without informing either Lucas or Carr of their intentions. In response to the continued complaints of both Carr and Lucas, Secretary Gallatin sent a new and more detailed set of instructions to guide the commission.

Unhappy with the rigid restrictions placed upon the board's right to confirm titles, Donaldson decided to go to Washington to seek a new and more favorable law for the land claimants. After his departure from the territory sometime in the fall of 1806, the business of the board of commissioners came to a virtual standstill. Since many of the board's original decisions had still not been revised in accordance with the Attorney General's ruling, Commissioner Lucas angrily denounced Donaldson for having returned pertinent original papers and documents to their owners before he left the territory. Without this evidence, Lucas maintained that the commissioners would not be able to reconsider the cases in question. He refused, therefore, to join Penrose in submitting to the Secretary of the Treasury a report of the decisions handed down by the board of commissioners until all necessary changes had been made. Even though he offered to meet with the remaining commissioner to record new claims, Lucas declined to render any additional decisions in specific cases.

When Penrose and Donaldson demonstrated continued reluctance to adhere strictly to instructions from Washington, the President revised his evaluation of their conduct. His disgust with the two commissioners was obvious when he wrote to Gallatin, "I have never seen such a perversion of duty as by Donaldson & Penrose." Jefferson consequently removed Donaldson from his position as recorder and replaced him with Frederick Bates of the Michigan Territory, and Secretary Gallatin recommended that the commissioners suspend any further decisions on cases until Congress had completed action on the new act then under consideration for adjusting Louisiana land claims.

Thus, the status of the Spanish land claims remained substantially unchanged when Wilkinson left the territory in the summer of 1806. No final decisions had been handed down by the board; numerous petitions had been circulated and opposing politicians had maneuvered frantically to take advantage of the situation; tempers had flared and the emotional fervor had grown so intense that one prominent politician-speculator, angered by the remarks of Donaldson, had burst into the proceedings of the board of commissioners and publicly caned him. Obviously, the dispute had only intensified existing divisions, and the land claims remained mired down in a morass of conflicting attitudes and interests.

Although Governor Wilkinson's excessive interference in local politics and his meddling in the land-claims controversy consumed much of his time, he often did have to turn his attention to the military and defensive problems which Jefferson had assumed would be the Governor's major preoccupation. When he arrived in St. Louis in July, 1805, Wilkinson found a band of approximately 150 disgruntled Sac and Fox Indians awaiting him. They had come to inquire about the fate of the Sac warrior accused of taking part in the Cuivre River murders whom they had turned over to Governor Harrison the preceding year. In an attempt to promote improved Indian relations Harrison had suggested that Jefferson pardon the guilty warrior, and the President had granted his request, but before the pardon reached St. Louis the Indian reportedly had been killed while attempting to escape. Wilkinson produced the presidential pardon for the Indians to examine and tried to explain the unfortunate situation to them.

In the course of his discussions, the Governor learned of the widespread dissatisfaction among the tribes created by the treaty which Harrison had negotiated with them. Already aware of this growing disaffection, federal officials hoped that the opening of a factory that would provide trade goods for the Indians at reasonable prices, as promised by the treaty, might alleviate the most serious discontent. Secretary of War Dearborn instructed Governor Wilkinson to give prompt attention to the selection of a site for the proposed trading factory and adjacent fort. Since Dearborn had specified that the location should be convenient for Indians residing along both the Missouri and Mississippi rivers, Wilkinson chose a spot on the Missouri four miles above the Mississippi junction. Construction on the post, known as Fort Belle Fontaine, began in the summer of 1805, but Governor Wilkinson had little time to oversee its progress.[3]

One of the most serious matters requiring the Governor's attention was the problem of the growing volume of British commerce in the trans-Mississippi west. Not only did British traders

3. Following its completion, Fort Belle Fontaine served as the major military fortification in the Far West for nearly twenty years.

control the lucrative trade, but they also sought to turn their Indian allies against the United States. Consequently, in late July, 1805, Wilkinson ordered Lt. Zebulon Montgomery Pike to lead a military expedition to the source of the Mississippi. Pike's instructions called for him to note the best sites for locating military posts in the Upper Mississippi Valley, to seek to cultivate friendly relations with the Indian tribes in the region, inviting their chiefs to come to St. Louis and, though not explicitly stated, to seek to check British activity wherever possible. Pike's expedition departed on August 9, 1805, as the initial phase of the Governor's efforts to diminish British influence in the area.

After consulting the officers of the territory for advice, the Governor issued a proclamation providing stringent regulations covering the conduct of the Indian trade in the Missouri Valley. In an attempt to eliminate the British traders, licenses to trade with Indians went exclusively to American citizens, who received them only after they had subscribed to a loyalty oath. Wilkinson also succumbed to pressure from the leading St. Louis fur magnates and agreed to permit the use of firearms in the trade. Despite the Governor's efforts, British influence remained largely undiminished. Like most frontiersmen, General Wilkinson believed that the maintenance of strong military posts in the interior was the only effective means of establishing American hegemony in the region, but the economy-minded national administration vetoed any such plans.

The rejection of Wilkinson's proposal to establish fortifications in the Upper Missouri-Mississippi valleys came too late to cancel an expedition, under the command of the Governor's son, which had allegedly been dispatched in October to construct a fort at the mouth of the Platte River. The party failed to accomplish its avowed objective after hostile Indians forced them to return to Fort Belle Fontaine in December, 1805. Seth Hunt later contended that in reality the venture had been a trading expedition. He charged that, under the guise of a military mission, the Governor had dispatched a public boat to transport $2,000 worth of trade goods owned by friends and associates of Wilkinson. Whatever its purpose had been, Secretary Dearborn strongly reprimanded Wilkinson for the unauthorized venture, but Wilkinson continued to defend his own actions.

Lingering hostilities between the Osage and a confederation of eastern Indians led by the Sac and Fox remained a serious problem for territorial officials. Governors Harrison and Wilkinson ordered representatives of the various tribes involved in the conflict to come to St. Louis to discuss the situation. By September, 1805, the first delegations had begun to arrive, but Governor Wilkinson found little room for optimism. At the same time that the Sac sent a party to St. Louis to negotiate an end to the fighting, they also dispatched a band of warriors to renew the attack against the Osage. Wilkinson blamed the continuing Sac depredations on dissatisfaction with the terms of the 1804 treaty and the influence of British traders.

Representatives from the Delaware, Miami, Potowatomi, Kickapoo, Kaskaskia, Sioux of the Des Moines River, Iowa, Sac, Fox, and Osage tribes met in St. Louis in response to the call of the government in October. Bowing to heavy pressures from the American officials, the tribal representatives agreed to sign a treaty pledging to end all hostilities, but they scarcely had departed when the fighting resumed. Both Harrison and Wilkinson remained apprehensive about the safety of their respective territories and urged the federal government to send a military force to Prairie du Chien to subdue the belligerent Indians. During the ensuing winter and spring the Sac continued their raids against the Osage, at times turning against isolated white settlers when they failed to find their Indian adversaries. Several deaths in the Louisiana Territory were attributed to the Sac warriors. In view of the continuing seriousness of the situation, Governor Wilkinson again summoned representatives of the Sac tribe to St. Louis in December, 1805, and delivered the strongest possible warning to the errant tribesmen stating that, unless they ceased their depredations and returned all Osage prisoners, the United States government would cut off all trade and supplies from the tribe. Despite these repeated threats, the Indian situation remained precarious.

The President had instructed Wilkinson to investigate the possibility of transferring the residents of the scattered settlements on the Mississippi below St. Louis to other more settled portions of the United States. Because of his desire to see a gradual orderly settlement of the nation's western regions, Jefferson continued to advocate the restriction of settlement in Upper Louisiana. By removing settlers from sparsely inhabited regions, the President hoped to make the existing settlements more compact, to facilitate the administration of justice, and to strengthen western outposts against possible attacks.

Even the usually aggressive Wilkinson recognized the need for caution in initiating any such program. He recommended that the relocation could best be accomplished by discouraging further settlement in the area and by offering inducements to those already there to move elsewhere. Having contacted several influential persons in the area in question, Governor Wilkinson informed Secretary of State Madison that the objective appeared attainable, provided that the government adopted the necessary measures and that all territorial officers cooperated, but he conceded that securing the assistance of the other territorial officials would not be easy.

Although in theory Jefferson's proposal may have had substantial merit, it was, in fact, so contrary to the frontier mind and the firmly established pattern of the American settlement process that it never stood even a remote chance of success. Moses Austin spoke for the territory when he warned federal officials of the futility of the proposal and admonished them to abandon the project before it jeopardized relations between the national government and the territory.

The President also had proposed to transfer the Indians from the southeastern part of the United States to unsettled portions of Louisiana, but resettlement became less and less feasible as the influx of American settlers into the territory continued. In the face of growing tension between neighboring Indians and the newly-arrived frontiersmen, all plans for the introduction of more Indians into Louisiana had to be quietly dropped.

Unfortunately, Wilkinson's interest in territorial affairs did not extend to routine administrative and legislative matters. During the first stage of territorial government the Governor was expected to take the lead in the preparation of new laws, but Wilkinson failed to press for any major revisions in Louisiana's legal code. He repeatedly had postponed the opening of the territorial legislature because of his dispute with the judges, even though they insisted that the local statutes needed attention. In fact, nearly a year elapsed before Wilkinson finally called the legislature into session. Meeting during the spring and early summer of 1806, the Governor and Judges Lucas and Meigs enacted a series of laws encompassing such varied topics as the appointment of an attorney general, the sale of liquor to Indians, marriages, prisons, public roads and highways, the regulation of ferries, the prevention of stallions from running at large, and the regulation of taverns. These long-overdue additional statutes remedied some of the most serious deficiencies in the territorial laws, but on the whole the Wilkinson administration, like most other first-class territorial governments, compiled an unimpressive over-all legislative record.

Political animosities within the territory remained strong. Following Samuel Hammond's refusal to support the move to back Wilkinson's confirmation by the Senate, relations between the Governor and the commandant of St. Louis rapidly deteriorated. The feud intensified after Wilkinson's attempt to arrest Hammond's nephew, Samuel Hammond, Jr., for the murder of an Indian in St. Louis. A coroner's inquest subsequently cleared young Hammond of any wrongdoing, but the St. Louis commandant never forgave Wilkinson for the manner in which he had handled the affair.

Slowly and painfully the Jefferson Administration had to revise its estimate of the situation in the Louisiana Territory. The unrelenting political hassle made it necessary to reconsider Governor Wilkinson's role, particularly in view of reports the President had begun to receive early in 1806 suggesting the possible existence of a western conspiracy under the leadership of Wilkinson and Aaron Burr. Keenly aware of his tenuous situation and obviously disturbed by rumors circulating in the territory that predicted the imminence of his removal, the Governor wrote to the President and to his close friend Senator Samuel Smith of Maryland concerning the possibility of such action.

As late as May 4, 1806, Jefferson, anxious not to alienate the general's influential friends, assured Senator Smith that no immediate change was contemplated in Wilkinson's status. Nevertheless, it seems obvious that the decision to remove Wilkinson as governor already had been made, for only two days later on May 6, 1806, Secretary of War Henry Dearborn ordered General

Wilkinson to leave Louisiana and to report to the Territory of Orleans to take command of the troops in that area as a consequence of threatened hostilities with Spain.

Worsening relations between Spain and the United States, caused by a dispute over the still-unresolved Louisiana-Texas boundary, provided Jefferson with the perfect opportunity to extricate himself from a very difficult political situation. Under the pretext that military necessity dictated Wilkinson's departure from the territory, the President successfully transferred him from Louisiana without formally having to remove him as governor of the territory. At least partial credit for this solution to the President's dilemma must be given to Congressman Matthew Lyon of Kentucky, who had suggested such a plan to Jefferson only a short time earlier.

Although Wilkinson's departure did not necessarily mean that his tenure as governor had ended, most Louisianians interpreted it to mean that. Upon receiving his orders to go to New Orleans, the Governor expressed strong displeasure to the Secretary of War that rumors emanating from Washington had anticipated his instructions far in advance of their actual public disclosure. He clearly feared that the widely-accepted view that his reassignment had been designed to get him out of the way was in fact true. Although he acknowledged his orders on June 16, Wilkinson remained in the territory for two more months, apparently waiting to see what materialized in the rapidly developing Burr intrigue. In July he ordered Lt. Zebulon Pike and a small band of soldiers, including his son Lt. James B. Wilkinson, on an expedition to the Southwest. The exact purpose of this venture remains a mystery, but it has frequently been suggested that Wilkinson wanted to relay some important information to Spanish authorities.[4]

Wilkinson's long-awaited departure from St. Louis, delayed until August 16, 1806, ended his active participation in the affairs of the territory.[5] As governor, Wilkinson had allowed himself to

4. Even though Wilkinson's purpose in sending out his mission remains obscured, it is clear that Lieutenant Pike was an innocent pawn who knew nothing of Wilkinson's intrigues.

5. After his departure Wilkinson never again returned to Missouri. By betraying his friend Aaron Burr, he managed to escape official cen-

become caught up in local factional squabbles and as a result had emerged as the central figure in the territory's party divisions. His high-handed manner and intense personal ambition made him a constant source of friction and contributed substantially to his failure as a territorial administrator.

Wilkinson's administration, while short in duration, had greatly increased the level of political activity in the territory. There can be no question about either the importance or the intensity of the feud between Wilkinson and his opponents, but for the most part the struggle actively involved only two small groups of people. Despite the deluge of petitions and letters that circulated throughout the territory, the greater part of these outpourings appears to have been the work of a comparatively few influential individuals residing in the principal villages. Characteristic of frontier communities, the average settler in Louisiana was preoccupied with his own personal advancement, and only when he believed that his interests were threatened did he take an active part in local politics.

---

sure for his role in the conspiracy, and, until his death in Mexico in 1825, continued his unfulfilled search for fame and fortune.

CHAPTER VII

THE TRANSITIONAL YEARS

SHORTLY after Wilkinson's departure, the citizens of St. Louis turned out in force to greet the returning members of the Lewis and Clark expedition. As the explorers approached the village on September 23, 1806, they fired a salute to the cheering crowds gathered along the bank to welcome them. That evening the two keen observers provided their friends in St. Louis with a brief synopsis of their observations and experiences from the past two years. No doubt their audiences listened with particular interest as they described the rich furs found along the Upper Missouri. Likewise, the wearied pair sought to be brought up to date on important developments that had occurred during their trip.

In Governor Wilkinson's absence the territorial secretary, Joseph Browne, had assumed the duties of Acting Governor, and Browne's brother-in-law, Aaron Burr, continued to look to the Louisiana Territory for assistance in carrying out his secretive project. In October, Burr sent his Chief of Staff, Col. Julien de Pestre, to St. Louis to distribute commissions and proclamations that some prominent residents, including Auguste Chouteau, refused to accept. Reports of an imminent revolution in the western states continued to circulate in the territory. In view of the Acting Governor's close association with Burr, the Administration had grave doubts about the wisdom of continuing him in that office. In an attempt to reassure his superiors in Washington, Browne informed Secretary of State Madison that he had been unable to find any basis for recent rumors concerning a contemplated separation of the western states from the Union. Browne's report proved very unconvincing, however, in the face of mounting evidence implicating Burr and his associates in some type of dubious project.

The end of the year saw a marked upswing in Burrite activity within the territory. While his recruiters sought to attract volunteers in the vicinity of New Madrid, Burr and his party reached that settlement on January 1, 1807, following their descent down the Ohio River. They remained in New Madrid only a short time before continuing down the Mississippi. When word reached St. Louis of Burr's arrival in the territory, Dr. Andrew Steele and Maj. Robert Westcott, Browne's son-in-law, rushed to Ste. Genevieve to join John Smith T and Henry Dodge; together they went in search of Burr. The four men failed to join up with him, possibly because they learned that a presidential proclamation had been issued on November 27, 1806, ordering Burr's arrest.

The return of this group to Ste. Genevieve created a great deal of local excitement. In their absence, Judge Otho Shrader had issued warrants for the arrest of Smith T and Dodge, charging conspiracy. Dodge submitted to arrest, posted bail, and then personally informed the grand jurors who had prepared the indictments of his displeasure. Smith T forcibly refused to permit authorities to arrest him, and no further action was taken in the matter.

The arrest of Major Westcott in St. Louis on charges of organizing a military expedition against Spain added to the local doubt. A resolution drafted by the citizens of St. Louis proposed that the territorial militia should be alerted as a precaution against any possible western conspiracy. The Acting Governor expressed his appreciation to the citizens for their promises of support, but reiterated that he thought no real danger to the territory existed.

By the early months of 1807, Joseph Browne had apparently lost much of his local support. Prior to his departure from the territory, Governor Wilkinson had attempted to use his influence to secure Browne's appointment as his permanent successor, and in accordance with the Governor's wishes Auguste Chouteau had spearheaded a drive to promote Browne's candidacy. The anti-Wilkinson forces had countered with a proposal that the post should go either to Return J. Meigs, Jr., or Samuel Hammond. However, in February, Chouteau's growing doubt about Browne's intentions had caused him to join Hammond and other St. Louis residents in calling upon the Acting Governor to take steps to combat the threatened conspiracy.

Although President Jefferson did not appoint a successor for

Wilkinson immediately, he did remove Browne as acting governor. Unwilling to risk the possible consequences of continuing him in office, the President commissioned Frederick Bates on February 4, 1807, to replace Browne as secretary of the Louisiana Territory. In addition, he also named Bates to succeed James Donaldson, another former Wilkinson associate, as Louisiana's recorder of land titles and as a member of the board of land commissioners.

Desirous of placing the territory in competent hands during this critical period, Jefferson selected Bates because of his background in territorial administration. Originally from Virginia, Bates had gone to the frontier outpost of Detroit in 1797 as an appointee in the quartermaster's department of the United States Army. In 1800, Bates established himself as a Detroit merchant, but his business venture collapsed after a great fire swept through that village in 1805. While in Detroit Bates occupied various local offices, including positions as deputy postmaster, receiver of public monies, and commissioner of land titles. Following the creation of the Territory of Michigan in 1805, the President appointed him to serve on the newly-established superior court. Unquestionably Bates's previous administrative experience made him a good choice for the Louisiana posts.[1]

The President had not yet designated Wilkinson's successor, and Representative Matthew Lyon urged Jefferson to act on this matter immediately so that his political enemies could not charge him with planning to retain Wilkinson in the position. Having considered the possibility of naming his close friend and

---

1. The decision to move an official from one territory to another was not uncommon. William C. C. Claiborne had been shifted from his post as governor of the Mississippi Territory to fill the same office in the Territory of Orleans. Winthrop Sargent, Secretary of the Northwest Territory, later served as governor of the Mississippi Territory. William Henry Harrison had been both secretary and territorial delegate prior to his nomination as governor of the Indiana Territory. Transfers were even more common among the ranks of territorial judges. At least three of Missouri's superior court judges, Return J. Meigs, Jr., Alexander Stuart, and William Sprigg, held similar posts in other territories. Reasons for the reassignments varied. Bates undoubtedly preferred service in the rapidly-developing Territory of Louisiana, with all of its concomitant opportunities, to continued assignment in the remote and still-isolated Michigan Territory.

former personal secretary, Meriwether Lewis, to fill the post as early as the preceding October as a reward for his successful mission, Jefferson made his appointment as governor of the Louisiana Territory official on March 3, 1807.

Because of the intense factionalism in Louisiana, Jefferson had decided to seek Wilkinson's replacement outside of the territory. In his judgment, Lewis was particularly well-equipped to cope effectively with the region's mounting frontier problems. Lewis probably accepted the appointment only because Jefferson had urged him to do so. Reluctant to move to St. Louis permanently, the new Governor originally hoped to administer the territory *in absentia.* At the same time, Jefferson named Lewis's friend and partner, William Clark, to be Indian agent for all tribes in the territory, except the Osage, as a reward for his services.

Since Governor Lewis did not plan to report to Louisiana immediately, he also designated Clark to head Louisiana's territorial militia. At the Governor's request, Clark, who had received a commission as a brigadier general, departed at once for St. Louis to assist Secretary Bates in launching the new administration. Reflecting the federal government's special concern about the Burrite threat in Louisiana, Governor Lewis instructed Clark to watch carefully the activities of Smith T, Dodge, Westcott, and Browne. A myriad of other problems also awaited the arrival of Louisiana's new administrators. The steady deterioration in American relations with both Spain and Great Britain intensified anxieties arising from problems of Indian hostilities, deficient frontier defenses, and inadequate communication. Moreover, the unresolved questions concerning land titles and lead mines continued to generate local controversy. The task assigned to Bates and Clark was not an easy one.

Frederick Bates arrived in St. Louis on April 1, 1807, confident that he would be able to eliminate the divisions that had existed during the previous administration. Having found Joseph Browne reluctant to surrender his positions, Bates did not formally take over as secretary until April 7. The immediate press of public business and the heavy responsibilities of the office temporarily overwhelmed the new Acting Governor.

During his first few weeks in Louisiana Bates remained undecided about the extent of his authority in the absence of the

Governor, but in response to urgent local needs he quickly assumed full responsibility for territorial administration, with apparently little local resistance to his actions. Insofar as frontier conditions permitted, Bates attempted to cooperate fully with the absentee Governor and to keep him informed on important local matters, but he often had to act without securing Lewis's prior approval. Although minor differences did arise between the Governor and the Secretary during this period, it was not until after Governor Lewis arrived in the territory that strained relations between the two men threatened to interfere with routine territorial administration.

Bates immediately attempted to root out the last vestiges of Burrism in Louisiana and to end the territory's deep factional divisions. Having decided that the discord would be permanently stilled only after the territorial administration had dealt effectively with its most prominent detractors, Bates initiated action against John Smith T, the prototype of Louisiana's troublemakers. The Acting Governor believed that Smith T, a suspected Burrite, had been largely responsible for fomenting the violence and resistance to legal authority prevalent in the district of Ste. Genevieve, and consequently he ordered Smith T's removal as judge of the court of common pleas, lieutenant colonel of the district militia, and commissioner of rates and levies. Bates also ousted a few other minor local officials from their posts, but he allowed others accused of Burrite connections to remain.[2]

The initial consequence of Bates's actions against Smith T increased rather than diminished the political turmoil in Ste. Genevieve. Some of the officers in the militia even resigned to protest Smith T's ouster, but Bates refused to reconsider. By refusing to return Smith T's archrival Moses Austin to the vacant post of judge of the court of common pleas, the Secretary sought to avoid identification of the territorial government with any particular faction.[3] Evidently his policies of neutrality proved at

2. Bates decided against removing Henry Dodge as sheriff of Ste. Genevieve because he believed that John Smith T had misled him. Bates's decision proved a wise one, for Dodge subsequently enjoyed a successful career as governor of the Wisconsin Territory.

3. Governor Wilkinson had originally removed Austin from that post in order to make room for the appointment of Smith T.

least partially successful, because Ste. Genevieve's exaggerated party fervors gradually subsided.

Elsewhere in the territory the party divisions also disappeared following Wilkinson's departure. Realizing that a continuation of the Franco-American divisions within the territory would be suicidal for them, many prominent Frenchmen quietly initiated a campaign to gain acceptance among the more influential American newcomers. Likewise, the specter of large profits from the ajudication of land titles caused many of the young attorneys who had strongly opposed Wilkinson to join forces with the Spanish land claimants in what they hoped would be a mutually profitable partnership. Gradually an elite coalition of territorial leaders emerged and dominated the territory socially, politically, and economically until the struggle for statehood again forced a realignment of factions.

As acting governor, Bates convened the territorial legislature on April 27, 1807, and it continued to meet regularly until early summer. A second session followed in October of that year. In contrast to the Wilkinson administration, relations between the judges and the executive seem to have been amiable and they worked together to revamp the territory's confused and inadequate statutes. In most territories an inefficient and often contradictory system of laws hampered local administration during the first stage of government, and Louisiana was no exception. Judge John Coburn reported finding a hodgepodge of laws combining English, French, Spanish, and American usages. This bewildering legal maze proved totally inadequate for the needs of a rapidly-growing territory.

Seeking to bring order out of this legal chaos, the territorial legislators enacted a substantial amount of new legislation covering such diverse subjects as divorce and alimony, insolvent debtors, mortgages, orphans, local government, and courts of justice. In their legislation, they paid particular attention to judicial proceedings and the structure of the court system. One of the more controversial bills passed by the legislature removed the May session of the superior court to Ste. Genevieve, much to the consternation of the residents of St. Louis. Although the modifications in the judicial system brought needed improvements, subsequent sessions of the territorial legislature found it necessary to constantly redraw these statutes in order to accommodate changing local needs.

Of the numerous tasks he performed as acting governor, Secretary Bates encountered his greatest difficulties in handling the intricate Indian problems. In accordance with Governor Lewis's recommendation, whenever possible he turned the management of Indian affairs over to the territory's Indian agents, William Clark and Pierre Chouteau. Clark's arrival in the territory in early May, 1807, temporarily relieved the overworked Acting Governor of the burden of dealing with those difficult problems. Clark immediately began making arrangements for a military expedition to escort the Mandan chief, Shahaka, to his home on the Upper Missouri. Shahaka had accompanied Lewis and Clark on their return journey and had gone with them to Washington, but the homesick chieftain now longed to rejoin his people. A short time later a military party under the command of Ens. Nathaniel Pryor left St. Louis assigned to oversee the chief's safe return.

Other matters also required Clark's prompt attention, as he distributed gifts among a party of visiting Sioux, admonishing them to live peacefully with their neighbors and not to harm American traders. Clark joined Pierre Chouteau in listening to the complaints of Chief White Hair and a band of his Osage tribesmen who had been in the territorial capital for some time to protest the failure of the United States government to build a mill and a trading factory at their villages. As territorial Indian agent, Clark handled numerous cases involving isolated Indian depredations, and, at the request of the Acting Governor, he helped draft a new territorial militia law. However, after two and one half months in the territory, Clark left for Kentucky to visit friends and relatives.

After Clark's departure, Bates once again found himself confronted with serious Indian problems. During the summer of 1807 reports of the steadily deteriorating Indian situation in the Upper Mississippi Valley produced widespread apprehension among territorial residents. The most ominous accounts concerned the rumored attempts by Tecumseh and the Prophet to organize the Shawnee for an attack against the Americans. Although Bates considered the local rumors exaggerated, he ordered all men to arm themselves in compliance with the new militia law.

Worsening relations between the United States and Great Britain made stories of British attempts to incite the Indians against Americans seem even more foreboding. Unconfirmed and often distorted reports of Indian hostilities circulated daily on the streets of the various territorial villages. When word reached the territory in August, 1807, of the British assault upon the *Chesapeake*, local tensions increased. Residents remained restless in anticipation of the British directed attack that many assumed would follow an American declaration of war against Great Britain.

Bates continued to believe that anxious local inhabitants magnified the immediate dangers, but, in view of the tense international situation, he took the precaution of ordering about one third of the territorial militiamen to muster at their respective parade grounds ready to march at a moment's notice. Although the Acting Governor felt that his action would reduce the growing fears of his constituents, the unexpected return of Ensign Pryor and the men assigned to accompany Shahaka to the Mandan villages again revived the local gloom. A band of hostile Arikara and Sioux warriors had forced them to turn back before they could deliver the Mandan chief to his intended destination.

While the delicate Indian situation continued to demand most of his attention in the fall of 1807, Frederick Bates made an attempt to resolve the lingering dispute involving conflicting claims to the district of Ste. Genevieve's richest lead lands. Since it had adopted a policy of reserving mineral lands, the American government had been greatly disturbed by reports of unauthorized diggings on public lands. In an attempt to end this practice and at the same time to enable the government to share in the anticipated lucrative returns from the mines, Congress in 1807 empowered the President to lease mineral lands for a term not in excess of three years under conditions he deemed appropriate.

Acting under the provisions of the new law, Bates authorized several persons to operate lead mines on government-owned land for a three-year period. The leases, drawn up by the Acting Governor, stipulated that the United States government was to receive one tenth of all minerals taken from the mines. Bates predicted that the new policy would end speculation and also supply the American government with substantial monetary returns, but in order to ensure that the government received full value from these agreements, he suggested that it establish furnaces and a storehouse to process the lead it obtained.

Even though the President approved the contracts negotiated by Bates and indicated a willingness to endorse additional leases, he recommended that they be made to cover as short a period of time as possible. Furthermore, he rejected the suggestion that the United States erect its own furnaces, and instead proposed that in the future the government's share should be made payable in metal rather than mineral.

In actual practice the new leasing system proved a complete failure. The government's refusal to approve any Spanish land claims located on mineral lands had already aroused the unhappy claimants, and they led a fight against the new scheme. Unauthorized intruders, who had long operated mines on public lands with or without bona fide Spanish claims, refused to recognize the validity of the new leases and continued to operate illegally as they had in the past. Moreover, the intruders often harassed and intimidated those who had actually been authorized to engage in mining on the public lands. From his post in St. Louis, nearly sixty miles from the mines, the Acting Governor had neither the time nor the means at his disposal to enforce effectively the governmental leases. Failing to secure the additional assistance from the government which he considered necessary, Bates never succeeded in checking their flagrant disregard of governmental authority, and as a result the leaseholders failed to receive the protection to which they were rightfully entitled. While the lead-leasing system never functioned satisfactorily, the government did not officially abandon it until 1829.

Although he had been appointed governor on March 3, 1807, Meriwether Lewis did not arrive in Louisiana to take charge of the government until March 8, 1808. The Governor's long-awaited appearance brought welcome relief to the overloaded Secretary, but it also temporarily resurrected old political rivalries as the principal protagonists vied for the new executive's favor. Unlike Governor Wilkinson, however, Meriwether Lewis displayed little interest in political activity, preferring instead to concentrate upon western problems.

Alleviation of the territory's worsening Indian situation became a primary concern with Lewis. In response to the repeated encroachment on their lands by white settlers and by enemy tribes, the Osage repudiated their leader, White Hair, and began terrorizing white settlers in the territory. Renowned on the frontier for their ferocity, the rampaging Osage warriors stole horses, killed cattle, destroyed homes, and generally threatened isolated territorial residents.

The Governor, who also served as ex officio superintendent of Indian affairs, without hesitation initiated actions designed to force that tribe to come to terms with the American government. He declared that the Osage no longer enjoyed the protection of the United States government and invited other friendly tribes to make war upon them and drive them from the territory. He also suspended all trade with the errant nation. Anticipating that the Jefferson Administration might consider his measures unnecessarily harsh, Lewis wrote to Secretary of War Dearborn suggesting that in its concern for the welfare of the Indians, the federal government should not lose sight of the precarious position of the white settlers along the frontier.

The Osage were not the only tribe causing difficulties for the Governor. A Spanish council attended by representatives of the Kansa, Omaha, Ponca, and Pawnee tribes prompted Lewis to suspend all trade along the lower Missouri until a military force could be stationed in the area. Meanwhile, the Sac continued to commit hostile acts along the Upper Mississippi. Governor Lewis and Gen. William Clark, who had returned to St. Louis in June, 1808, with his new bride, were convinced that British traders were responsible for the widespread Indian unrest along the frontier. These two men spent much of the summer attempting to counter British efforts and to pacify the generally volatile situation.

Governor Lewis predicated his Indian policies upon the assumption that their love of merchandise and their fear of punishment afforded the most effective means for controlling them. Most local residents heartily endorsed his strong stand in handling Indian problems, but national officials remained more reserved in their assessment of the situation. While approving the Governor's course of action, the President advised him to avoid, if at all possible, any military coercion of the Indians. Jefferson held that "commerce is the great engine by which we are to coerce them, & not war."

Operating under this philosophy, federal officials hoped to regain the friendship of the Indians through the establishment of additional government trading factories in the troubled region to provide the Indians with good merchandise at reasonable prices. Because the existing factory at Fort Belle Fontaine had not been readily accessible to the various tribes, the Department of War decided to construct a new factory near the Osage villages and another one on the Upper Mississippi at the mouth of the Des Moines River. Secretary Dearborn instructed the commander of Fort Belle Fontaine to establish military forts, manned by enough soldiers to protect them, adjacent to each of the proposed new trading posts.

By late summer all of the necessary arrangements for the new posts had been completed. When Governor Lewis and General Clark objected to plans to build the proposed Osage factory on the Osage River because of its inaccessibility, Secretary Dearborn agreed to shift its location to a site on the Missouri River approximately 300 miles above its junction with the Mississippi. In early August, 1808, a keelboat expedition under the command of Capt. Eli Clemson set out from Fort Belle Fontaine carrying men and supplies for the new installation. A short time later, Clark and a company of dragoons from St. Charles began an overland march to join Captain Clemson's force at the site of the proposed post. Nathan Boone, son of the famed pioneer Daniel Boone,[4] guided the party to their intended destination.

Clark had selected a spot on a high bluff overlooking the winding Missouri that would provide an unobstructed view of

4. The elder Boone had come to Missouri in 1799 at the invitation of Lt. Gov. Zenon Trudeau, who had promised him a grant of 1,000 arpents of land. Like many residents, Boone encountered difficulty in securing confirmation of his grant from the American government, because he had failed to cultivate the tract in question. A special act of Congress finally confirmed the title for the famed pioneer.

many miles of the surrounding countryside. Immediately after Clark's arrival on the site he ordered construction on a block-house to begin. As the log buildings began to rise, Clark dispatched Nathan Boone and an interpreter to inform the Osage of his arrival and to invite them to take up residence near the new fort. When they received the good news the Osage, who because of their recent hostilities no longer enjoyed the protection of the United States government, rushed to meet Clark at the fort that was already beginning to take shape.

Clark found the Indians agreeable to the site he had chosen for the location of the factory and even more eager to re-establish themselves under the protection of the United States. Taking advantage of the Osage's favorable disposition, he negotiated a treaty in which they relinquished their title to nearly 200 square miles of land between the Missouri and Arkansas rivers in the Louisiana Territory. However, shortly after Clark returned to St. Louis with the treaty, an Osage delegation came to the territorial capital to protest the agreement. The appearance of the band of disgruntled Indians irritated Clark, who had carefully gone over every provision of the treaty with them before they had signed it. General Clark was convinced that Pierre Chouteau had encouraged the Indians to reject the treaty in the hope that a new agreement might contain a provision recognizing his Spanish land grant to 30,000 arpents of land in the ceded area.

Nevertheless, both Clark and the Governor agreed that whatever the reason for the Indians' sudden change of mind, the treaty should be renegotiated to avoid future problems. Consequently Governor Lewis drew up a new treaty designed to remove all Indian objections to the previous agreement. In drafting the document, Lewis consulted with Pierre Chouteau, the Osage Indian agent, but he rejected Chouteau's request to incorporate an article confirming his land grant. Lewis instructed Chouteau to submit the revised treaty to the Osage leaders for their approval, and they agreed to accept its terms on November 10, 1808. After the formal signing of the treaty in St. Louis on August 31, 1809, it was submitted to the Senate for ratification.

The basic provisions of the revised treaty did not differ significantly from those outlined in the original document prepared by Clark. The new version did contain additional articles concerning hunting grounds, the surrender and punishment of Indian and white criminals, and the recovery of stolen property. The land cession by the Osage remained unchanged. In return for title to the land, the American government agreed to establish a permanent factory to supply the tribe with merchandise, to erect a blacksmith shop and mill for use by the Indians, to grant annual stipends of $1500 to the tribe, and to restore to them the protection of the United States.

The signing of the treaty and the completion of Fort Osage marked the final return of the Osage to the American fold. Now they and members of other friendly neighboring tribes could come to this westernmost military post in the United States to exchange goods with the resident factor, George Sibley, whenever they desired. Dressed in their finery of beads, red ribbons, vermillion, silver ornaments, and scarlet blankets, they gathered to observe the official opening of Fort Osage on November 10, 1808. Hours after the brief formal ceremonies had ended, the joyous Indians continued to sing and dance in honor of the long-awaited establishment of a regular trading factory in their region. As dawn broke amidst the dying echoes of the lively chants and the smoldering embers of the previous night's fires, a stillness settled over the fort high atop the Missouri bluffs. At least momentarily, tranquility had seemingly been restored along one remote portion of the frontier.

Meanwhile, attempts to establish a similar post along the Mississippi at a site fifteen miles above the mouth of the Des Moines River had not gone so smoothly. Work on that post, known as Fort Madison, had proceeded much more slowly. Located in the heart of territory long dominated by British traders, the Americans found local Indians generally unreceptive. Despite their desire to secure a trading factory, the tribesmen in that region strongly disliked the presence of regular military forces in the region. An unusually harsh winter further retarded progress on the fort. When spring finally arrived, Fort Madison remained uncompleted. Alarmed by increasing Indian activity in the area, the commanding officer at the post sent an expedition to St. Louis requesting assistance, but before any reinforcements could arrive a band of Sac Indians, after pretending friendship, attempted unsuccessfully to storm the still-unfinished fortification.

From St. Louis the situation seemed ominous in the spring of 1809. The urgent pleas from Fort Madison offered graphic proof of the continuing Indian hostilities along the Mississippi. Reports that the Prophet was expanding his attempts to incite the Shawnee against the Americans added to the local uncertainty, and erroneous reports persisted in the territory that the United States had already declared war on both France and Great Britain. In response to these conditions, Governor Lewis took steps to strengthen territorial defenses. He dispatched two volunteer companies of militia to relieve the beleaguered garrison at Fort Madison. He also ordered the construction of a series of blockhouses in the district of St. Charles and as a final precautionary measure he placed the members of the militia in the districts of St. Charles and St. Louis on alert in case of an attack.

Although Lewis's measures struck a generally responsive chord in the territory, his attempts to control the Indians through trade restrictions occasionally roused protests from the local fur traders. They particularly objected to his temporary suspension of the issuance of licenses for trading with the Indians. Profits from the fur trade had been steadily declining since the late eighteenth century in the Louisiana Territory, and St. Louis's staid conservative merchants had gradually lost ground to their more aggressive British counterparts. With the notable exception of Jacques Clamorgan's ill-fated Company of Explorers of the Upper Missouri, the St. Louis traders had not attempted to expand their trade into new regions. Instead they had continued to operate in the same areas year after year.

Reports from the Lewis and Clark expedition of the rich supply of furs along the Upper Missouri had rekindled interest in the possibility of opening trade with some of the tribes in that region. One of the first of the St. Louis traders to catch a glimpse of the rich potential of that trade was Manuel Lisa. Considered to be something of a maverick by the small group of St. Louis merchants who had managed to monopolize the trade for many years, Lisa joined forces with another unorthodox trader, Jacques Clamorgan, in an unsuccessful attempt to open trade with Santa Fe in 1806. Although the venture failed, it convinced Lisa that a trading expedition to the rich beaver areas in the Rockies would be profitable.

Unable to secure financial support for the undertaking in St. Louis, Lisa entered a partnership with Pierre Menard and William Morrison, both prominent merchants in Kaskaskia. The three partners sponsored the first planned American trading and trapping expedition to the Upper Missouri. With many recruits from the recently returned Lewis and Clark expedition, Manuel Lisa organized and directed a force of more than fifty men that headed up the Missouri in the spring of 1807. After enduring the hardships and privations of living in the wilderness for over a year, Lisa returned to St. Louis in the summer of 1808 with enough beaver skins to show a modest return on the original investment. Based upon what he had seen, Lisa reported that tremendous profits awaited those willing to take the necessary risks. In fact many of his men had remained in the mountains for the upcoming hunt in the fall.

Lisa's successful venture created a dilemma for his St. Louis competitors. They now realized that they either must enter the race to capture the rich trade on the Upper Missouri or run the risk of losing their dominant position in the fur business. Already numerous American merchants, including John Jacob Astor, had expressed interest in entering the trans-Mississippi trade. Moreover, the St. Louis group, headed by the Chouteaus, faced the bleak prospect of a further reduction in the present revenues, as the unwelcome competition from the two newly-constructed government trading factories slowly eroded their long-time trade monopoly with the tribes along the lower Missouri.

After carefully considering the various alternatives open to them, the most prominent traders decided to join Lisa and his partners in the formation of the St. Louis Missouri Fur Company. With the additional capital that the new organization could provide, the founders hoped to fully exploit the rich trade in the Upper Missouri Valley. Under the Articles of Association and Co-Partnership drafted in St. Louis during the winter of 1808–1809, each member agreed to go on the first expedition or to provide an acceptable substitute. Some of the most prominent members of the St. Louis business community joined Lisa, Menard, and Morrison in launching the new company. They included Benjamin Wilkinson, nephew of the former governor; Pierre Chouteau; Reuben Lewis, brother of the current governor; William Clark; Auguste Chouteau, Jr.; and Andrew Henry. The group designated William Clark to act as the firm's agent in St. Louis.

Even before the final Articles of Agreement had been approved, the company had signed a contract with Governor Lewis to escort Shahaka the Mandan chief to his home. In return for a payment of $7,000, the company agreed to supply a force of 120 men to guarantee the chief's safe return. If the trade did not go as well as the members anticipated, they still could count on the substantial payment from the government. As an added incentive, the Governor promised not to grant any licenses to trade in the area above the Platte River until after the company's scheduled departure date, thereby assuring the Missouri Company's traders a head start. Altogether the company dispatched approximately 350 men up the river in May and June, 1809, with the knowledge that they enjoyed the Governor's confidence.

When it learned of the Governor's actions, the Administration had serious reservations about the large payment to the company in view of the expedition's quasi-commercial nature. Secretary of War Eustis agreed to pay the amount stipulated in the contract, but he declined to approve payment of an additional $500 authorized by Governor Lewis for purchasing gifts for the Indians. In refusing to pay the amount in question, the Secretary reprimanded Lewis for having failed to secure authorization in advance for this costly project. The federal government required local officials to seek prior approval for all large expenditures so that it could closely regulate territorial expenses. Economy-minded federal officials tended to be very conservative in the amounts that they authorized local officers to spend. In 1808, Secretary Eustis informed General Clark that the expenses of the Indian department in the Territory of Louisiana had exceeded the War Department's estimates by more than $20,000, and Eustis consequently trimmed Clark's requested budget for 1809.

The War Department's decision to reject additional sums that Governor Lewis had approved for payment prompted him to urge that territorial officials be given broader discretion in handling local problems in view of the distance separating them from Washington. Lewis pointed out that it required at least two months for him to receive a reply to his most urgent inquiries. Under such circumstances, unexpected situations frequently made it necessary for him to act without consulting his superiors in the executive branch.

The absence of regular channels of communication in frontier communities posed a perennial problem for territorial administrators, and more than any of his predecessors Governor Lewis sought to alleviate this deficiency in Louisiana. Irregular and undependable postal service proved a constant source of irritation to territorial residents and also to officials. Post riders, under contract, carried the mails on horseback. Working under difficult and sometimes dangerous conditions, these frontier couriers often failed to make their scheduled rounds. The territory was supposed to receive mail once a week from the East, but to the dismay of local residents several weeks sometimes elapsed between deliveries. Despite Governor Lewis's attempts to obtain improvements in the system, postal service in the territory remained unsatisfactory.

The Governor was also primarily responsible for establishing the first newspaper in the territory. Recognizing the need for a territorial printer who could publish Louisiana's newly-enacted statutes, Lewis advanced money to Joseph Charless to come to St. Louis to establish a newspaper. As a result of the Governor's efforts, issue number one of the *Missouri Gazette*, the first newspaper published west of the Mississippi River, went on sale in St. Louis on July 12, 1808.

The appearance of a newspaper was only one of many changes in the rapidly-growing territory. Since its transfer to the United States in 1804, Upper Louisiana had undergone a gradual transformation in appearance and in outlook. An atmosphere charged with excitement, and a sense of expectancy and frenzied activity had slowly replaced the leisurely pace of the Spanish period. American immigrants of all types and descriptions flocked to Louisiana expecting to profit from the tremendous opportunities just then unfolding. The steady stream of settlers boosted the territorial population from slightly more than 10,000 in 1804 to more than 20,000 by 1810. Land values rapidly appreciated as speculators rushed to buy up all of the available Spanish grants for later resale to the swelling tide of newcomers.

Land speculation was not the only profitable pursuit for the enterprising Louisianian. The expanding population created a boom for the local businessmen who found the task of supplying territorial needs an increasingly lucrative proposition. However, as the volume of business increased, so did the number of merchants. Long-time French mercantile firms encountered growing competition from the numerous American merchants who had recently opened for business. In contrast with their French counterparts who sold goods from their residences, American merchandisers opened stores in which they displayed their wares for customers to examine. These new American establishments could be easily identified by the signs prominently attached to the front of their buildings, and local buyers were delighted with the larger stocks inside from which they could make their selections. American manufactured goods—from the wholesale markets of Philadelphia and Baltimore—comprised a larger portion of the merchandise offered for sale, whereas the French and Spanish merchants had secured most of their goods from New Orleans and Canada.

The effects of the sudden influx of Americans were most noticeable in the territory's principal villages. An intense rivalry for the business of providing for the needs of the strangers that arrived daily replaced the generous hospitality that had characterized the earlier less complex Spanish period. Existing facilities were inadequate and competition for them was keen. A visitor in St. Louis in 1810 reported that "every house is crowded, rents are high, and it is exceedingly difficult to procure a tenement on any terms." The problems were by no means confined to that village since each of the territory's five districts experienced similar growth and expansion between the years 1804 and 1810.

Slowly the quaint French villages began to look more like American towns. Newly constructed brick and frame buildings, reflecting the American type of construction, intermingled with the older French style buildings. American modes of fashion and dress also gained wide acceptance, especially among the younger people. English replaced French as the principal language; the *Missouri Gazette* carried only occasional notices in French. Perhaps Washington Irving's colorful description of St. Louis in 1810 best captured the spirit of the cultural blend:

> ... Here were to be seen about the river banks, the hectoring, extravagant, bragging boatmen of the Mississippi, with the gay, grimacing, singing, good-humored Canadian voyageurs. Vagrant Indians, of various tribes, loitered about the streets. Now and then, a stark Kentucky hunter, in leathern hunting-dress, with rifle on shoulder and knife in belt, strode along. Here and there were new brick houses and shops, just set up by bustling, driving, and eager men of traffic from the Atlantic States; while, on the other hand, the old French mansions, with open casements, still retained the easy, indolent air of the original colonists; and now and then the scraping of a fiddle, a strain of an ancient French song, or the sound of billiard balls, showed that the happy Gallic turn for gayety and amusement still lingered about the place.

The Louisiana Territory's rapid development produced a growing impatience among local residents with the American government's failure to resolve perennial frontier problems: unresolved land claims, disputed mining rights, inadequate defenses, poor postal service, and insufficient transportation facilities. Their dissatisfaction and the growing awareness of the current system's inadequacies contributed to increased criticism of the existing territorial government, and in the years following 1808, Louisianians began to press for advancement to a second-class territory as the most promising means of alleviating their difficulties. The dual attractions of greater self-government and new opportunities for local public office brought added support to the movement.

As early as January, 1808, Frederick Bates referred to local desires for a second-grade territorial government, but the campaign to advance Louisiana's territorial status appears not to have begun in earnest until 1809. The editor of the *Missouri Gazette*, Joseph Charless, reported in January that he intended to publish in an upcoming issue a letter he had received proposing that application be made by Louisianians to the general government for advancement to a second-grade territory, but he also cautioned his readers to give careful consideration to the consequences of such a step. The editor suggested that the change would increase taxes and extend the Governor's powers in the territory while lessening his responsibility to the national government. Charless's arguments provided the basis for much of the later campaign against the proposed shift.

Two weeks after Charless's opening blast, the *Gazette* printed a copy of a petition to Congress, seeking the change in territorial status. Basing its demands upon the Treaty of Cession and the Constitution, the petition claimed that Louisiana's current system of government excluded its residents from the full enjoyment of the rights and privileges guaranteed to all American citizens. Furthermore, the petition reminded Congress that the Territory of Orleans already had been granted the rights which Upper Louisiana now sought.

The editor's opposition to the proposed change set off a major debate in the columns of the *Gazette* over the assets and liabilities of second-class status for the territory. "A Subscriber" accused Charless of resisting modifications in Louisiana's government because, as territorial printer, he feared loss of executive patronage. After questioning the editor's motives, the author of this letter then enumerated the advantages that the higher grade of government would provide. Appealing to the growing demands for representative government, "A Subscriber" argued that local residents were best equipped to solve their own problems, and that this measure would pave the way for even further advances in self-government.

Charless refused to budge from his original position, insisting that the changes would not be worth the greatly increased costs. Using arguments similar to those that had been advanced by opponents of second-class status in other territories, he contended that the increased costs of the new government would discourage additional immigrants from coming into the territory. Like Charless, the chief antagonists of the second-grade government continually stressed that such a change would necessitate a large increase in local taxes. Whereas the territorial legislators currently received their salaries from the federal treasury, the costs of the new legislature would have to be borne by the local tax-payers, particularly the property holders.[5]

While the debate continued to rage, copies of the petition printed in the *Gazette* had been circulated throughout the territory for signatures and were forwarded to Congress in January, 1810. Since Louisiana's organic act of 1805 had not provided for automatic advancement to second-class status when the territory reached a population of 5,000 adult males, congressional authorization was necessary prior to this step. However, a bill introduced in the House of Representatives on January 22, 1810, calling for the creation of a second-class government for the Territory of Louisiana failed to gain approval at that session. A shortage of time rather than any organized opposition apparently caused Congress to postpone action on the measure. Despite the temporary setback, the movement for the higher classification had introduced a new dimension into Louisiana's territorial politics.

As had been the case since Upper Louisiana had passed under American control, land claims continued to be the chief political issue, but the scope of the struggle had broadened. Many of the young American attorneys who had come to the territory after 1804 had joined forces with the large claimants whom they now represented in the complicated legal proceedings, while a growing number of opposing speculators who stood to benefit from the rejection of the large claims lined up solidly in opposition to confirmation. At the center of the storm of controversy was the board of land commissioners.

Because of the absence of James Donaldson, the board had discontinued all regular proceedings during the winter of 1806–1807, but following the arrival of Donaldson's replacement, Frederick Bates, in the spring of 1807, the commission resumed its deliberations. In the meantime, Congress had passed new

5. Prior to 1822, with one minor exception, all legislative costs in second-class territories had to be paid for locally. Widespread dissatisfaction with this system and a growing awareness of the burden it placed upon local resources caused the normally economy-minded national legislature to reconsider. In 1822 Congress agreed to pay territorial legislators in Florida, and gradually it extended the same consideration to all other territories. These changes, however, came too late to aid the Missouri Territory.

legislation liberalizing certain restrictions previously placed upon confirmation of titles. No longer did the claimant have to produce written permission for claims of less than 800 arpents if he could demonstrate that he had occupied and cultivated the lands for not less than ten years prior to December 20, 1803. Subsequently, Congress increased the amount allowable from 800 to 2,000 arpents. In addition it granted the board of commissioners full power to confirm titles in accordance with the laws and the established usages and customs of the French and Spanish governments over the strenuous objections of Secretary Gallatin, who contended that such so-called usages and customs were merely deviations from the very restrictions the board was supposed to enforce.

Upon resuming its regular proceedings the board made several important decisions. It replaced the controversial clerk, Charles Gratiot, with William Christy; following Christy's resignation, Thomas Riddick assumed his duties. Furthermore, in order to expedite the land-claims proceedings and to accommodate claimants in remote regions of the territory, the commissioners decided to hold regular sessions in various parts of the territory to record claims and to receive testimony. The originally-scheduled hearings, however, had to be postponed to a later time, probably because of inclement weather. This gave the board an opportunity to reconsider its decision, and its members decided that only one of them need visit the outlying regions to take testimony. As a result, Frederick Bates was designated to make the trip. The recorder went to Cape Girardeau in late May of 1808 and subsequently visited the districts of New Madrid and Arkansas. While in Arkansas, Bates encountered numerous difficulties in carrying out his assigned duties. Because of the isolation and almost total lack of education of the more remote settlers, he found them unable to comprehend even the most elementary legal procedures.

Following Bates's return from his journey, the board settled down to serious consideration of the claims that had been registered during the preceding two and one-half years. The commissioners issued their first formal decisions on December 8, 1808. An indication of the slow progress made by the board came in a report submitted to the Secretary of the Treasury on February 1, 1810, in which the commissioners reported that they had recorded 3,056 claims, including 2,699 cases in which they had taken testimony. They further disclosed that they had issued certificates of confirmation on only 323 claims, while an additional 167 had been authorized for survey. A total of 139 claims had been rejected by the board to date.

The board's tardiness in acting upon land claims and the still unpopular guidelines it had to follow in making its decisions precipitated an increasing impatience among the territory's claimants. In January, 1808, a group holding unapproved land grants petitioned Congress to order the confirmation of every title issued by the Spanish government except for those that could be proved to be antedated or fraudulent. A second petition, submitted in December of the same year by substantially the same group, again appealed for Congress to revise the conditions it had set down for the approval of titles. Its signers particularly objected to provisions requiring actual habitation and cultivation of lands claimed, limiting the maximum size of grants, and voiding all grants made after October 1, 1800.

Having failed to elicit any congressional action with their petitions, the land-claimant group decided to try a common frontier political device—the creation of an *ad hoc* committee. This technique previously had been used with moderate success in Upper Louisiana after its attachment to the Indiana Territory in 1804. Again seeking to present an impression of unity and broad support, a St. Louis group spearheaded the formation of a new general committee representing all districts of the territory to petition Congress for action on land claims.

As a product of their efforts, a general convention met in Ste. Genevieve in August, 1809, to consider the land-claims problem. The group, composed primarily of Louisiana's largest land claimants, designated the notorious John Smith T, Edward Hempstead, a popular attorney who often represented land claimants, and Hugh McDermed as members of a select committee to draft a memorial to Congress in behalf of the citizens of the territory. The convention adopted two resolutions: one recommending that their fellow citizens join them in seeking a second-class government and the other calling for the removal of John B. C. Lucas. Under the guise of petitions and special committees, the special-interest group attempted to create an appearance of widespread public approval for its objectives. In this case, by mixing their large and fluid claims with the moderate, bona fide claims of the majority of the territory's residents, the big land claimants hoped to secure confirmation of them all.

The committee appointed by the convention met in St. Louis in October, 1809, and drew up a petition calling for the establishment of a more generous policy for the confirmation of land claims. Departing from their original plans, they decided against preparing a resolution seeking the removal of Lucas from the board of land commissioners, because they believed that the petitions that were already being circulated for that purpose would be more effective and would also make any further actions on the subject unnecessary.

The concerted effort to oust Lucas from his place on the land-claims commission reflected a widely-held belief among the claimants that he had been personally responsible for blocking confirmation of most of the land claims. As early as 1807, Lucas reported sporadic attempts to secure his removal as a commissioner, but the campaign against the judge that materialized in mid-1809 obviously had been planned thoroughly and was well-organized. The *Missouri Gazette* contained a notice naming the persons in the various districts to whom petitions opposing Lucas should be returned. A slanderous attack against him had also been posted on the church door in St. Louis calling upon the people of Louisiana to oust this "little Robespierre."

In response to this and other equally vitriolic attacks, Lucas wrote to various members of the Administration defending himself against such charges. The judge invited President Madison to institute an inquiry into his official conduct if he believed it was necessary. Lucas insisted that he had been attacked simply because he had held the least favorable opinion of the land claims of any of the commissioners. He reported that he had resisted all attempts at bribery, and added wryly that, had he succumbed to such offers, Madison would never have heard any complaints against him. The President must have agreed since Lucas remained on the board of land commissioners until it had completed its work.

While the spotlight focused upon the land claimants' disputes, a smaller but very important division had arisen between Governor Lewis and Secretary Bates. Unfortunately the Governor left no account of his side of the controversy, and the story must be reconstructed entirely from Bates's sparse though heated references to their differences. Relations between the two men had been strained since shortly after the Governor's arrival in the territory. They disagreed on most major policy matters, including the removal of officials, the handling of lead leases, and the issuance of trading permits, and a clash of personalities made it difficult for them to resolve their differences amicably. Governor Lewis's preference for relying upon the advice of others in handling especially important matters must have intensified the Secretary's antipathy toward him. The Governor's inclination to depend upon William Clark for assistance in crucial matters particularly angered Bates. He complained that Lewis requested Clark to handle executive business in his absence that properly should have been assigned to the territorial secretary. Moreover, Bates lamented that Lewis never confided the Administration's wishes to him.

Both the Governor and the Secretary sought to avoid any public airing of their disagreement. Only once, at a ball in St. Louis which both men attended, did they fail to adhere to an agreement to keep their differences private. Thus, despite their inability to develop a harmonious working relationship, neither man sought to organize a personal following against the other, and their conflict remained largely a private matter.

Already disturbed by the strained relations between himself and the Secretary, Governor Lewis grew even more despondent when he learned that certain of his expenditures had not been approved for payment by the federal government. In order to clear himself of any possible taint of improper conduct and to secure approval of the protested bills, the Governor left the territory in early September, 1809, bound for Washington, D. C. Lewis never arrived at his destination because of his unexpected death in Tennessee. A major debate has raged over the cause of the Governor's death, but the preponderance of the evidence seems to suggest suicide.

Lewis apparently never enjoyed his duties as governor, and, even if he had lived, it is doubtful he would have returned to the post. Governor Lewis had not been a particularly good administrator. Unsatisfactory communications had doomed his attempts to direct the territory from Washington; he had been unable to develop a harmonious working relationship with the territorial secretary, and his failure to secure proper authorization in advance for territorial expenses threatened to bankrupt him. Nevertheless, the Lewis administration had produced some important gains. Thanks to the efforts of Frederick Bates the threat of a western conspiracy within the territory had been laid to rest; relative political calm had been re-established, and the Governor had at least acquainted national officials with the territory's most pressing problems.

CHAPTER VIII

THE WAR OF 1812
COMES TO MISSOURI

THE THREAT of a full-scale Indian war created a tense and uncertain atmosphere in the territory between 1810 and 1815. Although frontier residents needed always to remain alert to the possibility of Indian attacks, the danger now was increased greatly by a steady deterioration in relations between the United States and Great Britain and the resulting War of 1812.

Governor Lewis's Indian policies had been reassuring, but his unexpected death in 1809 renewed local anxieties. In the interim Frederick Bates again became Acting Governor of Louisiana, while the Madison Administration initiated a search to find a permanent replacement for Lewis. When compared with other early nineteenth-century territories, Louisiana seems to have been especially attractive to would-be office seekers. The territory's good climate, favorable location, and acceptance of slavery accounted for much of its popularity. Despite the low salaries paid territorial officials, the number of applicants for posts in Missouri always exceeded the number of positions available. Motives for seeking these offices varied, but persons who solicited territorial appointments generally looked upon them as a means to improve their circumstances. Not only did these offices provide limited financial security, but aspiring politicians believed that they also offered an opening for rapid political and economic advancement.

President Madison proceeded slowly in choosing a successor for Governor Lewis, perhaps in part because of the large number of persons who expressed an interest in securing the nomination. At least thirteen persons were recommended to fill the vacant post, but some of those considered were not willing to serve. William Clark may have been offered the post, and if so he apparently turned it down because he believed he lacked the necessary experience in political matters. Frederick Bates, whose name was also mentioned for the office, indicated privately that he preferred to retain his positions as territorial secretary and recorder of land titles because of the more lucrative remuneration he received from those combined posts. Nevertheless, most of those whose names had been recommended eagerly sought the office, including at least two men personally acquainted with Louisiana's problems—John B. Scott[1] and John Coburn. Scott was a Virginian who had served for a short time as military commandant in Cape Girardeau. Coburn, a territorial judge with strong local backing, waged a particularly intensive campaign for the post.

The President, however, decided to offer the position to Benjamin Howard, a popular Kentucky lawyer who understood frontier problems. Madison's reasons for appointing Howard are not entirely clear. Undoubtedly political considerations were involved, but Howard's military experience probably tipped the balance in his favor in view of the growing threat of a general Indian uprising along the frontier. Howard seemed a good choice for the governorship of Louisiana; a member of the United States House of Representatives at the time of his nomination, he resigned from that body on April 10, 1810, in order to take the post. Although Howard may have considered the governorship a step forward politically, he apparently later regretted his decision. He always preferred living in Kentucky rather than Louisiana, and when his term as governor expired, he declined reappointment.

Governor Howard administered the territory during a very crucial period, and he was necessarily preoccupied with matters of Indian policy and frontier defenses. During the summer of 1810, British traders had been particularly active among the tribes located east of the Mississippi. Their activity, combined with the work of the Prophet and his brother Tecumseh, threatened to turn the major tribes of the Northwest against the United States. The Shawnee, Potawatomi, Winnebago, Kickapoo, and Sac all showed signs of restlessness. A short time be-

1. John B. Scott should not be confused with the more prominent John Scott, also from Virginia, who later became Missouri's territorial delegate to Congress.

fore Howard made his first official visit to the territory a Sac murdered four settlers above the Missouri, reviving the fears of an Indian war.

Howard was commissioned on April 18, 1810, but he did not reach St. Louis until September 17. After his arrival, the tense residents of the territory heaved a temporary sigh of relief and feted Howard with a large public dinner followed by a dance in the Assembly Room which reportedly lasted until dawn. However, the Governor remained in the territory only a short time before returning to Kentucky.

The level of Indian activity declined during the winter months, but the arrival of spring signaled the beginning of a new wave of depredations. While settlers east of the Mississippi bore the brunt of the revived attacks, residents in the Louisiana Territory remained apprehensive. Governor Howard returned to the territory in July, 1811, to take charge of local defensive preparations and to inspect Missouri's northern frontier. With the assistance of William Clark, who was reappointed brigadier general of the territorial militia, the Governor directed the organization of militia companies and the construction of blockhouses in remote sections of the territory. Having put the territory in a state of military readiness, Howard once again left for Kentucky in September, 1811. In November, Acting Governor Bates ordered the territorial militia to be ready to repel a possible Indian invasion. Only four days after Bates alerted the militia, General Harrison clashed with Tecumseh's forces at Prophet's Town in the Battle of Tippecanoe. Although Harrison later successfully capitalized upon the battle to help win his way into the White House, the contest proved indecisive, thereby making the situation even more unsettled.

Fearing that Harrison's encounter with Tecumseh in the Indiana Territory might trigger a general Indian uprising along the frontier, Governor Howard hurried back to St. Louis to take charge. In February, 1812, a band of Indians from east of the Mississippi, after pretending to be friendly, murdered nine members of one family in the district of St. Charles. Conditions had become so serious in early 1812 that Governor Howard recommended a major campaign against the marauding savages. Both Howard and Clark consistently advocated the use of force against the Indians and their British partners, who were credited with instigating the unrest.

In reality the rising tide of Indian depredations was the inevitable result of the United States's inept Indian policy. Despite a lukewarm commitment to safeguard the interests of the Indians, governmental officials ultimately always acquiesced to the demands of the more powerful white settlers. An ill-conceived and poorly administered plan to teach the Indians the white man's ways never had a chance. Capitalizing on the Indians' dependence upon the white man for weapons and merchandise, the United States systematically deprived them of millions of acres of land through negotiations with their leaders, whom they bribed with gifts and annuities. Failing to understand the Indians' natural resentment, frontier officials routinely attributed Indian unhappiness to British provocation. Steeped in a tradition of racial superiority, the recalcitrant frontiersman refused ever to consider the Indian anything more than an obstacle to be removed as quickly as possible.

To help subdue the warring tribes, Governor Howard, on his own initiative, authorized the formation of a company of rangers, and then requested the President to approve his actions. Rangers were special groups of militia raised for stipulated periods of time at federal expense to assist in the defense of frontier regions. Subsequently, the Secretary of War gave full approbation to the measures Howard had adopted to protect the frontier, including the organization of the special force. This company of rangers, under the command of Captain Nathan Boone, patrolled Missouri's northern frontier and aided regular troops from Fort Belle Fontaine in erecting additional blockhouse forts in the area. Following the expiration of their original enlistment period of three months, the men refused to sign up again unless they were given an opportunity first to visit their homes.

Recruitment posed a particularly difficult problem for frontier officials seeking to raise troops locally, especially since it was common knowledge that men previously called to duty had not received pay for their services. The federal government's failure to pay the troops sent by Governor Lewis to relieve Fort Madison in the spring of 1809 had led to a widespread notion that men called into service could be certain of payment only if the Governor had received advanced authorization to recruit them. Consequently, they were reluctant to volunteer their services, and Governor Howard reported that he had been forced to give his personal pledge that the men would be paid.

The growing danger of war and the constant problems of Indian defense in the Louisiana Territory led to a stepped-up campaign for a second-class government. Most Louisianians believed that the new form of government would offer them a more satisfactory means for securing a hearing of their problems. In their renewed efforts to build popular support for the measure, proponents of the change in status pointed out that it would give the residents a voice in making their own laws through the creation of a popularly-elected territorial House of Representatives. Other desirable features which they stressed included the right to send a delegate to Congress and the separation of legislative and judicial authority locally.

Much of the renewed impetus for a second-grade government must be attributed to the widespread belief that the general government was badly misinformed about actual conditions in the territory. Since the existing territorial government provided no means of direct contact with the government in Washington, except through appointed officials, the prospect of having a congressional delegate appealed strongly to Louisianians. They believed that their own elected representative would be able to keep Congress better informed of the actual situation in the territory, thereby enhancing prospects for the settlement of problems caused by unconfirmed land titles, inadequate defenses, unsatisfactory mail service, and other similar problems.

As in the earlier attempt to secure higher territorial classification, a major part of the debate in 1811 centered around territorial finances. "An Old Farmer" revived Charless's earlier charge that the proposed change in government would require a substantial increase in local taxes and that this would ruin property holders. Predictions that the search for additional revenue might cause officials to levy a tax on uncultivated lands must have alarmed individuals with extensive holdings. "Alknomack" attempted to quiet all such fears with a complex series of statistical calculations that purported to show that the costs of the higher stage of government would not be prohibitive. He argued that the revenues needed to cover the added expenses of a second-class government could be raised without imposing any additional hardships upon local residents because the expected increase in population would provide sufficient added monies to offset the higher costs.

Despite the argument that the advanced status would increase the flow of federal funds into the territory, the fear of heavier tax burdens continued to generate some opposition to the proposed change. By far the most serious objections came from the local French population. The extensive tracts of uncultivated lands held by many of these "ancient inhabitants" accounted for much of their hostility. For the most part these large land claimants felt that the added tax burden would not be worth the benefits to be derived from having a territorial delegate in Congress. Unlike those individuals with smaller claims, the holders of extensive claims had always been successful in the past in communicating their views to Congress through private agents. Moreover, as the territorial population increased, the French minority recognized that the proposed change would ultimately diminish their voice in territorial affairs. Like the French residents in other territories who also opposed the second grade of government, Louisiana's leading Frenchmen clearly preferred the existing system.

All efforts to postpone the change any longer failed. In retrospect, the American commitment to the ideal of self-government and the already firmly-established pattern of territorial advancement virtually had assured the ultimate success of those seeking to raise Louisiana to the higher classification. In November, 1811, Congress again took up consideration of a bill granting Louisiana a second-class government. Numerous petitions from Louisiana were introduced in support of the proposed measure. Aside from a debate over whether the act should grant freehold or universal suffrage, the major provisions of the bill encountered little opposition. Congress passed the bill, and President Madison signed it into law on June 4, 1812. Congress normally responded promptly to local demands for the second grade of government, and although Upper Louisiana had to wait slightly longer for the change in status than the average first-class territory, preoccupation with the ominous international situation undoubtedly accounted for some of the delay.

With the final approval of this act, the Territory of Louisiana became the Territory of Missouri. This change in names had been made in order to avoid unnecessary confusion with the new state of Louisiana. The former Territory of Orleans was admitted to the Union in 1812 as the state of Louisiana.

If, as Missourians generally believed, the advancement in territorial status would lead to improved defenses, the measure came none too soon. Only two weeks after President Madison signed the bill advancing Missouri to a second-class territory, Congress approved a formal declaration of war against Great Britain. When word of the congressional action reached the territory in early July, 1812, local residents received the news with mixed feelings. Because of their isolated yet exposed location on the edge of the frontier, they were understandably apprehensive about the future, but they also hoped that this decisive step would now clear the way for the permanent removal of the Indian menace from the territory. Hastily organized meetings in St. Louis and St. Charles unanimously adopted a series of resolutions in support of the war, but they also called upon the United States government to provide additional military and financial assistance to supplement local resources.

During the opening months of the war the situation along the frontier failed to improve. Only a short time after they had learned of the declaration of war, local residents received reports that at an Indian council held at the Rock River Sac villages the Winnebago, Kickapoo, Potawatomi, Shawnee, and Miami Indians had declared war on the United States, while several other tribes remained undecided. To make matters worse, a large party of well-armed Indians reportedly had begun to organize for an attack upon the Missouri Territory. By late summer the news of the failure of Maj. Gen. William Hull's attempt to invade Canada and of the surrender of several key military posts in the Upper Mississippi further discouraged Missouri's worried inhabitants. In desperation the St. Louis trustees even suggested that Governor Howard invite the Osage to declare war on all tribes hostile to the United States.

In the fall of 1812, Missourians undertook an intensive campaign to acquaint federal officials with their precarious plight. They requested Governor Howard to go to Washington, D. C. as their spokesman and to urge greater federal participation in the western campaigns. Although Howard agreed, he altered his plans and remained in Kentucky. Howard offered no explanation, but he may have been considering returning to Kentucky permanently. Judge John B. C. Lucas reported from Louisville, Kentucky, that the Governor had been sizing up prospects for a seat in the United States Senate. The Governor did, nonetheless, write a lengthy letter to Secretary of War John Armstrong strongly urging positive steps to improve the territory's defensive position as a means of averting a possible military disaster.

Howard further recommended that a major offensive campaign be waged against the belligerent tribes in order to end their depredations once and for all. He thought that such a plan would prove very effective, and that it would not exceed in cost the amount spent annually by the nation for frontier defenses. However, the Secretary of War rejected the Governor's proposed campaign on the grounds that it was not expedient at that time to undertake such a venture.

The hesitancy of the national government to move strongly against the Indian menace became a subject of widespread discussion. Most Missourians argued that a force adequate to defend the territory could not be obtained locally. Although they expressed a willingness to meet their responsibilities in this matter, they definitely felt that additional federal help would be necessary to achieve a victory. Most of all they were bothered by the federal government's failure to station a sizable number of regular troops in the territory permanently. At the outbreak of the war, there were fewer than 250 regular soldiers serving west of the Mississippi. Because of the unrest, Missouri's newly-elected delegate to Congress, Edward Hempstead, took pains to assure his constituents that he had labored to secure a vigorous prosecution of the war in the remote frontier regions and to gain increased governmental support for the territory.

Predictions that an attack was about to be staged by a combined force of British and Indians circulated throughout the territory in early 1813, and residents of St. Louis became particularly disturbed at the prospect. A group of them met on February 15, 1813, to discuss the problem as it related to that city, and decided to appoint a committee to draft a series of resolutions for consideration by the whole community. Two days later a second meeting received the committee's hastily prepared report, which suggested creating a local committee of safety and vesting it with unlimited power to adopt the most effective measures for defending the town. Those in attendance at the second session agreed to all the proposed resolutions, and included an unconsciously ironical proviso declaring that since they constituted a free and voluntary association for objects of mutual concern, those who failed to cooperate would be considered enemies of the territory.

Shortly after its formation, the committee of public safety, headed by Col. Auguste Chouteau, conferred with Acting Governor Bates, who informed the members that he had taken steps to obtain accurate information concerning the rumored attack. Bates also cautioned the committee that he had not been empowered to authorize the expenditure of any additional funds for immediate defense of St. Louis. Perhaps at least part of Bates's reluctance to sanction any emergency appropriation stemmed from the earlier unhappy experience of Governor Lewis, who had been unable to get the federal government to pay the costs of such unauthorized commitments.

Having failed to receive any real assistance from Bates, Chouteau and his committee next appealed to the St. Louis board of trustees, who replied that they lacked authority to compel citizens to act in such a situation. As a result of its futile initial efforts, the committee of public safety concluded that the chances of securing adequate local or federal governmental help were slight. Seemingly, the burden of defending the city would have to rest primarily upon its local inhabitants, and so the committee initiated plans to dig trenches around the outskirts, to repair the three or four dilapidated blockhouses remaining from the Spanish period, to mount the few available cannons, and to surround the village with a stockade of pickets.

Meanwhile, the St. Louis board of trustees asked the Acting Governor to station a force of militia or regulars in St. Louis to assist those already collected there in defending the town against the impending attack. Bates, however, declined to take such action immediately because it still had not been definitely established that an assault would be made on the city. While acknowledging the importance of protecting the territorial capital, he doubted the advisability of surrounding the town with a large body of militia before it had actually been threatened. The Secretary did order the various volunteer militia companies to muster on March 20, 1813, and instructed them to be ready at any time thereafter to be called into immediate service.

In the midst of the adversity and uncertainty produced by the War of 1812, the territory needed a strong and effective leader at the helm. Had Governor Howard remained in the territory for longer periods of time, he might have provided that leadership, but his frequent absences often disrupted administrative operations. Howard may have been a more serious offender than most of his counterparts, but absenteeism was a perennial territorial problem, aggravated by the practice of appointing outsiders to fill territorial offices. Attempts to mitigate the difficulty by designating the territorial secretary to serve as acting governor in the absence of the regular executive brought only partial relief.

None of Missouri's territorial executives remained in the territory during his whole administration, and Governors Lewis and Howard were absent for particularly long periods of time. While Governor Lewis's absences had been a nuisance, Governor Howard's frequent absenteeism proved even more exasperating because of wartime conditions. Acting Governor Bates wrote to the Governor early in 1813, "We are almost in despair on account of your silence." Howard's periodic departures apparently stemmed from his desire to be with his friends and family in Kentucky. Throughout his term as governor he never lost his preference for Kentucky over Missouri.

While some residents criticized Governor Howard for his frequent absences from the territory, his otherwise satisfactory conduct in office seems to have shielded him from outright local hostility. Missourians particularly liked his strong stand in favor of military action against the Indians. For the most part, territorial inhabitants attributed their continuing problems to inaction by the federal government rather than to inattention from the Governor.

Following Howard's return to Missouri in the spring of 1813, he and Colonel Bissell took steps to evacuate Fort Osage, since they believed that its isolated location made it unwise to continue its operation at the current site. In a move to strengthen further local defenses, Howard and Bissell decided to construct a blockhouse fortification at Portage des Sioux. Additional encouragement came when word reached the territory in April that Congress had authorized the organization of ten new companies of rangers to defend those regions exposed to attack with the stipulation that Missouri Territory was to be given permission to recruit three of the companies. By early June the hysteria that had temporarily gripped the territory had subsided. In view of the slightly improved situation, the residents of St. Louis decided to abandon their costly plans to picket the village, much to the relief of local citizens who would have financed the project.

To strengthen the nation's defensive forces, the national government completely reorganized the structure of military administration. The new system divided the United States into nine military districts. The eighth military department, which encompassed the states of Kentucky and Ohio, and the territories of Indiana, Illinois, Michigan, and Missouri, was placed under the command of Gen. William H. Harrison. To provide supervision of the military operations in the western part of the eighth district, President Madison issued a special commission to Gov. Benjamin Howard, making him a brigadier general in the United States Army in charge of all forces in the territories of Missouri and Illinois. Having previously decided not to seek reappointment as governor, Howard accepted the nomination and resigned from Missouri's top executive post to devote full attention to his new responsibilities. In accordance with the President's wishes, William Clark replaced Howard as Missouri's territorial governor in 1813.[2]

A flurry of activity followed the change in assignments. Gen-

2. The President sent Howard blank commissions for the governorship and for the newly-created military post with instructions for him to accept the one he preferred and to offer the other position to Clark.

eral Howard organized a military expedition which he dispatched up the Mississippi and Illinois rivers to subdue warring tribes in those regions. At about the same time, the government supervised the resettlement of a band of friendly Sac and Fox Indians in present-day Moniteau County. Before moving to the Missouri Territory, those Indians had promised to remain at peace with all tribes including their traditional enemies, the Osage, and, to keep the Indians within the territory satisfied, the United States government built trading factories at Arrow Rock and Little Moniteau Creek to supply them with the merchandise they required.

Designation of General Howard to superintend the defense of the territory and assignment of the First Regiment of the United States infantry to St. Louis had brought renewed hope to the war-conscious residents. Nevertheless, fears occasioned by their relative isolation caused them to follow the conduct of the war closely, both locally and on the national scene, and their mood fluctuated in accordance with the changing tide of combat. The news of Oliver Hazard Perry's naval victory on the Great Lakes temporarily revived the territory's sagging spirits. John B. C. Lucas reported that gloom and despondency had been replaced by gladdening prospects as the result of that great naval feat. The successful return of Howard's expedition and the death of Tecumseh temporarily overshadowed the abandonment of Fort Madison by the American troops. In October, reports circulated in the territory that General Harrison had arranged a truce with many of the warring tribes. Those hopeful events caused local residents to conclude in the fall of 1813 that the end of the war would not be far away.

Unfortunately the temporary euphoria produced by the positive developments of late 1813 gradually subsided and was superseded by renewed anguish and alarm. Missourians generally favored the expulsion of the British from all of North America as the only permanent solution to the struggle.

In contrast with the improvements of the previous year, the events of 1814 particularly exasperated Missouri's war-weary residents. In January, 1814, General Howard received orders to report to General Harrison at Cincinnati. The removal of the popular and successful general, and, more importantly, the withdrawal of a portion of the regular troops recently stationed in St. Louis, once again left the territory heavily dependent upon its own limited forces. Residents of the territory reacted immediately to news of the new orders. Utilizing a public meeting to express their displeasure with the recent changes, several disaffected citizens of St. Louis met on February 2, 1814, to remonstrate against the general government for its failure to provide adequately for their defense.

Primary responsibility for the unpopular changes must be assigned to General Harrison rather than to officials in Washington. Harrison had recommended that Howard be sent to Detroit to replace Gen. Lewis Cass on the grounds that Howard could be spared from the Missouri Territory. General Harrison had informed Secretary of War John Armstrong that Gov. William Clark's military talents and his superb knowledge of Indians qualified him to direct operations in that territory. Furthermore, he suggested that one company of rangers at St. Louis would provide sufficient local protection. The Secretary of War had agreed to Harrison's recommendations, but had decided to consult Howard concerning the number of rangers that should be kept in service in Missouri.

In response to the rising tide of territorial discontent, Missouri's delegate to Congress, Edward Hempstead, prodded the Administration to inform him concerning its plans for protecting the panic-stricken territory. Hempstead worked closely with the territorial delegates from Illinois and Indiana to improve the inadequate frontier defenses, but he had a particularly difficult time satisfying his constituents. A combination of the efforts of the territorial delegate, urgent communications from Governor Clark, growing manifestations of local unrest, and a letter from General Howard stressing Missouri's precarious situation caused the government to countermand its earlier order and return the general to St. Louis.

In the absence of General Howard, Governor Clark assumed responsibilities for directing military operations in the territories. He pressed for the organization of an expedition to be sent up the Mississippi River to capture Prairie du Chien, a post located on the river about 500 miles above St. Louis in what is today southern Wisconsin. The Governor argued that the location of an American military garrison at that site would effectively isolate the Indians on the lower Mississippi from their British allies in Canada. Convinced that his plan provided the most satisfactory means of forestalling renewed Indian hostilities in the spring, Clark, acting under his own authority, outfitted an expedition for a journey up the river. In informing Secretary of War John Armstrong of his actions, Governor Clark reported that he had most of the necessary provisions on hand and that all other expenses could be paid out of the Indian fund. Armstrong privately questioned the advisability of establishing a post in the heart of enemy country because of the tremendous efforts and expense required to maintain it, but he made no move to stop the force which by that time had already departed from St. Louis.

Governor Clark personally accompanied the group, which reached Prairie du Chien on June 2, 1814, and directed the early stages of construction of a fort on the site. The Governor departed from the northern outpost shortly thereafter, leaving Lt. Joseph Perkins in command. Soon after Clark's return to St. Louis, General Howard, who had backed the Governor's plan for stationing a military garrison at Prairie du Chien, requested authorization to send reinforcements to guarantee the safety of the troops assigned there. Before a force sent to alleviate the fort's hazardous situation could reach Prairie du Chien, word arrived in St. Louis that it had fallen on July 19, 1814, to a combined force of British and Indians.

Meanwhile the situation in the territory also had worsened. A rash of Indian hostilities in the spring of 1814 had forced the abandonment of the newly-established trading factories at Arrow Rock and Little Moniteau Creek. The rampaging Indians stole large numbers of horses and cattle and generally terrorized the inhabitants in the territory's sparsely-settled areas. When Manuel Lisa visited the Boonslick region along the Missouri River in August, 1814, he reported that the Indians roamed about the countryside while the frightened settlers remained barricaded in forts that had been constructed for their protection.

The unexpected death of General Howard in September, 1814, came as an added blow to the territory. Howard had been popular with the territorial residents, who had considered him highly competent to direct military operations. Because of the loss of the general's services and the recent reverses along the frontier, it was widely believed that unless prompt action were taken the territory would fall to the combined forces of the enemy sometime during the following spring. To avert any such possible catastrophe, Governor Clark once again called upon the national government to render immediate additional assistance.

While Clark urged stronger action from his post in Missouri, the territory's newly-elected delegate to Congress, Rufus Easton, lobbied in Washington for relief from the heavy burden resting on the territory. Easton, making a political comeback after his defeat during the Wilkinson administration, had replaced Edward Hempstead, who had declined to seek re-election as the delegate to Congress in 1814 for personal and business reasons. Keenly aware of the current territorial sentiment, Missouri's new delegate was especially anxious for his constituents to be kept informed of his exertions in their behalf. Likewise, the territorial assembly took cognizance of the mounting dissatisfaction and prepared a memorial to Congress calling for the dispatch of a force of regular troops sufficiently large to protect the territory.

Although in terms of its limited resources the federal government had done everything possible to assist the territory, local residents strongly resented its failure to station a body of regular troops there permanently. By 1814, it had become almost impossible to raise a fighting force locally because of the frequency of troop requisitions and militia musters during the preceding years. Moreover, rangers and militiamen strongly resented the government's failure to pay many for their services in 1812 and 1813. Nevertheless, it seems safe to conclude that while officials of the national government may not have fully appreciated the problems of the frontier, territorial inhabitants greatly overestimated the abilities of the central government under the difficult circumstances produced by the conflict.

The sudden announcement of the end of the war caught territorial residents off guard. Missourians rejoiced at the news of Jackson's victory in New Orleans, but the provisions of the Treaty of Ghent, signed with Great Britain at the close of the war, did not occasion similar popular acclaim. Article IX of the treaty, which called for immediate cessation of hostilities against the Indians and a return of the rights and privileges to which the Indians had been entitled before the war—providing that they also refrained from any further belligerence—aroused particularly strong criticism in Missouri. The idea of suspending all further military operations against the Indians ran counter to convictions held by both the military and civilian sectors of the population. St. Louis merchant Christian Wilt's candid observation to his uncle that " . . . it is the Opinion of the People here that we shall not have peace with the Indians until we drub them soundly into it" described perfectly the attitude of the Missouri frontier in 1815. Reports of continued depredations only further confirmed the already prevalent outlook and increased the unpopularity of the government's Indian policies.

The close of the conflict left the warring Indian tribes bewildered as well. They had expected their British allies to continue the fight until the Americans had been driven back to their earlier boundaries. Britain's surprise withdrawal from the contest greatly altered their situation. In their confused state, the tribes debated what course of action to follow. Some remained determined to push ahead with the fight against their adversaries; others displayed uncertainty.

The government assigned Clark, Gov. Ninian Edwards of the Illinois Territory, and Auguste Chouteau to negotiate a settlement with the various Indian tribes. The continuation of the hostilities made the task of the commissioners more difficult. They issued a call for the Indians to meet in July, 1815, at Portage des Sioux. The government supplied the commissioners with $20,000 worth of presents to facilitate the negotiations with the tribes who came to discuss their future relations with the United States. Some signed treaties immediately; others required longer to come to terms, but gradually most of the warring Indian nations had reached an agreement with the United States.

Most Missourians strongly resented the presents the Indians received from the commissioners. Unfortunately for Clark, his close association with the government's policy in the public mind greatly lessened his personal popularity. However, contrary to the opinion held by most local residents, the fate of the Indian in the Missouri Territory had already been sealed. Having lost their British allies, the Indians could not resist the encroachment of the hordes of settlers who poured into the territory following the end of the War of 1812. "You need not be alarmed about the Indians—they will never venture upon this quarter of the world—the country is populating too rapidly to fear them," wrote land speculator Justus Post from the Missouri Territory in November, 1815. Post's prediction proved remarkably accurate. Although sporadic Indian outbursts would continue in the territory during the succeeding years, a steady influx of population accomplished what inadequate military forces had been unable to achieve. After 1815 the Indian menace in Missouri steadily declined.

The years of uncertainty, intermittent fighting, and general confusion had taken their toll. Between 1804 and 1810 the territorial population had doubled, but the threat of war with Great Britain and the concomitant fear of renewed Indian raids greatly impeded territorial development and expansion between 1810 and 1815. A few hardy souls had come to the territory during the war years, but others left Missouri because of their fear of the Indians. The diminution of immigration was not the only change produced by the hostilities.

The level of economic activity in the territory mirrored the changing tides of the conflict, as wartime conditions intensified the problems of the frontier businessman. The repeated demands imposed upon local inhabitants for service in militia and ranger units aggravated the territory's perennial labor shortage. Prices fluctuated wildly in response to the general economic dislocations produced by the war, while unsettled conditions both nationally and locally made it difficult to secure supplies and to conduct routine business transactions. Specie, always in short supply on the frontier, grew even scarcer during the war years.

Like other members of the business community, Missouri's lead producers had to deal with these complex problems. Despite the increased demand for lead and lead shot created by the war, Moses Austin reported in late 1812 that the labor shortage coupled with unusually severe weather conditions had brought leadmaking in the territory to a virtual standstill. Gradually the situation improved, permitting a return to the diggings, and Missouri mines again produced large quantities of this important metal. Nevertheless, unstable local conditions continued to interfere with routine mining operations throughout the war.

The war also profoundly affected Missouri's important fur trade. After an attempt to revive its lagging fortunes through a general reorganization in 1812, the strife-torn Missouri Fur Company formally went out of business in 1814. Although serious internal problems had hampered its effectiveness, the company labored under added burdens created by the war. Growing Indian hostilities, an increasing difficulty in securing trade goods from hardpressed local merchants, and a shortage of *engagés*[3] were among the most serious handicaps confronting all traders. The war forced a general retrenchment in trading operations until, by the war's end, Missouri traders found themselves confined to regions they had occupied prior to 1804.

To offset the losses produced by the shrinking fur trade, many territorial merchants turned their attention to the task of supplying the local needs of the United States government. In addition to the normal federal expenditures for routine frontier operations, the greatly expanded military efforts opened new opportunities for the business community. Equipping the militia was an especially profitable venture. Since the law required each member of the militia to provide himself with a good musket or rifle, a knapsack and pouch, cartridges or powder horn, powder and balls, and other miscellaneous items, territorial merchants did a landoffice business whenever companies formed to go out on patrol, often selling the merchandise at higher prices than usual. The territory also purchased provisions for the militia locally.

Although territorial residents chronically complained about the inadequacy of the national government's contribution to the war effort, it is clear that federal subsidies played a vital role in

3. An *engagé* was an individual under contract as a boatman or a hunter.

sustaining the local economy during these troubled years. The payment of the troops always stimulated business activity in the territory, and local merchants complained bitterly when the monies were delayed.

During peacetime the situation was somewhat different. Federal authorities constantly sought to minimize territorial expenditures. The national government paid only the salaries of officials appointed by the President. It also paid for miscellaneous clerical and office expenses, but the combined costs of civil administration seldom exceeded $10,000 a year in the Missouri Territory. Congress tended to be more liberal in authorizing expenditures for adjusting land claims and, although allocations proved adequate for that purpose, they could hardly be termed excessive. Indian expenses and frontier defense always constituted the bulk of federal expenditures in the territory. Since the Army maintained only a small number of regular troops in Missouri under normal circumstances, those expenses remained limited. William Clark estimated that the federal government spent approximately $34,000 per year for all Indian expenses in the Missouri Territory.

Administration officials in Washington frequently warned territorial officers not to exceed the amounts appropriated by Congress for their expenses, and they sometimes refused to approve payment of expenditures authorized by local officials without prior clearance. Territorial residents, who always overestimated the resources of the national government, undoubtedly exaggerated the paucity of federal assistance. Nevertheless, it is clear that except during the war years, direct federal subsidies played a proportionately lesser role in the settlement and development of Missouri than in later territories where governmental expenditures sometimes became the mainstay of the local economy.

The long-awaited upturn in economic activity closely followed the end of the war, and the year 1815 witnessed a dramatic reversal in Missouri's economic fortunes. The flow of incoming settlers, which had slowed to a trickle after 1810, suddenly became a virtual tidal wave. Rangers who had roamed through the hills of mid-Missouri in pursuit of Indians during the war came back with glowing tales of the richness of the land; many now returned there to settle permanently. Land prices rose so rapidly that even land speculators wished for a temporary leveling off in the boom so they could acquire additional lands and take full advantage of the situation. By the end of 1815 it was clear that Missouri had turned a corner and that the territory had entered a new and final phase prior to achieving statehood.

CHAPTER IX

POSTWAR EXPANSION
AND DEVELOPMENT

THE END of the War of 1812 initiated a period of accelerated expansion and growth in the Missouri Territory that transformed the region and paved the way for eventual statehood. The territorial population increased from an estimated 25,000 in 1814 to more than 65,000 in 1820. With the danger from serious Indian depredations greatly reduced, large numbers of settlers ventured for the first time into Missouri's interior regions.

Drawn to the territory by the prospect of securing valuable lands, the majority of Missouri's new immigrants came from Virginia, Kentucky, Tennessee, and North Carolina. The absence of any restriction on slavery made the region especially inviting to prospective settlers from the upper South who often brought their slaves with them. Almost daily caravans of heavily laden wagons followed by a procession of assorted livestock rumbled through the streets of the Mississippi River towns raising a cloud of dust as they headed for the territory's unoccupied lands.

Prior to 1815 most of Missouri's inhabitants had chosen to live in the areas adjoining the Mississippi River between the settlements of St. Louis on the north and New Madrid on the south. Until that time only a few adventurous persons had dared settle further west than the village of St. Charles, located on the Missouri River a short distance above St. Louis. Postwar conditions, however, dramatically altered that situation. All along the Mississippi the newcomers advanced inland to find vacant lands. Many headed for the Salt River country north and west of St. Charles. Others moved up the Missouri River occupying the regions adjacent to that stream. The booming town of Franklin, established in 1817 along the north bank of the Missouri, reflected central Missouri's rapid development in the postwar period. Only three years after its founding, Franklin had become a thriving settlement boasting numerous stores, a federal land office, and its own newspaper. By 1820 the Boonslick country had a population in excess of 20,000 persons.[1]

Everywhere the story was the same. As the population grew, the territorial legislature created additional counties to administer the newly-settled areas, and by 1820 the territory contained fifteen such administrative units, in contrast with the original five. St. Louis, the territorial capital, proudly claimed 5,000 residents by 1818. A leisurely excursion through many of that city's nearly forty retail stores revealed the increasing wealth and affluence of its residents. From the well-stocked shelves of those establishments the shopper could choose from a wide selection of luxury items including fancy silk shawls, parasols, elegant glass bowls, fine china cups and saucers, high quality stationery, and such palatable delicacies as figs and raisins. The thriving frontier metropolis also contained several manufacturing concerns, a post office, a federal land office, two banks, a courthouse, a theatre, three churches, a museum, some paved streets, and even a few sidewalks.

On August 2, 1817, a large crowd turned out in St. Louis to welcome the *Zebulon M. Pike*, the first steamboat to ascend the Mississippi above the Ohio. A party of Indians who had gathered to observe the proceedings fled in fright when they sighted the vessel and the huge clouds of black smoke belching forth from its single smokestack, but the remaining onlookers, amused by the response of the unsophisticated Indians, vigorously cheered as the boat docked at the foot of Market Street. In comparison with the later steamboats that regularly plied the western waters, the *Pike* would seem rather dinky; its low-pressure engine sometimes required assistance from the crew using poles to move it against the Mississippi's swift current, but its arrival in St. Louis on that hot summer day marked a momentous occasion in the history of the city and of the territory.

Less than two years later the *Independence* headed up the Missouri for Franklin to inaugurate the traffic on that stream, but its more treacherous waters made regular service along the

1. The Boonslick country refers to a largely undefined area generally regarded as encompassing the counties of Chariton, Saline, Howard, and Cooper in central Missouri.

river's upper reaches impractical for another decade. By 1819, however, steamboat arrivals and departures had become commonplace in St. Louis, as the splash of the churning paddlewheels increasingly replaced the songs of the hardy boatmen straining to propel the heavy boats upstream against the strong river currents. The promise of speedy and economical transportation further brightened the prospects of the rapidly developing territory.

As the steady stream of immigrants continued to flock to the territory, Missourians gleefully reaped the benefits of the dramatic growth. The local economy flourished; land prices soared in value. Since the federal government did not open the sale of public lands in the territory until 1818, the contest over the confirmation of Spanish land titles continued to divide the territory. The perennial complaints against the commissioners and the national government for their failure to approve all of the Spanish claims could be heard in all parts of Louisiana. New petitions demanding additional concessions circulated throughout the territory, and the columns of the local newspaper were filled with letters on the subject.

Confronted with these persistent outpourings of territorial discontent, Congress labored to reach a satisfactory solution to the problem. In January, 1812, the board of land commissioners had issued its final report containing a résumé of its actions, including a list of every claim that had been filed with the recorder and a summary of the verdict on each claim. The board had examined a total of 3,300 claims, and it had confirmed 1,340 of them. Most of the claims approved by the board were small, with only five containing more than 500 acres. In submitting the report to the Secretary of the Treasury, Clement Penrose, a member of the board, explained that the board's task had been greatly complicated by the failure of Spanish officials to adhere to any systematic procedures in making land grants. He outlined various types of claims which the board had not been authorized to confirm, but which he believed should be granted.

Congress had acted speedily on the subject after the board's report. Less than a month after the board's decisions had been officially communicated to the House of Representatives, the President approved a bill for the further settlement of land

claims in the Missouri Territory. The act confirmed most of the
classes of claims that Penrose had recommended for approval.
It also empowered the recorder of land titles to review once
again all claims still not confirmed and to issue a final opinion
on these. In its eagerness to settle the land-claims question fairly,
Congress adopted a more liberal policy of confirmation. An additional law approved by the President on April 12, 1814, confirmed most French and Spanish concessions made prior to
March 10, 1804, except for those judged antedated or fraudulent, but even this did not satisfy completely many Missouri
claimants.

As a consequence of the growing congressional liberality,
many claimants greatly extended their confirmed holdings.
Auguste Chouteau's real estate increased from 9,000 acres and
7 town lots in St. Charles and St. Louis to more than 23,000
acres as a result of the revisions. His brother Pierre's possessions
went from a total of 500 acres to more than 22,700 acres. Philip
Marie Leduc expanded his confirmed holdings from a single
town lot in New Madrid to nearly 13,000 acres. Similar increases
were experienced by other large claimants.

Frederick Bates, the recorder of land titles, had spent nearly
four years re-examining the unsettled claims before presenting
his final report to Josiah Meigs, commissioner of the General
Land Office, on February 2, 1816. Although the recorder had
approved for confirmation a great many additional Spanish
titles, he had rejected a large number of others. Therefore,
following the conclusion of Bates's lengthy investigation, the
clamor from the remaining claimants continued largely unabated.

Still confronted with a barrage of petitions and memorials
demanding further action on the subject, the United States
House of Representatives requested the Secretary of the Treasury to submit copies of all reports compiled by the various commissioners appointed to settle and adjust land claims in the
Missouri Territory. Secretary William H. Crawford forwarded
copies of all such communications to the House on February 5,
1816, but, after only a brief consideration of the problem, the
House decided to refer the whole matter back to the Secretary
of the Treasury. It instructed Secretary Crawford to re-examine

all pertinent memorials and petitions and then to prepare a suggested plan for the final adjustment and settlement of the Spanish claims.

At the next session of Congress the Secretary of the Treasury, in accordance with his instructions, submitted a report to the House of Representatives which concluded that "it is extremely improbable that injustice has been done by the rejection of claims which ought to have been confirmed." Crawford noted that Congress had consistently relaxed the requirements for confirmation in the past, and therefore he believed that no further concessions were necessary. However, the Secretary did suggest that one final opportunity be given claimants to file previously unrecorded claims for consideration. After receiving Crawford's recommendations, the House decided against taking any further action on the matter.

The absence of any authoritative records made it virtually impossible to determine the number of bona fide claims that remained unconfirmed. Some legitimate claims may not have been approved, but even if Congress had approved every known title, many of which were fraudulent, it is unlikely that the problem would have been resolved. Such an action would only have encouraged the filing of a large number of additional claims and would have brought further demands for greater leniency from Congress. Thus, when Missouri's territorial period came to a close in 1820, the Spanish land-claims controversy remained a hotly-contested issue, and it would continue to stir up dissension for years to come. All frontier territories encountered serious problems arising from foreign land titles, but the contest in Missouri had been particularly intense.

In addition to the difficulties stemming from the Spanish land-claims controversy, the disposition of public lands in Missouri had been further complicated by the New Madrid claims. In December, 1811, a devastating earth tremor, more intense than the one that destroyed San Francisco a century later, had struck the southeastern portion of the territory. Centered in the vicinity of New Madrid, the shock waves uprooted large trees, split the earth apart creating giant crevices, and shattered the banks along the Mississippi. The effects of the convulsion on that stream impeded the normal flow of river traffic for many months. Hardest hit were the settlements at New Madrid and Little Prairie, where most of the buildings were destroyed, but the tremor toppled chimneys and damaged brick structures as far away as Cape Girardeau. Fortunately, despite the quake's severity, the number of casualties and the amount of property destroyed both had been small, principally because of the sparsity of the local population.

Immediately after the tragedy, most of the settlers fled the region and headed across the river where the damage had been less serious. Although they gradually returned to reclaim their few remaining possessions, many moved to other parts of the territory. Pleas for relief went unheeded because of the preoccupation with wartime problems, until 1815, when Congress belatedly enacted a measure for their benefit. The act authorized those persons owning damaged lands to relocate at no charge the same quantity of land on any of the public lands of the United States approved for sale. The law limited all such New Madrid claimants to a maximum of 640 acres and also prohibited relocation on mineral lands.

Upon receiving word that this measure had been approved, speculators poured into the New Madrid area in the spring of 1815 to purchase titles to damaged lands from unsuspecting residents before they learned of the new law. Even Governor Clark had been unable to resist the temptation to take advantage of the situation, and had authorized Theodore Hunt and Charles Lucas to purchase titles to damaged lands shortly after the new act had been adopted. Speculation in New Madrid claims became so widespread that United States Attorney General William Wirt finally ruled in 1820 that New Madrid claims could not be transferred from the original owner, except by death and then only to his heirs.

Although the measure had been intended to relieve the hard-pressed residents of New Madrid, most Missourians believed that it had benefited only the speculator. Attempts to claim the choicest lands in central Missouri with New Madrid certificates aroused the wrath of those persons already residing there. The situation became particularly critical when Secretary of the Treasury Crawford ruled that the right of pre-emption, extended to the Missouri Territory by Congress in 1814, did not apply to Howard County. By denying residents already established in the region any priority in the purchase of land, the ruling in effect opened all lands in central Missouri to claims by the holders of New Madrid titles including those presently occupied. Samuel Hammond reported that, as a result of the Secretary's ruling, claims had been filed to cover the best improved farms in Howard County and the already flourishing villages of Franklin and Boonville.

Opposition to Crawford's interpretation was immediate and intense. A memorial to Congress by the territorial assembly argued that Crawford's instructions were ". . . not only arbitrary and unauthorized by law, but most unjust, cruel and oppressive, towards a people who have fought and bled for the Soil they cultivate." The hostility became so strong in Howard County that an itinerant Baptist preacher, John Peck, who had arrived in the area during the height of the crisis, reported that he "could not call at a cabin without being accosted: 'Got a New Madrid claim?' 'Are you one of these land speculators stranger?'"

In the face of such opposition Secretary Crawford quickly retreated from his original ruling. He informed the Commissioner of the Land Office on December 14, 1818, that since Congress was considering the possibility of extending the right of pre-emption to Howard County, all lands so claimed should not be offered for sale, thereby removing them from the potential grasp of the New Madrid claimants. On January 21, 1819, the Secretary completely reversed his original opinion and agreed that the provisions of the 1814 law had applied to Howard County. Taking no chances, Missouri's delegate to Congress, John Scott, had secured the passage of a law, finally approved on March 3, 1819, which formally extended the pre-emption provisions of the earlier act to include Howard County specifically.

As competition for available lands in the territory grew, the pressure upon the federal government to open Missouri's public lands for sale rapidly built up. Although in 1811 Congress had authorized the President to take such a step whenever he thought it necessary, not a single acre of Missouri's public lands had been offered for sale by 1816. Several factors accounted for the Administration's hesitancy to approve the sale of lands in Missouri, including a preoccupation with the War of 1812, the continued failure to settle old Spanish land claims, difficulties in extinguishing Indian titles, an inability to complete surveys in the territory, and a lingering reluctance to encourage settlement west of the Mississippi.

Unable to secure titles to lands which they desired, a growing number of frontier farmers settled illegally upon the public lands and began to make improvements upon them. Unauthorized settlement on the public domain created major problems for local officials throughout the territorial period, but the increasing incidence of this practice in Missouri made some type of special action imperative. Hoping to remedy this situation, Congress had adopted in 1814 a nebulous statute which, in effect, extended the right of pre-emption to persons residing in the Missouri Territory on April 12, 1814.

The partial extension of the right of pre-emption still did not eliminate the basic problem of squatters on the public domain. Concerned with the growing encroachment upon Indian lands, Governor Clark, who also served as ex officio superintendent of Indian affairs, ordered the removal of all intruders from such lands in a proclamation promulgated on December 4, 1815. Only a week later President Madison issued a directive calling for the eviction of all unauthorized settlers from all of the public lands. Already disturbed by Clark's proclamation, the President's executive order further alarmed Missouri settlers. Their protests against the presidential proclamation were among the most intense in the nation, and in response the territorial legislature adopted two resolutions on January 22, 1816, suggesting that neither of the recent orders be enforced immediately.

Actually, Missouri's territorial officials could not have enforced either of the decrees if they had desired to do so. Col. Alexander McNair flatly stated that the territorial militia would refuse to march against the intruders. Furthermore, it would have been extremely difficult for local authorities to have determined which persons had legal authorization to remain on the public lands. Forced to back down from his initial order, President Madison approved a law on March 25, 1816, permitting settlers to remain on the public lands until they were offered for sale.

As the land hunger pushed speculation in private holdings to new heights, the campaign to bring Missouri's public lands into the market also gained momentum. Proponents of the sale of the public lands in Missouri predicted that their proposal would enrich the national treasury, bring an end to intrusions on the public domain, and increase the population to the point that the region could defend itself against any enemy. The long-awaited announcement of the opening of public land sales in Missouri appeared in the *Missouri Gazette* on June 5, 1818. President Monroe ordered the sales to begin in St. Louis on the first Monday in August, 1818, and in Howard County on the first Monday in September. In accordance with the provisions of federal land statutes, Missouri's public lands were offered for sale at public auction to the highest bidder. Federal law fixed the minimum price at two dollars per acre, and although the smallest quantity that could be purchased was 160 acres, the government granted liberal terms of credit to prospective buyers.

The first sales opened on schedule in St. Louis, but they had to be postponed in Howard County because of the tardy arrival of that region's land-office officials. As soon as the sales got underway local newspapers reported feverish bidding and high prices. In 1819 improved lands in the vicinity of St. Louis averaged between four and twelve dollars an acre. One particularly good section of land near Franklin in central Missouri brought over twenty-six dollars an acre. The easy credit system that permitted purchasers to obtain sizable tracts of public lands with only minimal down payments added to the already widespread speculation that previously had been confined to private holdings. The extent of land speculation prompted President Monroe to suggest that the minimum price of public lands should be raised, but local residents strongly protested any such move.

While the lure of cheap lands attracted growing numbers of settlers to the territory, the scarcity of labor remained a serious local problem. During the war years the shortage had been especially acute, but even after the conflict had ended competition to hire the limited supply of laborers remained keen. "Smart young men are the scarcest articles to be found in this place," Christian Wilt had informed his uncle in 1814. Employers complained about having to tolerate incompetent and unreliable hired hands; skilled workers were particularly difficult to find. By 1817, bricklayers, masons, and carpenters received three dollars per day for their services, while unskilled workers generally commanded at least half that amount.

To help alleviate the chronic labor shortage, territorial residents continued to rely on black workers. Many immigrants brought slaves with them when they came to the territory. Negroes, who comprised roughly 15 per cent of the population, performed a wide variety of tasks ranging from domestic chores to skilled occupations, but most worked as field hands and general laborers. The percentage of blacks in the total population remained fairly constant throughout the territorial period, but the number of free Negroes in Missouri drastically declined. In 1810 there were approximately 600 free blacks among the territory's more than 20,000 inhabitants, but by 1820, even though the territorial population had jumped to 66,000, the number of free Negroes had dropped to about 375. During that same period, Missouri's slave population had increased from 3,000 to nearly 10,000.

Fear of Negro insurrections caused territorial officials to adopt strict black codes regulating the activities of both slaves and free blacks. The American code adopted in 1804 proved to be even more restrictive than the French and Spanish codes, because, unlike its predecessors, it prohibited blacks from testifying against whites in court, and from administering medicine, and it failed to include the provisions designed to prevent slave abuse contained in the Spanish code.

Reports of physical mistreatment of slaves caused the editor of the *Missouri Gazette* to query, "Is there no punishment for such crimes?" Only in the most extreme cases, usually involving the murder of a slave, were masters held accountable for their actions, and even then the scales of justice seem to have been weighted heavily in favor of the white owner.

Few whites in the territory condoned excessive physical abuse of blacks, but like the vast majority of their countrymen they considered both Negroes and Indians as inferior beings. Most whites accepted slavery without question. Not until the very end of the territorial period did any audible objections to the peculiar institution arise within the territory, and few of the critics based their objections on humanitarian grounds.

Forced to perform the least desirable chores without compensation for their services, Missouri's slaves found numerous ways to remonstrate against their unhappy lot. One form of protest was running away. The columns of the *Missouri Gazette* occasionally contained notices advertising for the return of missing slaves. With slaves valued at between $300 and $500 each, the loss of a bondsman represented a serious financial blow to the owner. In 1816, John B. C. Lucas offered twenty-five dollars for the return of a bilingual slave whom he described as "artful and plausible." Lucas cautioned that the runaway probably carried a forged pass identifying him as a free Negro. Not all slaves were so subtle in their attempts to express their dissatisfaction. Pierre Chouteau attributed the loss of his lavish St. Louis home by fire in 1805 to the action of a disgruntled slave, and in 1818 officials charged a slave named Elijah with conspiracy to poison his master's family.

Most blacks labored in the fields, but a small fraction found employment in the territory's infant industries. Moses Austin leased a number of slaves to help operate his lead mines, while his archrival John Smith T kept two Negroes who manufactured flintlock rifles and pistols. Christian Wilt paid a free black man, Henry Cauld, thirty-five dollars a month to perform the hazardous and difficult job of coloring lead at his factory.

Manufacturing in the Missouri Territory remained limited and small-scale, with a lack of capital proving to be the greatest single deterrent to the development of local industry. Conservative monied interests generally considered commerce and real estate better investments than manufacturing. Designed only to supply the local market, most early factories grew up in conjunction with merchandising operations in the territory, and remained small concerns.

The heavy demands for building materials led to the construction of sawmills to provide lumber and brickyards to supply bricks. Since its bulkiness made furniture a costly item to import, local craftsmen began to produce chairs and other pieces to satisfy territorial needs. Tinsmiths and coppersmiths sold kettles and miscellaneous utensils. Even though most areas enjoyed the services of one or more blacksmiths, the vast majority of the iron that they worked came from outside of the territory. The only ironworks established in Missouri prior to statehood opened near Pilot Knob in the southeastern portion of the territory in 1816.

Ready-made clothing did not reach the area until the 1820's, but shortly after the United States acquired the territory, tailors and hatters offered their services to local residents. Jewelers opened shops in which they made jewelry and repaired watches and clocks, and flour millers, bakers, meat packers, soap and candle makers, tanners, brewers, and distillers also operated within the territory.

Lead production reached new highs during the postwar years. Herculaneum, founded by Moses Austin in 1809, had quickly replaced Ste. Genevieve as the primary territorial lead depot. The two shot towers constructed atop the high Mississippi River bluffs below Herculaneum had produced substantial commodities of lead shot before the end of the War of 1812, and their output further increased after 1815.

The fur trade made a less dramatic comeback after the war. Because of the tremendous amounts of capital necessary to reopen operations in the Upper Missouri Valley, the St. Louis merchants continued to trade primarily with the more accessible tribes along the lower Missouri. President Monroe's announcement of plans to erect a military post on the Yellowstone River in order to establish American control in the area temporarily rekindled interest among the St. Louis traders in 1819, but the failure of the specially constructed steamboat, the *Western Engineer*, to reach its destination doomed the project and once again dashed hopes for a quick return of American traders to the Upper Missouri.

The continuing scarcity of capital on the Missouri frontier frequently hampered local development, and the absence of a regular financial institution within the territory complicated even the most routine financial transaction with eastern merchants. Hoping to remedy these difficulties, Auguste Chouteau spearheaded a drive by St. Louis businessmen to establish a bank within the territory. In response to this campaign, the territorial legislature granted a charter authorizing the creation of the Bank of St. Louis in 1813.

Because of the wartime dislocations, the bank failed to secure enough subscriptions for its stock to enable it to begin operations. Following its long-awaited opening on December 13, 1816, the popular new institution began to make sizable loans for real estate transactions by issuing large amounts of its own bank notes to borrowers. In a short time the bank had overextended itself and appeared to be headed for certain disaster. A small faction of the bank's directors, representing the more conservative local interests, charged the officers with mismanagement. They particularly attacked the activities of the bank's cashier, John B. N. Smith, who had issued large amounts of bank notes without proper authorization. Although the disgruntled minority succeeded in securing Smith's removal as cashier, they failed to win support from a majority of the directors for any fundamental alteration in the bank's policies. To dramatize their disaffection with the current practices, three dissenting directors resigned in protest.

The dispute among the directors soon widened to include many of the bank's stockholders. On February 11, 1818, a group led by Joshua Pilcher, Thomas Hart Benton, and Elias Rector gathered in front of the bank and held an impromptu stockholders meeting at which they adopted a resolution authorizing their leaders to demand the keys from bank officials. When the officers refused to surrender the key to the safe, the protestors promptly ordered everyone out of the bank and padlocked its doors. After taking this step, the insurgents announced that the bank would not be permitted to reopen until the directors had taken steps to safeguard the interests of the stockholders. Prompt legal action by the directors secured a return of the keys and a court-enforced ban against any further interference with the bank's operations, but the institution remained closed while the officials attempted to put its troubled affairs in order. The Bank of St. Louis finally reopened early in 1819, but after operating only a few months it had to close its doors permanently in the summer of 1819. A combination of internal divisions, poor management, and overextension of credit had finally forced its liquidation.

Although the Bank of St. Louis's speculative policies had been popular with land speculators and rising young entrepreneurs in need of substantial amounts of capital, many of the territory's established businessmen and small farmers had been hurt by the freewheeling issues of paper money. Auguste Chouteau and Manuel Lisa, two of the bank's original backers, had withdrawn their support from the institution shortly after its organization. Representing the community's more conservative financial interests, they sought permission to establish a second bank in the territory. Directors of the Bank of St. Louis did everything possible to block the chartering of a rival institution, but even a series of last-minute parliamentary maneuvers by opponents in the territorial legislature failed to prevent the enactment of a measure authorizing the creation of a new bank.

The Bank of Missouri actually had been operating on a limited basis since the fall of 1816, but early in 1817 it opened for business under its new charter in the basement of Auguste Chouteau's home. Reflecting the more conservative policies of its backers, the bank, in contrast with its local competitor, offered to redeem its notes in specie. As the westernmost depository for the United States government the bank seemed destined for success, but even this solidly based financial institution found itself in trouble when the Panic of 1819 belatedly reached Missouri. Extensive loans to its directors, in violation of the charter, compounded the bank's woes and forced its closing in 1821. The unhappy experience of Missouri's two territorial banks produced a strong public reaction against all banks that delayed the creation of another state chartered financial institution until 1837.

The swift and largely uncontrolled expansion that Missouri experienced between 1815 and 1820 brought together widely disparate elements. Enterprising young settlers who came to the territory expecting to make their fortunes through diligence and hard work were joined by the less reputable segments of society bent on exploiting their fellow citizens with fraudulent schemes to get rich quick. The blending of these diverse groups produced occasional violence and lawlessness that greatly disturbed the solid citizens of the community. A rash of counterfeit bank notes being circulated in the territory led to the formation of a company of regulators determined to restore law and order. Organized in St. Louis County in 1815, the regulators sought to punish culprits whose misdeeds they believed had gone unpunished. As often happens with self-appointed vigilante groups, the regulator movement threatened temporarily to get out of hand as members expanded their activities. They conducted trials and assessed punishment in a variety of cases involving such dissimilar offenses as hog stealing, arson, counterfeiting, and gambling. However, most local residents doubted that local conditions justified such drastic measures as those adopted by the regulators, and opponents of regulation repeatedly stressed the dangers inherent in this type of extralegal activity.

Although the Missouri frontier had its share of lawlessness and vice, the territory never verged on the brink of savagery. The territory's long-established upper-class citizens continued to enjoy the comforts of polite society, and the vast majority of territorial residents remained hardworking, law-abiding citizens. In addition, the rapidly growing Missouri Territory provided a fruitful field for religious organizations. Prior to the War of 1812 both the Baptists and the Methodists had actively recruited members for their newly-organized congregations in the territory. Their simple and direct doctrines and democratic organization appealed to frontier settlers. Both groups concentrated their early efforts among the widely-scattered American immigrants in outlying areas of the territory, bypassing the larger villages that remained nominally Catholic.

The Baptists, who did not require their ministers to have a formal education, sometimes "raised up" their preachers from the local congregation. Since Baptist ministers normally had to support themselves by working during the week, usually as farmers or hunters, they often joined other settlers moving westward. Consequently, several Baptist preachers accompanied the swelling tide of American immigrants to the territory.

Baptists were particularly active in the district of Cape Girardeau because of the heavy concentration of American settlers there. The earliest Baptist church formed in Missouri was the Twappity Baptist Church established in that district in 1805.

The following year a group of Baptists constructed the first Protestant meetinghouse west of the Mississippi—the Bethel Church located near the settlement of Jackson. Mrs. William Murphy, wife of a Baptist minister and sister of noted Missouri political figure David Barton, taught one of the first Sunday school classes in the territory at the Murphy Settlement beginning around 1807. Gradually the Baptists expanded their activities to other parts of the territory. As the number of churches increased, they voluntarily joined together to form associations. Six Baptist churches in the Jackson area formed the Bethel Association in 1816.

Along with the Baptists, the Methodists entered Missouri at an early date. John Clark, whose switch in religious affiliation from Methodist to Baptist has enabled both groups to claim him, had preached in Upper Louisiana prior to American acquisition. Shortly after the transfer of Louisiana to the United States, the Western Conference of the Methodist Church sent Joseph Oglesby to the territory to determine the need for preachers west of the Mississippi River, and, on the basis of his report, they appointed John Travis to form a Missouri circuit in 1806. After his first year's work in Missouri, Travis reported a membership of 100. By 1810, the Methodist Church had established five circuits with 528 members.

Unlike Baptist ministers who normally lived in the communities they served and who had to support themselves, early Methodist preachers were itinerants paid by church conferences in more settled areas to preach full-time on the frontier. The church assigned each of these frontier ministers to a specific area to serve. Known as circuit riders, they traveled from settlement to settlement preaching and ministering to the people in the region they had been designated to serve. Once the circuit had been completed, the minister returned to his original point of departure to begin the journey again. Between visits from the circuit rider, local groups often met to worship and to study.

Circuits were long and difficult—one Missouri circuit encompassed an area 100 miles in length and 200 miles in width. Frequently roads connecting the isolated settlements were virtually nonexistent. In addition to the hardships of frontier travel, many circuit riders endured personal privation. The pay, only eighty dollars a year plus traveling expenses, barely provided enough for minimal personal necessities. Even though settlers frequently opened their homes to them for the night, traveling ministers could not always find accommodations and on those occasions they had to sleep in the open. Because they lacked regular meeting places, the circuit riders preached wherever they could—outdoors, in barns, in taverns, and in courthouses. Drunks and troublemakers sometimes attempted to disrupt the meetings, as did rowdies employing a crude form of humor. Circuit riders often lacked formal education. Some gained their training by riding with an experienced minister who tutored the young recruits in the basic teachings of the church. These "brush college graduates," as they styled themselves, then received circuits of their own to cover. Through this system, the Methodists attempted to serve Missouri's widely-scattered settlements.

Occasionally, itinerant ministers representing various denominations conducted camp meetings in the territory. John Clark and John Walker organized one of the earliest of these gatherings in 1805 in the Coldwater Creek area north of St. Louis; the meetings normally lasted several days. People traveled for miles to attend these frontier revivals, bringing provisions with them to camp out. After the crowds had assembled, ministers often tried to arouse the emotions of their listeners and to keep them at a high pitch with the graphic portrayals of "hell-fire and damnation," which they employed in their sermons. In the noise and confusion, as preachers preached and members of the audience exhorted and prayed, the proceedings occasionally bordered on chaos.

The camp meeting served as a social gathering as well as a religious meeting. It provided lonely people on the frontier with a chance to visit their widely-scattered neighbors and to make new acquaintances. Many people came to camp meetings for disparate reasons, including some of a more worldly nature. Often politicians came to electioneer and merchants came to sell goods, but even though the effectiveness of the camp meeting as a religious device remains a matter for debate, it was an important frontier social institution.

Despite a temporary decline in the number of church members in the Missouri Territory during the war years, both the Baptists and the Methodists registered substantial gains after 1815. To augment the endeavors of local elements seeking to organize churches and to win the souls of their frontier brethren, eastern churches rushed to send additional missionaries to the rapidly-growing territory after the war. These clerical imports came to engage in evangelical activities and to combat the often exaggerated immorality and irreligion which they believed to be rampant on the American frontier.

The Methodists continued to send circuit-riding ministers to the territory, and in 1817 John Mason Peck and James Welch came to Missouri to preach the gospel under the sponsorship of a group of eastern Baptists. Peck, who became one of the most active of the frontier evangelists, also gained recognition for his literary and historical works. The appearance of Baptist missionaries in the territory precipitated a serious difference of opinion among members of that denomination. The condescending attitude of Peck and other missionaries toward the uneducated local clergymen helped produce an antimissionary faction within the Baptist Church.

Despite the divisions among the Baptists concerning the use of missionaries, many religious organizations dispatched preachers to the frontier. The Philadelphia Bible and Missionary Society sent Samuel J. Mills and Daniel Smith to the West in 1814. Mills and Smith, who were the first Presbyterian ministers to come to Missouri, drew large crowds to hear the sermons they preached in St. Louis. Before leaving the territory to visit other portions of the American frontier, they also attracted widespread support from among divergent segments of the local population for the establishment of a proposed Bible Society. Following their departure, Stephen Hempstead, whose son Edward already had become one of the most respected attorneys and political figures in the territory, took an active part in attempts to secure a permanent Presbyterian minister for the Missouri Territory.

Hempstead's appeals to churchmen in his native state of Connecticut produced results, and the Connecticut Missionary Society dispatched Salmon Giddings and Timothy Flint to the territory in 1816. Shortly after his arrival Giddings helped organize the Concord Church at the Bellevue settlement in Washington County, Missouri's first Presbyterian church. Subsequently the energetic minister helped organize other Presbyterian churches, including St. Louis's first Protestant church established in 1817. Emphasizing the need for an educated clergy and proclaiming the Calvinist doctrine of the elect, Presbyterianism found its greatest acceptance among the territory's upper classes.

Even more limited in its appeal on the frontier was the Episcopal Church, which did not come to Missouri until near the end of the territorial period. In October, 1819, the Reverend John Ward conducted the first Episcopal service west of the Mississippi in St. Louis. The following month Ward helped organize Christ Church in St. Louis, whose original members included many of territorial Missouri's most prominent citizens.

Following the transfer of Upper Louisiana to the United States in 1804, the Roman Catholic Church had steadily declined in Missouri. With the end of governmental support for the church, each congregation had to assume full responsibility for maintaining local operations. Once again parishes found themselves without the services of a regular priest, as most of the clerics left the territory in order to retain their salaries from the Spanish crown. As late as 1818 only the churches at Florissant and Ste. Genevieve had regular clergymen. The others had to depend upon the visiting priests who occasionally came to administer the sacraments. The prolonged period of neglect had a disastrous effect upon the Church. The widespread indifference and apathy among Missouri's Catholics shocked and saddened Bishop Benoit Joseph Flaget of Kentucky when he first visited the territory in 1814. Other priests who came to the area conveyed an equally dismal account of the general state of the Catholic Church in Missouri.

The arrival of Bishop William Louis Du Bourg in the territory in 1818 revitalized the floundering local parishes. Du Bourg, who had been consecrated Bishop of Louisiana and the Floridas in 1815, had decided to establish his residence temporarily in St. Louis because of the opposition in New Orleans to his appointment as bishop. No doubt much to his satisfaction, in view of the discouraging reports he had received concerning the situation in Missouri, the new bishop got an enthusiastic welcome in Ste. Genevieve and St. Louis. After he reached St. Louis, Bishop Du Bourg launched an energetic drive to revive the church and to establish an educational program. Work began almost immediately on a new church to replace the decaying log structure that had served the city since 1776. Although a shortage of funds prevented the completion of its interior, St. Louis's new cathedral opened for services on Christmas Day, 1819.

To assist him in the work of the church, Bishop Du Bourg had recruited a number of talented young European clerics, including Fathers Felix de Andreis and Joseph Rosati. With their assistance, members of the parish of St. Marys of the Barrens, located west of Ste. Genevieve, secured the establishment of a seminary of the Congregation of the Priests of the Mission of St. Vincent de Paul, which opened in 1818 to train badly-needed priests. Bishop Du Bourg actively encouraged the establishment of numerous educational institutions, including the St. Louis Academy, a Latin school for boys established in 1818 under the direction of Father Francis Niel. The next year Du Bourg approved the transformation of the academy into the College of St. Louis. Moreover, at Du Bourg's invitation, the Order of the Sacred Heart sent five of its members to establish a school for girls in the Missouri Territory. With Mother Philippine Duchesne in charge, the nuns arrived in St. Louis in August, 1818. From there the sisters traveled to St. Charles where they opened a school for girls, but it failed to attract many students. Handicapped by a scarcity of funds, the nuns lived and worked under the most primitive of frontier conditions during their first winter in St. Charles. In 1819 they moved their school to Florissant, where they also opened a novitiate.

The impact of the various religious groups is difficult to assess. Undoubtedly they provided an important stabilizing influence in the territory. Although the pioneer religious bodies were often inconsistent in the treatment of members who had violated their moral codes, the power of moral suasion exercised by the frontier preacher and the church carried great weight with the average territorial resident, and this important force undoubtedly complemented efforts to establish law and order. Moreover, the Church served as an important social agency, providing lonely territorial residents with a welcome opportunity to visit with friends and neighbors and to combat the isolation of frontier living. Since the concept of public, tax-supported education did not gain acceptance until later, the churches performed vital educational functions. Catholic priests and nuns and Protestant ministers played key roles in the development of educational opportunities in territorial Missouri.

In addition to the educational activities sponsored by Bishop Du Bourg, Protestant clergymen also encouraged education. Sunday schools often promoted learning by offering instruction in reading and writing. Many ministers, most of whom were superior to the lay teachers in the territory, organized schools. Salmon Giddings, Timothy Flint, John Peck, James Welch, and Jesse Walker all ventured into the educational field. The clergy also occasionally provided instruction for the territory's black population, but they normally confined themselves to matters of religion and morality, since it was generally known that educated slaves were more likely to cause their owners trouble.

Educational levels in the territory varied widely. Missouri boasted many highly educated and well-informed citizens, but it contained larger numbers of semiliterate pioneer farmers too busy with the daily tasks of frontier living to be concerned that their children were growing up in ignorance. Territorial residents looked upon education as a private matter. Except for a tacit agreement that some provision should be made for the education of indigent children, they expected parents to assume full financial responsibility for the instruction of their offspring. Consequently, the children of the well-to-do, prominent families enjoyed substantially greater educational opportunities than those of the average frontiersman. Likewise, the larger territorial cities offered a greater variety of educational experiences than could be found in the remaining portions of the territory where widely-scattered populations further complicated the problem of providing formal instruction.

Numerous private schools were created to offer instruction in a wide variety of subjects to territorial residents. St. Louis had the largest number of these educational institutions, but prior to statehood most settlements had some type of school offering to teach at least the basic fundamentals. Some were taught by competent, well-qualified teachers and provided a quality education, while others left much to be desired even by nineteenth-century standards. Stiff competition for the limited number of local scholars able to afford the tuition produced a rapid turnover among these fledgling schools. Because of the schools' uneven quality and the uncertainty of their duration, some wealthy residents continued to send their children outside of the territory to secure an education.

In addition to the schools founded by individuals or sponsored by churches, some communities attempted to provide academies to broaden local educational opportunities. Ste. Genevieve was the first of Missouri's settlements to undertake the creation of an academy. A subscription drive in 1807 netted pledges of nearly $3,000 for the establishment of a seminary of learning for the education of the young. The subscribers, including the most prominent residents in that village, elected Father James Maxwell as chairman of the board of trustees.

In 1808 the territorial legislature granted a charter to the academy, but that was the extent of its assistance to the struggling educational enterprise. The academy proposed to offer instruction in English and French along with such other languages and sciences as the funds of the institution would allow. Children of poor people and Indian children were to be educated without charge. Moreover, the articles of incorporation prohibited any discrimination on the basis of religion either in the instruction offered or in the selection of professors. Attempts to secure a land grant from the federal government to help finance the academy failed. Although the trustees built a large stone building to house the academy, a shortage of funds prevented it from becoming the type of institution that its founders had envisioned and forced its untimely closing. The territorial legislature also incorporated academies in Potosi, Jackson, St. Charles, and Franklin, but the story of these institutions differed little from the unhappy experience of the Ste. Genevieve Academy.

Attempts were also made to provide educational facilities for women. In the vicinity of St. Louis, several schools for girls offered instruction in scholastic subjects and in the domestic arts, with an emphasis on the latter. Outside of St. Louis the opportunities for young ladies were more limited. The trustees of the Ste. Genevieve Academy had promised to admit females whenever funds were available, but the needed monies never materialized. The expense of maintaining separate schools discouraged the creation of women's schools outside of the St. Louis area, and schools at Potosi, Jackson, and Franklin operated on a coeducational basis before the close of the territorial period.

Since the only prerequisites for creating a school were a teacher, a room, and some students, the quality of territorial educational institutions varied greatly. Standards were generally low, although in announcing the opening of the St. Louis Academy, the founders did stipulate that "none will be received before he can read at least tolerably well." Most schools could not afford to be so discriminating. The advertisements that regularly appeared in the *Missouri Gazette* promised techniques to make learning easier. Not inclined to understate their own abilities, most schoolmasters claimed European training and competence to offer instruction in many widely-divergent fields. Although Timothy Flint could hardly qualify as an unbiased observer since he had attempted to open a school himself, his caustic commentary on the frontier schools contains a good deal of truth:

> I have been amused in reading puffing advertisements in the newspapers. A little subscription school, in which half the pupils are abecedarians, is a college. One is a Lancastrian school, or a school of "instruction mutuelle." There is the Pestalozzi establishment, with its appropriate emblazoning. There is the agricultural school, the missionary school, the grammar box, the new way to make a wit of a dunce in six lessons, and all the mechanical ways of innoculating children with learning that they may not endure the pain of getting it in the old and natural way. . . .

Despite all the inadequacies and shortcomings of territorial Missouri's educational system, it probably compared favorably with that of other early nineteenth-century frontier areas.

Schools did not have a monopoly on cultural and intellectual activities in the territory. A small group of St. Louis residents organized an amateur Thespian society in 1814, and the following year they presented their first performance in a former blacksmith shop which they had converted into a theatre. They continued to offer amateur productions for the entertainment of local audiences throughout the territorial period, and in 1818 a company of professional actors further expanded the fare available to St. Louis theatregoers. In addition to the theatrical productions, territorial residents could also attend public debates, lectures, patriotic celebrations, concerts, and assorted programs.

Even though St. Louis's first commercial museum did not open until after the territorial period, William Clark often permitted visitors to view his extensive private collection. As one would expect, Clark's exhibits included many of the Indian relics that he had accumulated, along with a collection of unusual animal skins, but it also contained such oddities as a preserved pelican and elephant teeth.

Reading matter was not totally lacking on the Missouri frontier. After its establishment in 1808, the *Missouri Gazette* provided its subscribers with local news along with items reprinted from eastern periodicals. Near the end of the territorial period the rapidly-growing population spawned the establishment of a second newspaper in St. Louis, along with similar publications in Jackson and Franklin. At least some territorial Missourians continued to have access to a wide selection of books. Many St. Louis establishments offered books for sale to their customers, and a few Missourians maintained substantial personal libraries. Bishop Du Bourg opened his library of 8,000 volumes to students at the College of St. Louis. Attempts to establish a public library in St. Louis failed to materialize before statehood, but a group in Franklin did organize a semiprivate library in that settlement in 1819. Joseph Charless invited readers to come to the *Gazette* office, and in 1818 a "Reading Room & Punch House" opened nearby. While some Missourians undoubtedly availed themselves of these opportunities, reading was a luxury for which most residents had neither the time nor the inclination. Aside from a select group of well-established citizens, few persons had any book other than the Bible, and many even could not afford it.

Missouri's literary output was equally sparse. Henry Marie Brackenridge, who had been educated in Ste. Genevieve and had spent several years in the territory, probably ranks as the territory's leading literary figure. Timothy Flint, Henry Rowe Schoolcraft, John Bradbury, and Christian Schultz also published accounts of their travels in Missouri Territory. Pierre François Régnier, a minor French poet who lived in St. Louis and Ste. Genevieve between 1802 and 1821, wrote several French poems.

To label territorial Missouri as a cultural wasteland would be erroneous, but cultural and intellectual pursuits did remain the special province of a small segment of the territorial population. The world of poetry and drama would have been totally alien to Missouri's average pioneer farmer who toiled to clear his lands and raise his crops. These hardy frontiersmen preferred to leave such heady matters to the territory's social and cultural elite. In the tradition of the eighteenth century, they also deferred to territorial leaders in political matters. However, shortly after the rapidly-expanding territory joined the Union as a full-fledged state, the common man moved to reclaim his political prerogatives.

CHAPTER X

THE PROCESS OF
POLITICAL MATURATION

Missouri's advancement to second-class status in 1812 had marked an important step in its territorial history. Since 1805 the Territory of Louisiana had been administered by a governor, a secretary, and three judges, all appointed by the President. Under their direction, Louisiana's territorial government functioned much like most other first-class governments. The territory suffered from many of the same problems—disagreeing territorial officials, executive absenteeism, and statutes that failed to keep pace with changing conditions—that lessened the effectiveness of the first stage elsewhere. Moreover, like most territorial executives, Louisiana's governors found that the demands imposed upon them by land-claims controversies, Indian problems, and frontier defenses frequently left them little time to oversee routine civil administrative matters.

The major burden of managing local affairs fell to the district and county officials who received their appointments from the governor. Since these posts usually went to the most influential and often the wealthiest residents of the district, local government remained largely the prerogative of a select territorial elite. Although the county officers did not have the power to legislate, they did assess and collect taxes, supervise the construction of public works, license businesses, and administer local justice.

Government at the grassroots level generally reflected the conservative outlook of the men holding the key offices. For the most part they looked after the needs of their area satisfactorily, despite their inclination to limit public expenditures in order to hold taxes to a minimum. Occasionally, as in the case of the district of Ste. Genevieve between 1805 and 1807, the system completely broke down under the stress of intense local rivalries. Fortunately, the lawlessness and chaos that temporarily gripped that district were not typical, and the vast majority of Louisiana's territorial residents initially found no serious fault with their governmental system. In view of the territory's small population, its underdeveloped economy, and its limited financial resources, the first-class structure was well-suited to Louisiana's needs during the early years of American control.

As the rapidly-growing territory's problems became increasingly complex, local residents launched a successful campaign for advancement in territorial status. The law passed in 1812 that created the Territory of Missouri was based upon a combination of provisions taken from previous federal statutes for governing territories. Local citizens gained the right to elect members of the territorial House of Representatives. Representation in that body was to be apportioned according to the territorial population, with one representative allotted for each 500 inhabitants. The President appointed the nine members of the Legislative Council from a list of eighteen names selected by the members of the lower house of the territorial assembly. The measure also authorized territorial residents to send a nonvoting delegate to Congress.

Although the act made no direct reference to the Ordinance of 1787, Missouri's new government was patterned after the general form established by that act for second-class territories. There were, however, several minor differences between the two measures. The Missouri law, like an earlier act for the Mississippi Territory passed in 1808, provided for the popular election of the territorial delegate, as opposed to the selection of that officer by the territorial legislature, which was called for in the Northwest Ordinance; furthermore, in the Missouri statute Congress dropped the fifty-acre freehold suffrage qualification contained in the 1787 ordinance and substituted a requirement for the payment of a territorial or county tax, as it had done earlier for the Indiana and Illinois territories. Missouri's 1812 organic act also removed, for the first time in a territory, all distinctions between qualifications for voting and for officeholding.

The new Missouri law spelled out in greater detail the powers and duties of various territorial officials than the previous statutes for other territories had done, and, for the first time the territorial governor was not granted the power to prorogue the general assembly, although he did retain the power of absolute veto and authority to convene the legislature for special sessions.

All of these changes reflected a persistent congressional effort to revise the original provisions of the Northwest Ordinance, making them conform more closely to territorial needs and desires. In general, between 1787 and 1812, Congress attempted to make the territorial system more democratic and to grant local officials greater freedom in dealing with unique conditions in their particular territory.

With the new government scheduled to go into effect on the first Monday in December, 1812, Governor Howard announced that territorial elections would be held on the second Monday in November, 1812. Major interest centered on the race for territorial delegate. Edward Hempstead, Rufus Easton, Samuel Hammond, and Matthew Lyon all announced their candidacy for the post, but the real contest shaped up between Hempstead and Easton. Both men were young lawyers who had come to the territory shortly after the establishment of American control. In addition to their legal activities, both had engaged heavily in land speculation. Each had previously held public office, Easton having served for a short time as a superior court judge and as postmaster of St. Louis and Hempstead as clerk of the local legislature and as territorial attorney general.

In addition to having very similar backgrounds, both major contestants also substantially agreed upon the steps that should be taken to improve conditions in Missouri. They favored the speedy confirmation of land titles, land grants to reward citizens who had served in the militia, and increased federal assistance for territorial defense. Hempstead enjoyed greater support among long-time French and American residents, whereas many of the more recent American arrivals supported Easton.

In the hotly-contested election Hempstead won the right to represent the Missouri Territory in Congress. As Missouri's first territorial delegate, Hempstead compiled an impressive record during his one term in office. He labored to secure more adequate federal assistance in protecting the exposed frontier against attack, and partially because of his efforts Congress agreed to authorize the Missouri Territory to recruit three additional companies of rangers. Much to the satisfaction of the local holders of Spanish land titles, Hempstead helped secure congressional approval for a more liberal policy of confirmation, including an agreement to approve some grants made by Spanish authorities after 1800.

At the time of Hempstead's election, the voters in each district also selected their representatives for the lower house of the territorial legislature. In those contests, as in the race for delegate, a coalition representing the large land claimants and the established commercial and business interests easily controlled the new legislature. The same group that had dominated district government captured most of the seats in the territorial legislature. Even though the advancement in territorial classification had not altered the political power structure within the territory, it did give local leaders greater voice in shaping territorial laws and policies. Between its organization in 1812 and the creation of a state government in 1820, Missouri's territorial legislature struggled with the problems of governing frontier Missouri. The territory's continued growth and expansion made it imperative to revise outdated and unworkable statutes constantly in order to keep pace with rapidly-changing conditions.

In Missouri, as in other frontier territories, the problems of securing a satisfactory system of local government occupied a disproportionate amount of the legislature's time and often aroused political controversy. In 1813 the very first session of the General Assembly approved a measure that consolidated the functions formerly performed by the courts of common pleas, the courts of quarter sessions, the orphans courts, the probate courts, and the district auditors, placing them all under the jurisdiction of the newly-created courts of common pleas in each county.[1] Only two years later, the legislature once again revamped local governmental machinery by replacing the court of common pleas with two circuit courts. The controversial measure divided the territory into two circuits, with a judge to be appointed for each. The circuit judges, who received salaries of $1,200 a year, heard all cases formerly tried in the courts of common pleas. County business previously handled by the courts of common pleas was transferred to county courts composed of the justices of the peace in each county. Although advocates of the change in struc-

1. See Chapter V for a discussion of the functions of these earlier courts.

ture argued that it had been intended to regularize judicial proceedings, opponents of the plan accused the legislators of having created these two lucrative offices for their friends. The measure's foes oversimplified a complex problem, but their accusations seemed to gain credence when a legislator who had backed the measure resigned to accept one of the newly-created posts. Undoubtedly much of the opposition to the assembly's actions came from those local officials who had lost their positions as a consequence of the changes.

In addition to the attention which the territorial assembly gave to the structure of local government, it also enacted numerous new statutes and revised many others on such common local problems as public roads, militia, taxes, public offices, criminal punishment, and the creation of political subdivisions. In their attempts to meet the needs of a rapidly-growing territory, the members of the General Assembly employed the same financial conservatism that previously had characterized the efforts of district officials. Since they personally represented a substantial portion of the territory's wealth, the legislators sought to minimize expenditures in order to keep local taxes as low as possible. Consequently, the territorial legislature never attempted to formulate a comprehensive program to support internal improvements, education, or poor relief. Often the assembly did little more in these areas than refer the problems back to local authorities or petition Congress for federal assistance.

The territory's inadequate system of roads was a constant source of irritation to local residents who had to depend upon it for transportation. The problem became increasingly serious as large numbers of settlers began moving into Missouri's interior regions. In its legislation on the subject, the territorial assembly continued to make county authorities largely responsible for the establishment and maintenance of public roads. To help minimize the costs, the legislature authorized local officials to require able-bodied males between sixteen and forty-five to devote a specified number of days each year to road construction and upkeep. Some critics of the system contended that it placed a hardship upon the poorer residents who could not afford the fines levied for failing to render the required service, but many settlers performed their mandatory duties without serious complaint. Instead they organized social gatherings in conjunction with their roadwork, utilizing the occasion as an opportunity to catch up on the latest news from their neighbors who joined them in the "road bees."

In other areas the territorial assembly took an even more limited role for itself. It assigned full responsibility for poor relief to county authorities. Moreover, the legislators never accepted responsibility for the creation of a system of public education. Aside from granting charters to a number of academies, which failed because of insufficient financial support, and creating a board to oversee schools in St. Louis, the territorial legislature adopted a hands-off policy as far as public education was concerned.

While most residents looked to the territorial assembly for improved services, few wanted to bear the added costs necessary to provide them. Consequently the local legislators found themselves in the unenviable position of attempting to meet the needs of a rapidly-expanding territory with limited funds. In spite of the General Assembly's conservative fiscal policies, governmental expenses increased appreciably after the change in status. Since salaries paid to officials constituted a major portion of the territorial budget, critics leveled much of their criticism at the amounts expended for that purpose.

Prior to this time territorial revenue had attracted relatively little local attention, but the increasing costs of government necessitated new taxes. In its search for new sources of income the territorial legislature gradually extended the list of taxable property. The territory had no general property tax, relying instead upon special property taxes. In 1814, for the first time, the legislature added uncultivated lands in amounts up to 800 arpents to the list of taxable property in Missouri. The following year the General Assembly completely revised the territorial revenue system and imposed a tax on all land in the territory, including lands claimed under pre-emption rights. Fines and fees, license charges on certain occupations and activities, a poll tax levied on able-bodied single men with limited property, and taxes upon slaves, pleasure carriages, houses, and other similar improvements constituted additional sources of territorial income. Nevertheless despite the complaints from the legislature's critics, the over-all tax burden in the territory remained light.

Even though the costs of the higher classification were greater, most local residents preferred the second-stage government to its predecessor. They particularly applauded the assembly's constant efforts to keep the national government informed about local problems through its numerous petitions and remonstrances to Congress. Like their counterparts on other frontiers, territorial Missourians did not hesitate to ask the federal government for assistance when they believed it was needed, but at the same time they bitterly resented any attempts by federal authorities to limit in any way the scope of their private endeavors. Consequently, territorial residents strongly opposed the government's policy of reserving lead mines and saline lands for itself. Since the lead-leasing system had never operated satisfactorily, most Missourians favored its abandonment and the sale of the mineral lands to private interests.

Likewise, the leading St. Louis merchants led an attack upon the government-operated Indian factory system. The depressed state of the fur trade following the War of 1812 had caused Missouri traders to demand an end to government competition, but at the same time they had sought increased protection for their agents through the establishment of army posts in remote regions. Territorial residents also appealed to the national government for improved systems of transportation and communication, assistance in establishing schools, and aid for a myriad of other miscellaneous projects.

Aside from its increasingly liberal policy of land sales, the national government nonetheless displayed little disposition to increase the amount of its assistance to the local territory. Frustrated in their attempts to gain the desired changes in policy, territorial Missourians steadily increased their demands for statehood in the hope that the advancement in status would enable them to exert greater influence in determining national policies vital to local interests.

As the steady stream of immigrants continued to pour unabated into the territory following the end of the War of 1812, Missouri's prospects for a speedy admission to the Union brightened with each passing day. Largely as a consequence of the rapid increase in population, Congress approved the advancement of Missouri to a third-class territory in 1816. This action enabled Missourians to elect the members of the Legislative Council, and the elevation to the highest grade of territory represented the final step normally taken by Congress prior to granting consideration for admission to statehood.

Encouraged by the adoption of this measure, Rufus Easton, Missouri's second territorial delegate, reported from Washington in 1816 that the long-prevalent official disposition to discourage further settlement west of the Mississippi River and north of the state of Louisiana had at last been abandoned. "It is now admitted," he wrote, "with few exceptions that our settlements ought to be fostered to the extent of such district of territory as will form us into a State; and I rejoice that the period is not far distant, when we will form a free and independent State government."

Meanwhile, within the territory the tempo of local political campaigns had greatly intensified as competing factions waged a bitter struggle to win control of the territorial government. Local issues and personal rivalries determined Missouri's factional alignments and shaped the character of territorial politics during this period. Because of the territory's overwhelming Republican majority and the reduced level of party activity throughout the country during the so-called Era of Good Feelings, national party divisions failed to develop in Missouri prior to statehood. In the absence of a meaningful Federalist-Republican contest, local groups fought one another for the opportunity to direct the destinies of the territory and at the same time to enrich their own personal fortunes. Above all, the land-claims controversy was the dominant local issue.

One faction, commonly referred to as the St. Louis junto, drew most of its support from the coterie of French families who had long dominated affairs in that town. Auguste Chouteau, Charles Gratiot, and Bernard Pratte were among the more-prominent French residents who formed the nucleus of this group. Each of these men held unconfirmed Spanish land titles to sizable quantities of land. Following the removal of their strong ally, Gov. James Wilkinson, from the territory in 1806, these canny Frenchmen had realized quickly that without support from certain influential Americans they stood little chance of having their titles confirmed. Through the effective use of their wealth and influence, they had subsequently won the allegiance of some powerful American allies. Their most important support came from a group of enterprising young lawyers who entered the territory after the United States took control. Attracted by the prospective profits in handling land-claims cases, many of these aspiring attorneys were persuaded to cast their lots with the fortunes of those holding large claims. Edward Hempstead, John Scott, and Thomas Hart Benton thus chose to align themselves with the St. Louis junto. In addition, this group had also gained the backing of Gov. William Clark, whose considerable influence proved invaluable, and together this coalition constituted a formidable political force during the closing years of Missouri's territorial period.

The opposition came primarily from a rival group of land speculators who opposed confirmation of the large Spanish grants. Composed principally of Americans who entered the territory after 1804, the faction's most prominent members included William Russell, Rufus Easton, and John B. C. Lucas. This group could also count upon the support of Joseph Charless, publisher of the *Missouri Gazette*, Lucas's son Charles, and the extremely popular young frontier attorney, David Barton.

By 1816 the factional lines had been clearly drawn, and the two competing groups prepared for a showdown in the elections scheduled for that year. Although contests for the territorial legislature attracted intense local interest, the race for territorial delegate received primary attention both in the territorial press and in the contemporary correspondence. Eager to defeat the incumbent, Rufus Easton, who had always been *persona non grata* with the French population, the St. Louis junto nominated an attorney from Ste. Genevieve, John Scott, as its candidate for the post of territorial delegate.

Easton, a well-known land-speculator politician, had been elected in 1814 to succeed Edward Hempstead who had declined to seek re-election for personal reasons. As territorial delegate Easton worked hard in behalf of his constituents' interests and pressed for a variety of measures—most of them unsuccessfully. Overall, his achievements had been modest in contrast with the record of his predecessor.

As early as December, 1815, a full eight months prior to the election, John Scott's supporters were already reported to be hard at work in his behalf. Aiming for the widest possible appeal, Scott published a circular in March, 1816, designed to win support from all segments of the territorial population. Offering something for everyone, the aspiring candidate proposed to end the government's monopoly of lead and saline lands, to abolish the government-owned Indian trading factories, to press for the speedy admission of Missouri to statehood, to work for the prompt sale of public lands in the territory at reduced prices and in smaller quantities, to seek the establishment of new public schools and roads and, finally, to oppose the removal of squatters from public lands.

Meanwhile, Scott's friends attacked the record of incumbent Rufus Easton. They argued that, as a delegate, Easton had accomplished relatively little for the territory, especially when compared with Edward Hempstead who now actively supported Scott for the post. Not surprisingly, the pro-Scott faction particularly criticized Easton's record on land claims, suggesting that he had consistently opposed the legitimate interests of the Spanish land claimants. Furthermore, Easton's opponents attributed the postponement in the opening of land sales in the territory to his desire to sell the large tracts which he already had acquired through speculation.

On the other hand, Easton's supporters attempted to refute this unfavorable picture of their candidate's record as a first-term delegate. They credited him with having secured increased protection for the frontier, a new law to prevent the removal of settlers from the public lands, relief for the sufferers of the New Madrid earthquake, the advancement of Missouri to third-class territorial status, and a law confirming additional land claims. While accusing the opposition of misrepresentation and slander, Easton's adherents leveled equally-abusive charges against their opponent. They represented Scott as a gambler renowned primarily for his excessive profanity. Moreover, they accused him of having aligned himself with a faction of lawyers, colonels, and majors in St. Louis who sought only to dominate the territory and fleece the public of its money, goods, and offices.

Following the election, Governor Clark, whose preference for

Scott was well-known, certified that Scott had won the contest by fifteen votes over Easton. However, in designating Scott as the winner, the Governor had decided to accept a set of contested returns belatedly brought to St. Louis by the victorious candidate himself from the township of Cote Sans Dessein in St. Charles County. The *Missouri Gazette*, which had endorsed Easton, printed a barrage of protests against the Governor's actions.

Easton, who went to Washington to seek a reversal of the Governor's decision, prepared a lengthy report describing the irregularities and inaccuracies in the returns submitted by Clark. Following consideration of Easton's memorial, the Committee on Elections in the House of Representatives recommended that Easton be seated by the House in place of Scott. The committee's report triggered a lengthy debate, with some members arguing that territorial delegates were merely agents who had been afforded the courtesy to sit and speak in the House, and as such their elections did not come under the jurisdiction of the House.

Although a majority of the members rejected this interpretation, they did vote to recommit the report to the Committee on Elections for reconsideration. On January 10, 1817, the committee requested that it be relieved of further deliberation in the matter, since it could not accurately determine the validity of the disputed returns in the Missouri election. After rejecting the committee's original recommendation that Easton be certified to sit as the delegate from Missouri, the House voted to declare the seat vacant and to order a new election on the grounds that the original election had been illegally conducted.

Preparations for the special election began immediately after word reached the territory that the House had declared the seat vacant. Following a careful evaluation of the situation, both groups decided to back the candidates that they had supported in the original race. Amidst growing hostility generated by the renewal of the contest, a second election was held in August of 1817, but as in the earlier contest the results failed to placate the defeated faction.

"MILITARY ELECTION!!!" charged the *Missouri Gazette* immediately following the special election. "On Monday last," the editor wrote, "an election for delegate to congress took place in the several election districts of this territory. In this town, the election was conducted in the most violent, turbulent and savage manner." Joseph Charless listed a vast array of irregularities, including intimidation of voters, military interference, the use of liquor to secure votes, and unwarranted pressure by Governor Clark in behalf of John Scott.

Although the unhappy editor, disturbed because Scott had defeated Easton by a considerably larger margin than in the previous contest, obviously exaggerated the conditions in St. Louis on election day, the evidence does indicate that there had been unwarranted interference in the proceedings. Capt. John O'Fallon, a nephew of Governor Clark, boasted of his attack upon Dr. Robert Simpson, a supporter of Easton, at the courthouse during the election. Simpson's subsequent complaints, therefore, had substantial merit and at least partially confirmed the charges made by Charless. Nevertheless, Scott took his seat as territorial delegate in Congress. With Scott's election, the triumph of the St. Louis junto was complete, and they retained control of local politics during the few remaining years of territorial government.

As territorial delegate, Scott regularly pressed for the confirmation of additional Spanish land grants and the extension of the right of pre-emption. He also worked for the adoption of other popular local policies including the sale of the government-owned saline lands, the abandonment of the Indian factory system, the improvement of roads, the sale of additional public lands, and the discontinuation of the removal of squatters from public lands. Although he failed to secure approval for most of these programs, Scott's record apparently satisfied his supporters, who managed to continue him in office throughout the remainder of the territorial period. Scott also took a particularly active part in the campaign to secure Missouri's admission to the Union, and the voters rewarded his efforts by electing him as the new state's first congressman.

Governor Clark's active participation in local political proceedings in support of the St. Louis group enraged the members of the opposing camp. They viewed the Governor's undisguised assistance to the junto as a clear-cut example of unjustified executive interference. The Governor had not hesitated to use his influence, whenever possible, in support of the junto's candidate, and Scott's opponents attributed his selection over Easton in the election of 1817 largely to the territorial executive's influence. Not since the administration of James Wilkinson had a governor's actions created so much local controversy.

All of Missouri's territorial governors had been favorably impressed by the small group of Frenchmen who, because of their prestige and wealth, largely dominated social and economic activity in St. Louis and to a lesser extent in other parts of the territory as well. However, the individual governors differed markedly in the degree of their involvement in territorial politics. Although both Amos Stoddard and Governor Harrison had been predisposed to favor the French elements, they had escaped any serious criticism, largely because of the low level of political activity during the earliest years of American control. Likewise, Governors Lewis and Howard had been on friendly terms with the French faction, but generally had avoided any direct participation in local political feuds. Since their major interests had always remained outside of the territory, it had been much easier for them to remain aloof.

Only Governors Wilkinson and Clark had become deeply embroiled in the territory's internal squabbles. Wilkinson's determination to exercise absolute control in the territory and his desire to win the approval of the French inhabitants had precipitated his frequent meddling. Clark's involvement emanated not so much from selfish personal motives as from the natural tendency to assist long-time friends. Both Clark's public and private associations with many of the more prominent members of the St. Louis junto predated his appointment as governor by several years.

Despite his occasional unwarranted interference in local politics, William Clark was probably the best of Missouri's territorial governors. Although Clark exerted little influence in shaping government policy, he carried out orders from his superiors in Washington efficiently, and he kept them reasonably well-informed about local conditions. His intimate knowledge of Indian affairs, acquired through long years of service, made him one of the most successful Indian agents in the history of the

United States. Unfortunately the Governor's close identification with national Indian policies, not always popular locally, lowered his standing among the rank-and-file frontiersmen and probably cost him the governorship upon Missouri's admission as a state.

Clark's popularity is difficult to gauge, but, unlike most of his predecessors, he made Missouri his permanent home. Consequently, Governor Clark had a much greater interest in strictly local problems. Moreover, he demonstrated a facility for working effectively with the territorial assembly, and together they successfully revised the local laws. Overall, William Clark compiled a creditable record as governor.

Personalities played an important role in shaping the political climate of territorial Missouri, and Governor Clark became a favorite target for the barbs of the antijunto faction. Political partisans frequently resorted to name-calling and slander to discredit their opponents. Moreover, political disagreements invariably degenerated into bitter personal feuds.

Occasionally one of the disputants went so far as to challenge an opponent to a duel in order to obtain the satisfaction due a gentleman. Of the at least eight duels fought in territorial Missouri, the contest between Thomas Hart Benton and Charles Lucas in 1817 was by far the most important politically. The disputed election for territorial delegate in 1816 had intensified existing personal animosities and shortened tempers. Such was the case with Benton and Lucas, when Lucas challenged Benton to prove that he had paid the necessary tax before he cast his ballot in the special election of 1817. The proud Benton exploded, and in his rage he disdainfully referred to Lucas as a "puppy." Lucas then sought satisfaction, and arrangements for the affair of honor were set. The first encounter was inconclusive, but Benton later demanded a second contest at which the young Lucas was mortally wounded. The death of the prominent young politician merely increased the already deep divisions in the political arena.

In addition to its highly personalized character, political activity in territorial Missouri remained primarily the prerogative of a small elitist group. The number of men who actively participated in the local political maneuvers always remained small. The average frontiersman, preoccupied with his own personal economic advancement, usually willingly delegated responsibility for making political decisions to members of one of the competing cliques. The local politicians, for their part, employed a variety of techniques to elicit the support of local voters. While representing small special-interest groups, political candidates carefully conducted their campaigns to appeal to the widest spectrum of the territorial populace and to convey an impression of active popular participation. A disgruntled observer of a territorial election reported that, "The timid and uninformed *male* population were brought in like sheep to the slaughter, under convoy, many under the influence of fear, and more ignorant of the consequences of a vote." Such occurrences were not uncommon, and in most respects frontier democracy in Missouri did not differ significantly from that in other rapidly-developing regions of the United States.

The tempo of the statehood movement gradually gained momentum in Missouri and by 1818 had completely overshadowed all other issues in territorial politics, including the long-dominant land-claims controversy. Although the introduction of the slavery question into the congressional debates temporarily postponed Missouri's admission to the Union, local residents, whose ire had been raised by the territorial government's seeming inability to resolve long-standing problems, refused to be dissuaded from their insistent demands for complete equality with the older states. For most Missourians statehood represented the final step in their long struggle to gain full recognition of their rights as American citizens.

Angered by the attempts to further delay their admission into the Union, Missourians rallied behind statehood with a unanimity rarely seen in the territory previously. Undoubtedly, this local consensus provided the most logical explanation for the minimum of dislocation that accompanied the final transition from territorial status to statehood in Missouri. Yet, despite the quickening desire to escape the confines of territorial administration, it would be unwarranted to conclude on the basis of Missouri's experience that the American territorial system had been overly deficient. Admittedly there had been numerous problems within the system, but under its tutelage the territory had matured sufficiently to assume full responsibility for its own government. Missouri had progressed from a sparsely-settled and politically-backward frontier outpost in 1804 to a reasonably well-governed region ready for statehood in 1820.

ESSAY ON SOURCES

The purpose of this essay is twofold. First it is designed to indicate the sources consulted in the preparation of this study, and secondly it is offered as a guide for further reading. The list is necessarily selective, but an attempt has been made to include the most pertinent materials dealing with Missouri's early history.

LIST OF ABBREVIATIONS USED

The Bulletin for *Bulletin of the Missouri Historical Society*
MHR for *Missouri Historical Review*
MVHR for *Mississippi Valley Historical Review*
AHR for *American Historical Review*

GENERAL HISTORIES AND REFERENCE WORKS

Louis Houck's three-volume *History of Missouri from Earliest Explorations and Settlements Until the Admission of the State into the Union* (Chicago, 1908) remains a standard reference work on territorial Missouri. These volumes are encyclopedic in nature and short on interpretation, but they contain a wealth of factual information. The best general history of Missouri is David D. March's excellent *The History of Missouri*, 4 vols. (New York and West Palm Beach, 1967). Published by subscription, this outstanding work has not received the attention it properly deserves. Duane Meyer's *The Heritage of Missouri* (St. Louis, 1963) is an informative and readable one-volume general history of the state. Another recent book is Edwin C. McReynolds, *Missouri: A History of the Crossroads State* (Norman, Oklahoma, 1962). Older but still helpful is Eugene Morrow Violette's *A History of Missouri* (Boston, New York, and Chicago, 1918). *Missouri and Missourians: Land of Contrasts and People of*

Achievements, 5 vols. (Chicago, 1943) by Floyd C. Shoemaker continues to be a valuable source of information on Missouri history. Also useful as general references are *Missouri, Mother of the West*, 5 vols. (Chicago and New York, 1930), coauthored by Walter Williams and Floyd C. Shoemaker, and *Missouri: A Guide to the "Show Me" State*, rev. ed. (New York, 1954) compiled by the workers of the Writers' Program of the Works Projects Administration in the State of Missouri.

Frederick L. Billon's *Annals of St. Louis in its Early Days Under the French and Spanish Dominations* (St. Louis, 1886), and *Annals of St. Louis in its Territorial Days from 1804 to 1821* (St. Louis, 1888) are compendiums of miscellaneous items which their author, an early resident of the city, compiled from territorial archives, private manuscript collections, newspapers, and other sources—some of which are no longer extant. Another early work of value is John T. Scharf's *History of St. Louis City and County from the Earliest Period to the Present Day*, 2 vols. (Philadelphia, 1883). A recent popularly-written history of St. Louis is Ernest Kirschten's *Catfish and Crystal* (Garden City, New York, 1960).

Since Missouri's early history was closely associated with that of Illinois and Louisiana, general histories of those states are also helpful in reconstructing the events of Missouri's prestatehood years. For Illinois, see Clarence W. Alvord's *The Illinois Country: 1673-1818* (Springfield, 1920). Two standard works on Louisiana history are Alcee Fortier's *A History of Louisiana*, 4 vols. (New York, 1904), and Charles E. A. Gayarre's *A History of Louisiana*, 4 vols. (New York, 1854-1866). The *Dictionary of American Biography*, edited by Dumas Malone, 44 vols. (New York, 1933), and the *Biographical Dictionary of the American Congress, 1774-1927* (Washington, D.C., 1928), are two sources of biographical information for important territorial figures.

For purposes of comparing Missouri's American territorial experience with that of other territories, Jack Ericson Eblen's *The First and Second United States Empires: Governors and Territorial Government, 1784-1912* (Pittsburg, 1968) is a valuable recent study. Likewise, Richard C. Wade's excellent book, *The Urban Frontier* (Cambridge, 1959) makes it possible to consider the early history of St. Louis within the broader framework of frontier urban development. Finally, the first chapters of Jerena East Green's *First Ladies of Missouri* (Jefferson City, Missouri, 1970) contain interesting accounts of the wives of some of Missouri's early leaders.

MANUSCRIPT COLLECTIONS

MISSOURI HISTORICAL SOCIETY

The most extensive manuscript collections pertaining to territorial Missouri are located in the archives of the Missouri Historical Society in St. Louis. For information on the Spanish years, the Valle Papers, the Delassus Papers, the Ste. Genevieve Papers, the New Madrid Archives, the St. Charles Archives, the St. Charles Papers, and the Amoureux-Bolduc Collections all contain pertinent information. The sizable Chouteau Collection is disappointing as a whole, but it does contain useful items for both the Spanish and American periods, as do the Gratiot Papers. The Louisiana Purchase Transfer Papers and the Amos Stoddard Papers offer valuable data concerning the transfer of Upper Louisiana to the United States and the early years of American control in the territory. For the American period the Lucas Papers are indispensable, as are the Bates Papers and the Rufus Easton Papers. Each provides the researcher with a rich supply of material on many aspects of territorial Missouri, but they are particularly valuable for studying political developments after 1804. The Society's James Wilkinson Papers contain photostatic copies of documents pertaining to the controversial general's activities in Upper Louisiana. The Clark Papers, the Hempstead Papers, and the William C. Carr Papers are helpful to the historian of territorial Missouri, and the Christian Wilt Letters provide a rich source for exploring mercantile operations in early Missouri. Other smaller collections in the Society's archives containing items of interest related to the territorial period include the General Daniel Bissell Papers, the Governors' Papers, the Indians' Papers, the Justus Post Letters, the Louisiana Territory Papers, the Meriwether Lewis Papers, the Mines Envelope, and the Missouri History Papers.

LIBRARY OF CONGRESS

Of the numerous collections in the Library of Congress, the Thomas Jefferson Papers are particularly useful as a source of information concerning the acquisition of the Louisiana Territory and the problems of administering the newly-acquired region. Also helpful on this topic are the Breckinridge Family Papers, along with the James Madison Papers, and the James Monroe Papers, which contain occasional references to territorial Missouri.

Most of the pertinent documents on territorial Missouri found in the collections at the National Archives have been published in Volumes XIII, XIV, and XV of Clarence E. Carter's *Territorial Papers of the United States,* but the Auditor's Reports, Miscellaneous Letters Sent by the Comptroller of the Treasury, and other fiscal records provide useful information about the financial operations of territorial government not contained in the published papers. Moreover, the Letters of Appointment and Recommendation for the Administrations of Thomas Jefferson, James Madison, and James Monroe give the researcher added insight into territorial appointments in Missouri.

STATE HISTORICAL SOCIETY OF MISSOURI

The Thomas A. Smith Collection and a few miscellaneous Justus Post Letters in the Western Historical Manuscripts Collection contain selected items related to territorial Missouri.

PUBLISHED MANUSCRIPTS, PRINTED DOCUMENTS, AND CONTEMPORARY ACCOUNTS

Various printed documents and published manuscripts are available for the prestatehood years in Upper Louisiana. Louis Houck's *The Spanish Regime in Missouri* (Chicago, 1909) is a two-volume collection of documents pertaining to the Spanish period gleaned by Houck's researchers from the Spanish Archives in Seville. Another useful documentary collection is *Spain in the Mississippi Valley, 1765-1794,* Lawrence Kinnaird, ed., in *Annual Report of the American Historical Association, 1945,* Vols. II–IV (Washington, D.C., 1946). Equally important is the two-volume set edited by Abraham P. Nasatir, *Before Lewis and Clark: Documents Illustrating the History of Missouri, 1785-1804* (St. Louis, 1952). Nasatir's introductory narrative serves as an excellent summary of the period.

In addition to the work edited by Nasatir, the St. Louis Historical Documents Foundation has published two important collections edited by John Francis McDermott: *The Early Histories of St. Louis* (St. Louis, 1952), and *Old Cahokia* (St. Louis, 1949).

The Missouri Historical Society Collections contain additional selected items from the French and Spanish periods including "Documents Relating to the Attack Upon St. Louis in 1780," 2 (July, 1906), 41–54; "Letter of Instruction: Baron de Carondelet to Lieutenant Governor Don Carlos Howard," 3 (January, 1908), 71–91; "The Beginning of Spanish Missouri: Instructions of D'Ulloa to Rui, 1767," 3 (April, 1908), 145–69; "Letter and Sketch of Lieutenant Don Manuel Perez," 3 (1911), 307–12; "Fragment of Colonel Auguste Chouteau's Narrative of the Settlement of St. Louis," 3 (1911), 349–66; and "Journal of Jean Baptiste Trudeau Among the Arikara Indians in 1795," Mrs. H. T. Beauregard, trans. and ed., 4 (1912), 9–48. In addition, the *Bulletin of the Missouri Historical Society* published "Étienne Véniard de Bourgmont's 'Exact Description of Louisiana,'" Mrs. Max W. Myers, trans., 15 (October, 1958), 3–19.

Documents concerning Spanish Louisiana reprinted in the *American Historical Review* include "A Memorandum of Moses Austin's Journey, 1796–1797," 5 (April, 1900), 518–42, and "Documents—The Clark-Leyba Papers," Lawrence Kinnaird, ed., 41 (October, 1935), 92–112.

The *Mississippi Valley Historical Review* reprinted materials translated and edited by Abraham P. Nasatir in "Spanish Exploration of the Upper Missouri," 14 (June, 1927), 57–71. Nasatir also edited a series of documents for the *Missouri Historical Review*, most of them in conjunction with several articles that he prepared for that journal. See "Ducharme's Invasion of Missouri: An Incident in the Anglo-Spanish Rivalry for the Indian Trade of Upper Louisiana," 24 (October, 1929), 3–25, (January, 1930), 238–60, and (April, 1930), 420–39; "An Account of Spanish Louisiana, 1785," 24 (July, 1930), 521–26; and "John Evans, Explorer and Surveyor," 25 (January, 1931), 219–39, (April, 1931), 432–60, and (July, 1931), 585–608. In addition to Nasatir's contributions, *MHR* also published "A 1795 Inspection of Spanish Missouri," Jack D. L. Holmes, ed., 55 (October, 1960), 5–17.

Missouri's American territorial period provides an equally impressive array of published manuscripts and documents. By far the most comprehensive collection of documents for the Louisiana-Missouri Territory between 1803 and 1821 can be found in the twenty-six volume *The Territorial Papers of the United States*, edited by Clarence E. Carter. Specific volumes, all published in Washington, D.C., 1934 ——, are: *The Territory of Louisiana–Missouri, 1803–1806*, Vol. XIII (1948); *The Territory of Louisiana–Missouri, 1806–1814*, Vol. XIV (1949); *The Territory of Louisiana–Missouri, 1815–1821*, Vol. XV (1954). The carefully edited volumes in this series reproduce the most important previously unpublished materials located in the various governmental depositories in Washington, D.C.

The *Territorial Papers* is best used in conjunction with other government documents and public records. *The American State Papers: Foreign Relations, Indian Affairs, Military Affairs, Public Lands,* and *Miscellaneous* (Washington, D.C. 1832–1861) are particularly useful as a source of information concerning various facets of territorial operations. The *Annals of the Congress of the United States, 1789–1824,* 42 vols. (Washington, D.C., 1834–1836) provide an account of the congressional deliberations on questions concerning the territory; all federal laws enacted to govern the Louisiana-Missouri Territory can be found in the *United States Statutes at Large* (Washington, D.C., 1850). Laws passed by the early territorial legislatures are found in *Laws for the Government of the District of Louisiana* (Vincennes, Indiana, 1804), and *The Laws of the Territory of Louisiana* (St. Louis, 1808). All statutes adopted by the territorial legislature after 1808 were printed in the columns of the St. Louis *Missouri Gazette,* along with a record of legislative proceedings. Copies of these and all other known legislative and judicial records for the territory have been microfilmed and made available as a unit by the Early State Records project sponsored jointly by the Library of Congress and the University of North Carolina, under the direction of William S. Jenkins. In addition, the library of the State Historical Society of Missouri in Columbia has printed copies of numerous reports, memorials, petitions, and resolutions, both public and private, prepared for Congress concerning questions involving the Missouri Territory.

Several collections of published papers can be used to supplement the various government documents and public records. One of the most important of these is *The Life and Papers of Frederick Bates,* Thomas Maitland Marshall, ed., 2 vols. (St. Louis, 1926). Also useful are *Governors' Messages and Letters: Messages and Letters of William Henry Harrison,* Logan Esarey, ed., 2 vols. (Indianapolis, 1922), and *The Austin Papers: Annual Report of the American Historical Association for the Year 1919,* Eugene C. Barker, ed. (Washington, D.C., 1924).

William Plumer's *Memorandum of Proceedings in the United States Senate, 1803–1807* (New York, 1923), edited by Everett S. Brown, provides insight concerning the debates in the upper chamber of Congress pertaining to the acquisition and administration of the Louisiana Territory. A few items related to Upper Louisiana can be found in *Louisiana Under the Rule of Spain, France and the United*

States, 1785–1807, James A. Robertson, trans. and ed., 2 vols. (Cleveland, 1911).

The Missouri Historical Society's *Glimpses of the Past,* 2 (May-September, 1935), 78–122, contains the "Papers of Captain Amos Stoddard," reprinted from documents found in their archives. Similarly, Mrs. Dana O. Jensen edited the diary of Stephen Hempstead, Sr., for *The Bulletin*: "The Diary of a Yankee Farmer in Missouri, I At Home," Pt. I, 1811–1814, 13 (October, 1956), 30–56; Pt. II, 1815–1816, 13 (April, 1957), 283–317, Pt. III, 1817–1818, 14 (October, 1957), 59–96, Pt. IV, 1819, 14 (April, 1958), 272–88, and Pt. V, 1820, 15 (October, 1958), 38–48.

Other miscellaneous documentary items involving Missouri's early history include "Papers of Zebulon M. Pike, 1806–1807," Herbert E. Bolton, ed., in *American Historical Review,* 13 (July, 1908), 798–827; and Col. John Shaw's eyewitness account, "New Madrid Earthquake," *MHR,* 6 (January, 1912), 91–92.

Contemporary accounts furnish another valuable source of information for the territorial period. Most were written by travelers and other itinerants who came to the territory for varying periods of time. These works differ considerably in quality and in value and often reflect the biases and preconceived ideas of the men who compiled them. Nevertheless, they do add to our knowledge of general conditions in the territory at the time that they were written. Among the best of these accounts are the works of Amos Stoddard and Henry Marie Brackenridge. Stoddard's *Sketches, Historical and Descriptive, of Louisiana* (Philadelphia, 1812) provides a great deal of useful information about the territory at the time of its transfer to the United States. Likewise Brackenridge's *Views of Louisiana* (Pittsburg, 1814), and his *Recollections of Persons and Places in the West* (Philadelphia, 1834) are essential sources for the historian of early Missouri.

Other accounts include Victor Collot's *A Journey in North America,* 2 vols. (Paris, 1826); Perrin DuLac's *Travels Through the Two Louisianas and Among the Savage Nations of the Missouri* (London, 1807); Christian Schultz's *Travels on an Inland Voyage* . . . , 2 vols. (New York, 1810); John Bradbury's *Travels in the Interior of America, in the Years 1809–1810 and 1811* . . . (London, 1817); Henry Rowe Schoolcraft's *A View of the Lead Mines of Missouri* (New York, 1819), and his *Journal of a Tour into the Interior of Missouri and Arkansaw* . . . (London, 1821); Timothy Flint's *Recollections of the Last Ten Years* (Boston, 1826); and John Mason Peck's *Forty Years of Pioneer Life* (Philadelphia, 1864). Many of these accounts have been reprinted and are currently available for use by students of Missouri history.

NEWSPAPERS

Copies of most territorial newspapers can be found at the State Historical Society in Columbia. Those available are *Franklin Missouri Intelligencer and Boon's Lick Advertiser*, April 23, 1819–April 8, 1820; Jackson *Missouri Herald*, August 13, 1819–April 1, 1820; *St. Louis Enquirer*, September 4, 1819–March 29, 1820; St. Louis *Missouri Gazette* (published under various mastheads, as follows: *Missouri Gazette*, July 26, 1808–November 23, 1809; *Louisiana Gazette*, November 30, 1809–July 11, 1812; *Missouri Gazette*, July 18, 1812–February 19, 1814; *Missouri Gazette and Illinois Advertiser*, February 26, 1814–July 8, 1815; *Missouri Gazette*, July 15, 1815– May 1, 1818; *Missouri Gazette and Illinois Advertiser*, May 8, 1818–July 3, 1818; *Missouri Gazette and Public Advertiser*, July 10, 1818–April 12, 1820).

BOOKS AND ARTICLES

EXPLORATION AND SETTLEMENT

The number of books and articles on early exploration and settlement in the Mississippi Valley is extensive, but only a few selected titles have been included in this discussion. Charles E. Nowell's brief but well-written history, *The Great Discoveries and the First Colonial Empires* (Ithaca, 1954) provides a good general overview of early European exploratory and colonization activity. Various early explorers are discussed in "The Missouri Reader: Explorers in the Valley," Kate L. Gregg, ed., *MHR*, Pt. I, 39 (April, 1945), 354–88, and Pt. II (July, 1945), 505–44. Charles E. Burgess discounts the possibility that DeSoto ever set foot on Missouri soil in "The DeSoto Myth in Missouri," *The Bulletin*, 24 (July, 1968), 303–25. For an account of Missouri's first known European explorers, see Reuben Gold Thwaites, *Father Marquette* (New York, 1914), and "Jacques Marquette: 1673–1675," by John F. Bannon in *MHR*, 64 (October, 1969), 81–87. A recent biography of LaSalle is John Upton Terrell's *LaSalle: The Life and Times of an Explorer* (New York, 1968).

The story of the first attempted settlement in present-day Missouri (on the River des Pères) can be found in "First Settlement on the Site of St. Louis," in Gilbert J. Garraghan's *Chapters in Frontier*

History: Research Studies in the Making of the West (Milwaukee, 1934), and in John F. Bannon, "Black Robe Frontiersman: Gabriel Marest, S. J.," *The Bulletin*, 10 (April, 1954), 351–66. Early French activity on the Missouri River is described in M. F. Stipes, "Fort Orleans, The First French Post on the Missouri," *MHR*, 8 (April, 1914), 121–35; Gilbert J. Garraghan, "Fort Orleans of the Missoury," *MHR*, 35 (April, 1941), 373–84; and Henri Folmer, "Étiene Véniard de Bourgmond [*sic*] in the Missouri Country," *MHR*, 36 (April, 1942), 279–98. Francis J. Yealy provides an account of the establishment of Missouri's first permanent settlement in his study, *Sainte Genevieve* (Ste. Genevieve, Missouri, 1935).

The story of St. Louis and its founders has been told best by John F. McDermott. Articles prepared by him on that subject include, "Myths and Realities Concerning the Founding of St. Louis," in *The French in the Mississippi Valley*, John F. McDermott, ed. (Urbana, Illinois, 1965); "The Exclusive Trade Privileges of Maxent, Laclede and Company," *MHR*, 29 (July, 1935), 272–78; "Pierre Laclede, the Father of St. Louis," *Missouri Magazine*, 9 (March, 1937), 11–13; "Pierre Laclede and the Chouteaus," *The Bulletin*, 21 (July, 1965), 279–83; and "Paincourt and Poverty," *Mid-America*, 5 (April, 1934), 210–12.

The origins of New Madrid have been studied extensively by Max Savelle; see Savelle, "The Founding of New Madrid, Missouri," *Mississippi Valley Historical Review*, 19 (June, 1932), 30–56, and *George Morgan: Colony Builder* (New York, 1932). Floyd C. Shoemaker examines the settlement at Cape Girardeau in "Cape Girardeau, Most American of Missouri's Original Five Counties," *MHR*, 50 (October, 1955), 49–61, and Ben L. Emmons discussed the beginnings of St. Charles in "The Founding of St. Charles and Blanchette Its Founder," *MHR*, 18 (July, 1924), 507–20.

More general treatments of early settlements and settlement patterns can be found in Eugene M. Violette, "Early Settlements in Missouri," *MHR*, 1 (October, 1906), 38–52; and Jonas Viles, "Population and Extent of Settlement in Missouri before 1804," *MHR*, 5 (July, 1911), 189–213. In her article, "Missouri a Land of Promise," *MHR*, 30 (April, 1936), 227–53, Hattie M. Anderson describes some of the features that attracted settlers to frontier Missouri. In a related article, "Missouri 1804–1828: Peopling a Frontier State," *MHR*, 31 (January, 1937), 150–80, she discusses the settlement process following the American acquisition of Upper Louisiana. Jonas Viles examines one of territorial Missouri's later settlements in "Old Franklin: A Frontier Town of the Twenties," *MVHR*, 9 (March, 1923), 269–82.

UPPER LOUISIANA UNDER SPANISH RULE

For a general introduction to the Spanish role in North America, see John Francis Bannon, *The Spanish Borderlands Frontier, 1513–1821* (New York, 1970). A brief and rather unsophisticated account of Spanish rule in Upper Louisiana is presented in Walter B. Douglas, *The Spanish Domination of Upper Louisiana* (Madison, Wisconsin, 1914). On the subject of Anglo-Spanish relations in Upper Louisiana, the authoritative studies of Abraham P. Nasatir remain unsurpassed; in addition to his works cited elsewhere in this essay, see "The Anglo-Spanish Frontier in the Illinois Country During the American Revolution, 1779–1783," *Journal of Illinois State Historical Society*, 21 (October, 1928), 291–358, and "The Anglo-Spanish Frontier on the Upper Mississippi, 1786–1796," *Iowa Journal of History and Politics*, 29 (April, 1931), 155–232.

Less satisfactory as an authoritative source on Anglo-Spanish relations is the earlier "Spanish Influence in the West During the American Revolution," *MVHR*, 4 (September, 1917), 193–208 by James A. James. Several writers have dealt with the British attack on St. Louis in 1780, the best being Don Rickey, Jr., "The British-Indian Attack on St. Louis, May 26, 1780," *MHR*, 55 (October, 1960), 35–45. Also see James A. James, "The Significance of the Attack on St. Louis, 1780," *Proceedings of the MVHA*, 2 (1908–1909), 199–217, and Stella M. Drumm, "The British-Indian Attack on Pain Court (St. Louis)," *Journal of Illinois State Historical Society*, 23 (1930), 642–51.

Clarence W. Alvord deprecated the role of Spanish authorities in planning the attack and discounted the over-all importance of the entire campaign in "The Conquest of St. Joseph, Michigan, by the Spaniards in 1781," *MHR*, 2 (April, 1908), 195–210, while Frederick J. Teggart's "The Capture of St. Joseph, Michigan by the Spaniards in 1781," *MHR*, 5 (July, 1911), 214–28 credited the Spanish with organizing a highly successful assault. Lawrence Kinnaird presented the most satisfactory explanation of the attack in "The Spanish Expedition Against Fort St. Joseph in 1781, A New Interpretation," *MVHR*, 19 (September, 1932), 173–91.

Arthur P. Whitaker has skillfully traced the changing course of Spanish-American relations in his two important studies *The Spanish American Frontier, 1783–1795* (Boston, 1927), and *The Mississippi Question, 1795–1803* (New York, 1934). F. R. Hall's account, "Genet's Western Intrigue, 1793–1794," *Journal of the Illinois State Historical Society*, 21 (1928), 359–81 examines Genet's Louisiana schemes, while George W. Kyte in "A Spy on the Western Waters: The Military

Intelligence Mission of General Collot in 1796," *MVHR*, 34 (December, 1947), 427–42 describes the subsequent French activity in the Mississippi Valley. Jack D. L. Holmes's study, *Gayoso: The Life of a Spanish Governor in the Mississippi Valley, 1789–1799* (Baton Rouge, 1965), sheds additional light on Spanish problems and policies.

Spain's immigration policies are explained in Lawrence Kinnaird's "American Penetration into Spanish Louisiana," in *New Spain and the Anglo-American West*, I (Lancaster, Pennsylvania, 1932), 211–37, and in Gilbert C. Din, "The Immigration Policy of Governor Esteban Miró in Spanish Louisiana," *Southwestern Historical Quarterly*, 73 (October, 1969), 155–75.

DIPLOMACY AND THE LOUISIANA TERRITORY TO 1800

There are a variety of studies concerning Louisiana and international diplomacy. A general account of France's Louisiana policies can be found in E. Wilson Lyon's *Louisiana in French Diplomacy: 1759–1804* (Norman, Oklahoma, 1934). Concerning the transfer of Louisiana from France to Spain in 1762, William R. Shepherd argued in "The Cession of Louisiana to Spain," *Political Science Quarterly*, 19 (September, 1904), 439–58, that the Spanish were not particularly pleased with the prospect of assuming control of the province. However, Arthur S. Aiton, "The Diplomacy of the Louisiana Cession," *AHR*, 36 (July, 1931), 701–20, and Allan Christelow, "Proposals for a French Company for Spanish Louisiana, 1763-1764," *MVHR*, 27 (March, 1941), 603–11 both offer convincing evidence in support of their contention that Spain gladly received the cession of Louisiana.

Mildred Fletcher Stahl, "Louisiana As a Factor in French Diplomacy from 1763 to 1800," *MVHR*, 17 (December, 1930), 367–76 traces fluctuations in French interest in Louisiana. In explaining Spain's retrocession of Louisiana to France in 1800, Arthur Whitaker, "The Retrocession of Louisiana in Spanish Policy," *AHR*, 39 (April, 1934), 454–76, suggests that, although Spain had eagerly accepted Louisiana in 1762 in order to build a defensive barrier for her other possessions, the Spanish had concluded by 1795 that this was no longer feasible and Spain was prepared to get rid of the Louisiana Territory whenever the terms were right.

THE LOUISIANA PURCHASE

The American acquisition of the Louisiana Territory has received widespread attention. Marshall Smelser's recent book *The Demo-*

cratic Republic, 1801–1815 (New York, 1968) provides a succinct and authoritative general discussion of the subject. A more detailed examination of various aspects of the Louisiana Purchase can be found in Dumas Malone's definitive multi-volume biography of Thomas Jefferson, *Jefferson the President: First Term, 1801–1805*, IV (Boston, 1970). Although recent authors may disagree with some of its interpretations, Henry Adams's classic *History of the United States during the Administrations of Jefferson and Madison* (New York, 1889–1890), remains a valuable source of information. Also useful is Everett S. Brown, *The Constitutional History of the Louisiana Purchase, 1803–1812* (Berkeley, 1920).

Articles on the subject of the Louisiana Purchase include Floyd C. Shoemaker, "The Louisiana Purchase, 1803, and the Transfer of Upper Louisiana to the United States, 1804," *MHR*, 48 (October, 1953), 1–22; Charles Nutter, "Robert Livingston, the Forgotten Architect of the Louisiana Purchase," *MHR*, 48 (January, 1954), 117–33; Jerry W. Knudson, "Newspaper Reaction to the Louisiana Purchase: 'This New, Immense, Unbounded World,' " *MHR*, 63 (January, 1969), 182–213; "The Missouri Reader: The Louisiana Purchase," Alice La Force, ed., *MHR*, Pt. I, 42 (October, 1947), 50–71, Pt. II (January, 1948), 153–72; and Louis Pelzer, "Economic Factors in the Acquisition of Louisiana," *Proceedings of the MVHA*, 6 (1912–1913), 109–28.

THE LEWIS AND CLARK EXPEDITION

Since the actual Lewis and Clark expedition is only indirectly related to the story of Missouri's territorial development, no attempt has been made to survey the voluminous literature on this topic. *Lewis and Clark: Partners in Discovery*, by John Bakeless (New York, 1947) is a standard account. An excellent recent volume on the famous journey is Paul Russell Cutright's *Lewis and Clark: Pioneering Naturalists* (Urbana, Illinois, 1969). See also "The Missouri Reader: The Lewis and Clark Expedition," Helen Deveneau Finley and Ada Paris Klein, eds., *MHR*, Pt. I, 42 (April, 1948), 249–70; Pt. II (July, 1948), 343–66; Pt. III, 43 (October, 1948), 48–70; Pt. IV (January, 1949), 145–59.

GOVERNMENT AND POLITICS: 1803–1821

Floyd C. Shoemaker, "A Sketch of Missouri Constitutional History During the Territorial Period," *MHR*, 9 (October, 1914), 1–32, briefly traces Missouri's advancement through the various territorial stages. Likewise, Shoemaker's *Missouri's Struggle for Statehood, 1804-1821* (Jefferson City, Missouri, 1916) follows the attempts of Missourians to gain admission to the Union. Frederick C. Hicks studied the problems of financing territorial government in "Territorial Revenue System of Missouri," *Missouri Historical Society Collections*, 1 (1896), 25–40. Isidor Loeb provided a survey of early territorial statutes in "The Beginnings of Missouri Legislation," *MHR*, 1 (October, 1906), 53–71. Elizabeth Gaspar Brown briefly considered the status of laws during the transitional period in "Law and Government in the Louisiana Purchase: 1803–1804," *Wayne Law Review*, 2 (Summer, 1956), 169–89. For a look at legal proceedings and the role of the attorney in early Missouri, consult William Francis English, *The Pioneer Lawyer and Jurist in Missouri* (Columbia, Missouri, 1947).

Numerous biographical and other specialized studies provide additional information concerning political developments in the territory. Wilfrid Hibbert, "Major Amos Stoddard: First Governor of Upper Louisiana and Hero of Fort Meigs," *The Historical Society of Northwestern Ohio Quarterly Bulletin*, 2 (April, 1930), gives a brief account of Upper Louisiana's earliest American official. Two biographies are available for information on William Henry Harrison: Dorothy Burne Goebel, *William Henry Harrison: A Political Biography* (Indianapolis, 1926), and Freeman Cleaves, *Old Tippecanoe* (New York, 1939).

Stella M. Drumm, "Samuel Hammond," *Missouri Historical Society Collections*, 4 (1923), 402–22 examines the career of another prominent territorial figure. The early years of the controversial John B. C. Lucas are covered in John Francis McDermott, "John B. C. Lucas in Pennsylvania," *The Western Pennsylvania Historical Magazine*, 21 (September, 1938), 209–30; and Hugh G. Cleland, "John B. C. Lucas, Physiocrat on the Frontier," *The Western Pennsylvania Historical Magazine*, 36 (March, 1953), 1–15, (June, 1953), 87–100, (September–December, 1953), 141–68.

Two biographical studies provide a detailed picture of James A. Wilkinson's fascinating and controversial life. The better is James Ripley Jacob's *Tarnished Warrior* (New York, 1938), but Thomas Robson Hay and M. R. Werner's *The Admirable Trumpeter* (Garden City, 1941) is also useful. For Wilkinson's record in Upper Louisiana, see William E. Foley, "James A. Wilkinson: Territorial Governor," *The Bulletin*, 25 (October, 1968), 3–17. Thomas P. Abernethy examines the Burr Conspiracy in detail in both *The Burr Con-*

spiracy (New York, 1954), and Vol. IV of *The History of the South, The South in the New Nation, 1789–1819* (Baton Rouge, 1961), while Clarence E. Carter, "The Burr-Wilkinson Intrigue in St. Louis," *The Bulletin*, 10 (July, 1954), 447–64, provides a useful discussion of the role Upper Louisianians played in Burr's schemes.

An excellent biography of Wilkinson's successor is Richard Dillon's *Meriwether Lewis* (New York, 1965). Concerning the controversy surrounding Lewis's death, see Dawson A. Phelps, "The Tragic Death of Meriwether Lewis," *William and Mary Quarterly*, 13 (July, 1956), 305–18. Unfortunately, no full-length biographical study of William Clark has yet been published. In the absence of such a work, the student of early Missouri must consult John Bakeless, *Lewis and Clark: Partners in Discovery* (New York, 1947). Two very elementary sketches can be found in: Reuben Gold Thwaites, "William Clark: Soldier, Explorer, Statesman," *Missouri Historical Society Collections*, 2 (1906), 1–24, and Walter B. Smith, "General William Clark: Territorial Governor of Missouri," *Bulletin of Washington University Association*, 4 (1906), 49–69. A few unpublished theses and dissertations covering only certain portions of Clark's lengthy career are also available.

The life of Thomas Hart Benton and his role in early Missouri politics has been examined in detail. The best biography of Benton is William Nisbet Chambers, *Old Bullion Benton* (Boston, 1956). In addition, Chambers has examined Benton's role in territorial Missouri in "Young Man From Tennessee, First Years of Thomas Hart Benton in Missouri," *The Bulletin*, 4 (July, 1948), 199–216, and "Pistols and Politics: Incidents in the Career of Thomas Hart Benton, 1816–1818," *The Bulletin*, 5 (October, 1948), 5–17. Equally important for Benton's early career is Perry G. McCandless, "The Rise of Thomas Hart Benton in Missouri Politics," *MHR*, 50 (October, 1955), 16–29.

NEGROES AND MISSOURI SOCIETY

Black people constituted 15 per cent of the territorial population, but very little has been written concerning their role in Missouri's development. In the absence of a general history of the Negro in Missouri, Harrison A. Trexler's now-dated works remain the standard accounts for the territorial period: *Slavery in Missouri 1804–1865* (Baltimore, 1914), and "Slavery in Missouri Territory," *MHR*, 3 (April, 1909), 179–98. E. M. Violette, "The Black Code in Missouri," *Proceedings of the MVHA*, 6 (1912–1913), 287–316, surveyed the regulations governing blacks in early Missouri, while Emil Oberholzer's "The Legal Aspects of Slavery in Missouri," *The Bulletin*, 6 (January, 1950), 139–61, (April, 1950), 333–51, and (July, 1950), 540–45, provides a superior discussion of that topic. Benjamin Merkle's *The Antislavery Controversy in Missouri, 1819–1865* (St. Louis, 1942) devotes only a few pages to the territorial period.

INDIANS AND INDIAN POLICY

The best introduction to the study of Indians in Missouri is Carl H. Chapman and Eleanor F. Chapman, *Indians and Archaeology of Missouri* (Columbia, Missouri, 1964). Also helpful is Carl H. Chapman, "A Preliminary Survey of Missouri Archaeology," *The Missouri Archaeologist*, Pt. I, "Historic Indian Tribes," (October, 1946), and Pt. IV, "Ancient Cultures and Sequence," (December, 1948). Some information can be found in "The Missouri Reader: Indians in the Valley," *MHR*, Pt. I, 39 (October, 1944), 75–97, and Pt. II (January, 1945), 224–58. An excellent account of the Sac and Fox Indians is available in William T. Hagan, *The Sac and Fox Indians* (Norman, Oklahoma, 1958), and students of Missouri history will also find the same author's "The Sauk and Fox Treaty of 1804," *MHR*, 51 (October, 1956), 1–7 useful. For information on the Osage, see John Joseph Mathews, *The Osages* (Norman, Oklahoma, 1961). Various facets of the United States government's Indian policy are discussed in Francis Paul Prucha, *American Indian Policy in the Formative Years: The Indian Trade and Intercourse Acts, 1790–1834* (Cambridge, 1962); Reginald Horsman, *Expansion and American Indian Policy, 1783–1812* (East Lansing, 1967); and Annie Heloise Abel, "The History of Events Resulting in Indian Consolidation West of the Mississippi," *Annual Report of the American Historical Association*, 1 (1906), 235–450.

FRONTIER MILITARY OPERATIONS AND THE WAR OF 1812

James B. Musick's *St. Louis As a Fortified Town* (St. Louis, 1941) offers a comprehensive account of the numerous attempts to provide for the defense of St. Louis at various times during its early years, but it is particularly good for the Spanish period. On the same subject, see John Francis McDermott, "St. Louis as Military Headquarters," *The Bulletin*, 23 (January, 1967), 101–18. A brief sketch of the establishment and subsequent history of Fort Carondelet can be found in "Fort Carondelet," *MHR*, 35 (October, 1940), 92–95. Kate L. Gregg detailed the construction of Fort Belle Fontaine in "Building of the First American Fort West of the Mississippi," *MHR*, 30 (July, 1936), 345–64, and she also authored "The History of Fort Osage," *MHR*, 34 (July, 1940), 439–88. Donald Jackson discussed the history of Fort Osage's counterpart on the Upper Mississippi in his article "Old Fort Madison: 1808–1813," *The Palimpsest*, 47 (January, 1966), 1–62, and Kate L. Gregg's "The War of 1812 on the Missouri Frontier," *MHR*, Pt. I, 33 (October, 1938), 3–22, Pt. II (January, 1939), 184–202, and Pt. III (April, 1939), 326–48 offers the most comprehensive account of that conflict in the Missouri Territory. A general account of frontier military operations can be found in Francis Paul Prucha, *The Sword of the Republic: The United States Army on the Frontier, 1783–1846* (New York, 1969).

GENERAL ECONOMIC DEVELOPMENT

The best general account of economic development in Upper Louisiana during the Spanish years is J. Manuel Espinosa, "Spanish Louisiana and the West: The Economic Significance of the Ste. Genevieve District," *MHR*, 32 (April, 1938), 287–97. For the later territorial period, see Hattie M. Anderson, "Frontier Economic Problems in Missouri, 1815–1828," *MHR*, Pt. I, 34 (October, 1939), 38–70, Pt. II (January, 1940), 182–203. Marietta Jennings's *A Pioneer Merchant of St. Louis 1810–1820: The Business Career of Christian Wilt* (New York, 1939) is a well-documented case study of mercantile operations in the Missouri Territory. The story of the territory's unsuccessful banking ventures can be found in John Ray Cable, *The Bank of the State of Missouri* (New York, 1923); Timothy W. Hubbard and Lewis E. Davids, *Banking in Mid-America: A History of Missouri's Banks* (Washington, D.C., 1969); and Harry S. Gleick, "Banking in Early Missouri," *MHR*, Pt. I (July, 1967), 427–43. Dorothy B. Dorsey examined "The Panic of 1819 in Missouri," *MHR*, 29 (January, 1935), 79–91.

THE FUR TRADE

The two most comprehensive histories of the fur trade are by Hiram M. Chittenden, *The American Fur Trade of the Far West*, 3 vols. (New York, 1902), and Paul C. Phillips, *The Fur Trade*, 2 vols. (Norman, Oklahoma, 1961). Ada Paris Klein edited "The Missouri Reader: The Fur Trade," *MHR*, 43 (July, 1949), 360–80, 44 (October, 1949), 48–65, and (January, 1950), 168–78. An interesting account of the nature of the earliest Indian trade in the Upper Missouri is provided by John C. Ewers, "The Indian Trade of the Upper Missouri before Lewis and Clark: An Interpretation," *The Bulletin*, 10 (July, 1954), 429–46. A. P. Nasatir has studied various aspects of early Spanish attempts to capture the trade in Upper Louisiana. From his writings, see "Jacques D'Eglise on the Upper Missouri, 1791–1795," *MVHR*, 14 (June, 1927), 47–56; "Ducharme's Invasion of Missouri: An Incident in the Anglo-Spanish Rivalry for the Indian Trade of Upper Louisiana," *MHR*, 24 (October, 1930), 10–22; and "John Evans, Explorer and Surveyor," *MHR*, 25 (January, 1931), 219–39. Isaac J. Cox traces early interest in trade with the Southwest in "Opening the Santa Fe Trail," *MHR*, 25 (October, 1930), 30–66.

Biographical sketches and studies of several prominent traders offer additional information concerning Missouri's role in the early fur trade. Regretably, biographies of Pierre Laclede and the Chouteau brothers have yet to be published. For a brief sketch of the elder Chouteau, see John Francis McDermott, "Auguste Chouteau: First Citizen of Upper Louisiana," in *Frenchmen and French Ways in the Mississippi Valley*, John Francis McDermott, ed. (Urbana, Illinois, 1969). A. P. Nasatir outlines the career of the controversial Jacques Clamorgan in "Jacques Clamorgan, Colonial Promoter of the Northern Border of New Spain," *New Mexico Historical Review*, 17 (April, 1942), 101–12. Also helpful are Janet Lecompte's "Don Benito Vasquez in Early St. Louis," *The Bulletin*, 26 (July, 1970), 285–305; Julius T. Muench, "Jean Baptiste Roy, St. Louis Fur Trader," *The Bulletin*, 3 (April, 1947), 85–93; "Jean Gabriel Cerré," *Missouri Historical Society Collections*, 2 (1903), 58–76; Richard E. Oglesby, "Pierre Menard, Reluctant Mountain Man," *The Bulletin*, 24 (October, 1967), 3–19; and Charles E. Peterson, "Manuel Lisa's Warehouse," *The Bulletin*, 4 (January, 1948), 59–91. In addition to these shorter articles there are two excellent studies available in Richard E. Oglesby, *Manuel Lisa and the Opening of the Missouri Fur Trade* (Norman, Oklahoma, 1963), and John E. Sunder, *Joshua Pilcher: Fur Trader and Indian Agent* (Norman, Oklahoma, 1968). For the story of George Sibley, the factor at Fort Osage, see Charles T. Jones, Jr., *George Champlin Sibley: The Prairie Puritan (1782–1863)*, (Independence, Missouri, 1970).

LEAD MINING

The best general account of lead-mining activities in early Missouri is Ruby Johnson Swartzlow's "The Early History of Lead Mining in

Missouri," *MHR*, Pt. I, 28 (April, 1934), 184–94, Pt. II (July, 1934), 287–95, Pt. III, 29 (October, 1934), 27–34, Pt. IV (January, 1935), 109–14, and Pt. V (April, 1935), 195–205. Also helpful on this subject are John E. Rothensteiner, "Earliest History of Mine La Motte," *MHR*, 20 (January, 1926), 199–213; "The Missouri Reader: Lead Mining in Pioneer Missouri," Ada Paris Klein, ed., *MHR*, 43 (April, 1949), 251–70; Floyd C. Shoemaker, "Herculaneum Shot Tower," *MHR*, 20 (January, 1926), 214–16; and Brad Luckingham, "A Note on the Lead Mines of Missouri," *MHR*, 59 (April, 1965), 344–48. James A. Gardner's "The Business Career of Moses Austin in Missouri, 1798–1821," *MHR*, 50 (April, 1956), 235–47, recounts the activities of Missouri's most prominent lead miner, while Donald J. Abramoske examines the controversial lead leasing system in "The Federal Lead Leasing System in Missouri," *MHR*, 54 (October, 1959), 27–38

LAND CLAIMS

The task of unraveling the complicated land-claims controversy in Missouri is monumental, but several important studies provide useful information on the subject. See Lemont K. Richardson, "Private Land Claims in Missouri," *MHR*, Pt. I, 50 (January, 1956), 132–44, Pt. II (April, 1956), 271–86, and Pt. III (July, 1956), 387–99; Eugene M. Violette, "Spanish Land Claims in Missouri," *Washington University Studies*, 8 (April, 1921), 167–200; Louis Pelzer, "The Spanish Land Grants of Upper Louisiana," *The Iowa Journal of History and Politics*, 11 (January, 1913), 3–37; and Richard C. Arena, "Landholding and Political Power in Spanish Louisiana," *Louisiana Historical Quarterly*, 38 (October, 1955), 23–39.

NEW MADRID EARTHQUAKE

Brief accounts of this event are provided by Margaret Ross, "The New Madrid Earthquake," *Arkansas Historical Quarterly*, 27 (Summer, 1968), 83–104, and Francis A. Sampson, "The New Madrid and Other Earthquakes in Missouri," *MHR*, 7 (July, 1913), 179–99.

MISSOURI SOCIETY

The French role in shaping Missouri's early development has been widely studied. For an introduction to French life in early Missouri, see "The Missouri Reader: The French in the Valley," Dorothy

Penn and Marie George Windell, eds., *MHR*, Pt. I, 40 (October, 1945), 90–122, Pt. II (January, 1946), 245–75, Pt. III (April, 1946), 407–30, Pt. IV (July, 1946), 562–78, Pt. V, 41 (October, 1946), 77–106, Pt. VI (January, 1947), 192–216, Pt. VII (April, 1947), 305–14, Pt. VIII (July, 1947), 391–405. Also useful in assessing the French legacy are the two collections of essays edited by John F. McDermott, *The French in the Mississippi Valley* (Urbana, Illinois, 1965), and *Frenchmen and French Ways in the Mississippi Valley* (Urbana, Illinois, 1969). Ward Allison Dorrance's study, *The Survival of French in the Old District of Sainte Genevieve* (Columbia, Missouri, 1935) provides an authoritative account of French activity in that area. Rachel Fram Vogel describes home life in a French settlement in "Life in Colonial St. Louis: The French Mother and Housewife," Missouri Historical Society *Glimpses of the Past*, 1 (September, 1934), 85–91.

Three excellent studies assess the impact of Americanization upon particular aspects of French society. They are: Marshall Smelser, "Housing in St. Louis, 1764–1821: An Example of Cultural Change," *The Louisiana Historical Quarterly*, 21 (April, 1938), 335–48; Marshall Smelser, "The Food Supply of Creole St. Louis," *Mid-America*, 8 (October, 1937), 254–64; and Harvey Wish, "The French of Old Missouri (1804–1821): A Study in Assimilation," *Mid-America*, 12 (July, 1941), 167–89.

The American entry into the territory is chronicled in "The Missouri Reader: Americans in the Valley," Ruby Matson Robins, ed., *MHR*, Pt. I, 45 (October, 1950), 1–15, Pt. II (January, 1951), 158–69, Pt. III (April, 1951), 275–92, Pt. IV (July, 1951), 386–403, Pt. V, 46 (October, 1951), 46–63, Pt. VI (January, 1952), 162–71, Pt. VII (April, 1952), 262–75, Pt. VIII (July, 1952), 363–79, Pt. IX, 47 (October, 1952), 47–61, Pt. X (January, 1953), 148–62, Pt. XI (April, 1953), 251–65, Pt. XII (July, 1953), 364–75. Hattie M. Anderson discusses various facets of life for the late territorial period in "The Evolution of Frontier Society in Missouri, 1815–1828," *MHR*, 32 (April, 1938), 298–326, (July, 1938), 458–83, 33 (October, 1938), 23–44. Another useful account can be found in R. L. Kirkpatrick, "Professional, Religious and Social Aspects of St. Louis Life, 1804–1816," *MHR*, 44 (July, 1950), 373–86. Dorothy J. Caldwell examines the early celebration of Christmas in "Christmas in Early Missouri," *MHR*, 65 (January, 1971), 125–38. A general description of St. Louis at the time of its transfer to the United States is available in John F. McDermott, "Captain Stoddard Discovers St. Louis," *The Bulletin*, 10 (April, 1954), 328–35, while Jonas Viles provides a general description of the territory on the eve of statehood in "Missouri in 1820," *MHR*, 15 (October, 1920), 36-52.

ARCHITECTURE, ARTS, AND CRAFTS

Charles E. Peterson, a prominent architect and authority on historical restoration, has provided valuable discussions of French colonial architecture and crafts. See Peterson, *Colonial St. Louis: Building a Creole Capital* (St. Louis, 1949), and "Early Ste. Genevieve and its Architecture," *MHR*, 35 (January, 1941), 207-32. Additional information can be found in Charles Van Ravenswaay, "The Creole Arts and Crafts of Upper Louisiana," *The Bulletin*, 12 (April, 1956), 213-48.

EDUCATION, BOOKS, AND NEWSPAPERS

Students of Missouri history are profoundly indebted to John Francis McDermott for his masterful studies of early cultural and educational developments. The picture he presents is a positive one. In "The Confines of a Wilderness," *MHR*, 29 (October, 1934), 3-12, McDermott concludes that early St. Louis was neither primitive nor isolated, and instead finds it to be a cultural center unusual for its time and place. The same author elaborates on this theme in his excellent study of early St. Louis libraries, *Private Libraries in Creole St. Louis* (Baltimore, 1938), and his "Culture and the Missouri Frontier," *MHR*, 50 (July, 1956), 355-70 provides a general survey of early Missouri's cultural level.

Information concerning the educational system can be found in the following authoritative works: Ernest R. Liljegren, "Frontier Education in Spanish Louisiana," *MHR*, 35 (April, 1941), 345-73; Margaret McMillan and Monia C. Morris, "Educational Opportunities in Early Missouri," *MHR*, 33 (April, 1939), 307-25, and (July, 1939), 477-98; Hugh Graham, "Ste. Genevieve Academy: Missouri's First Secondary School," *Mid-America*, 4 (October, 1932), 67-79; John F. McDermott, "Private Schools in St. Louis, 1809-1821," *Mid-America*, 11 (April, 1940), 96-119; and Stafford Poole, "The Founding of Missouri's First College: Saint Mary's of the Barrens, 1815-1818," *MHR*, 65 (October, 1970), 1-22. John F. McDermott's "Museums in Early Saint Louis," *The Bulletin*, 4 (April, 1948), 129-38 provides additional useful information on that subject.

A very general account based largely on secondary sources is Eleanora A. Baer, "Books, Newspapers and Libraries in Pioneer St.

ESSAY ON SOURCES

Louis, 1808–1842," *MHR*, 56 (July, 1962), 347–60. Roy T. King offers a brief account of territorial newspapers in "The Territorial Press in Missouri," *The Bulletin*, 11 (October, 1954), 73–81. Other aspects of early Missouri journalism are covered in William H. Lyon's two works: "Joseph Charless, Father of Missouri Journalism," *The Bulletin*, 17 (January, 1961), 133–45, and *The Pioneer Editor in Missouri, 1808–1860* (Columbia, Missouri, 1965); and in William N. Chambers, "Thomas Hart Benton: Editor," *MHR*, 44 (July, 1952), 335–45.

Elijah L. Jacobs and Forrest E. Wolverton, *Missouri Writers: A Literary History of Missouri, 1780–1955* (St. Louis, 1955) is the most recent general work on the subject. Alexander N. DeMenil in "A Century of Missouri Literature," *MHR*, 15 (October, 1920), 74–125, and *The Literature of the Louisiana Territory* (St. Louis, 1904), provides brief sketches of selected Missouri literary figures. A study by Charles Guenther highlights a minor French poet who resided in the territory. See "An Early St. Louis Poet: Pierre François Régnier," in *The French in the Mississippi Valley*, John F. McDermott, ed. (Urbana, Illinois, 1965), 59–80.

RELIGION

John Rothensteiner's *History of the Archdiocese of St. Louis*, 2 vols. (St. Louis, 1928) is the standard reference for the role of the Catholic Church in early Missouri. Other useful studies on this topic include Joseph Donnelly, "Pierre Gibault and the Critical Period of the Illinois Country, 1768–1778," in *The French in the Mississippi Valley*, John F. McDermott, ed. (Urbana, Illinois, 1965), 81–91; William Barnaby Faherty, "The Personality and Influence of Louis William Valentine Du Bourg: Bishop of 'Louisiana and the Floridas' (1776–1833)," in *Frenchmen and French Ways in the Mississippi Valley*, John F. McDermott, ed. (Urbana, Illinois, 1969), 43–55; and Louise Callan, *Philippine Duchesne, Frontier Missionary of the Sacred Heart, 1769–1852* (Westminister, Maryland, 1957), and *The Society of the Sacred Heart in North America* (New York, 1937).

The introduction of Protestantism into Missouri is detailed in a variety of studies including Lucy Simmons, "The Rise and Growth of Protestant Bodies in the Missouri Territory," *MHR*, 22 (April, 1928), 296–306; John A. Hope, "More About Protestant Bodies in Missouri Territory," *MHR*, 23 (October, 1928), 85–90; and Joab Spencer, "John Clark, Pioneer Preacher and Founder of Methodism in Missouri," *MHR*, 5 (April, 1911), 174–77. Also useful are Lawrence E. Murphy, "Beginnings of Methodism in Missouri, 1798–1824,"

MHR, 21 (April, 1927), 370–94; Frank C. Tucker, *The Methodist Church in Missouri, 1789–1939* (Nashville, 1966); E. W. Stephens, "History of Missouri Baptist General Association," *MHR*, 7 (January, 1913), 76–88; R. S. Duncan, *History of Baptists in Missouri* (St. Louis, 1882); De Witt Ellinwood, Jr., "Protestantism Enters St. Louis: The Presbyterians," *The Bulletin*, 12 (April, 1956), 253–73; and Charles F. Rehkopf, "The Beginnings of the Episcopal Church in Missouri, 1819–1844," *The Bulletin*, 11 (April, 1955), 265–78. Two important manifestations of the frontier religious impulse are examined in Marie G. Windell, "The Camp Meeting in Missouri," *MHR*, 37 (April, 1943), 253–70, and James Hazlett, "The Troubles of the Circuit Rider," *MHR*, 39 (July, 1945), 421–37, while Leslie Gamblin Hill assesses Protestantism's role in taming the frontier in "A Moral Crusade: The Influence of Protestantism on Frontier Society in Missouri," *MHR*, 45 (October, 1950), 16–34.

Unpublished Theses and Dissertations

I would also like to mention a number of useful unpublished theses and dissertations covering a wide variety of topics relating to Missouri's early history. My own doctoral dissertation on which portions of this study are based may be consulted in order to secure more detailed documentation concerning political developments during the American period. See William E. Foley, "Territorial Politics in Frontier Missouri: 1804–1820." Ph.D. diss., University of Missouri, 1967.

The best account of William Clark's early career can be found in John Louis Loos' lengthy but otherwise well-written study, "A Biography of William Clark, 1770–1813," Ph.D. diss., Washington University, St. Louis, 1953. Robert Ralph Russell's "The Public Career of William Clark, 1813–1838," M.A. thesis, Washington University, St. Louis, 1945, provides a less comprehensive account of Clark's later years.

Sister Chelidonia Ronnebaum's "Population and Settlement in Missouri, 1804–1820," M.A. thesis, University of Missouri, 1936, brings together a great deal of information on that subject. Halvor Gordon Melom's "The Economic Development of St. Louis, 1803–1846," Ph.D. diss., University of Missouri, 1947, describes various aspects of early territorial economic growth. On another topic, Harold Dugger's detailed study "Reading Interest and the Book Trade in Frontier Missouri," Ph.D. diss., University of Missouri, 1951, is helpful.

Mary P. Adams's "Jefferson's Military Policy With Special Reference to the Frontier, 1805–1809," Ph.D. diss., University of Virginia, 1958, is useful in examining an often-overlooked phase of Jeffersonian policy, while John G. Westover traces "The Evolution of the Missouri Militia, 1804–1919," in his Ph.D. diss., University of Missouri, 1948.

Finally, the role of Missouri's territorial representative in Congress can be more completely understood, thanks to Nancy Jo Tice's long-needed examination of the role of the territorial delegate. See Tice, "The Territorial Delegate, 1794–1820," Ph.D. diss., University of Wisconsin, 1967.

INDEX

A

Agriculture: in Upper Lousiana, 15, 53, 58–59
American Revolution, 26
Andreis, Felix de, 185
Architecture: French colonial, 52–53; American influences on, 137
Arikara Indians, 41, 127
Arkansas, district of, 141
Armstrong, John, 158, 159
Arrow Rock, Missouri, 157
Astor, John Jacob, 134
Aubry, Charles Philippe, 20
Austin, Moses, 102, 104. 124, 163, 176, 177; and lead mining techniques, 59–60; dispute with John Smith T, 101

B

Bank of Missouri, 179
Bank of St. Louis, 178–79
Banking: in Missouri, 177–79
Baptists: in Missouri, 180–81, 183
Barbe-Marbois, Francois, 65
Barton, David, 199
Bates, Frederick, 112, 138, 140, 141, 145, 146–47, 169; background of, 122; as acting governor, 123–28, 146; and territorial defense, 126–27, 148, 154–55; dispute with Meriwether Lewis, 144
Bellevue, Missouri, 184
Bent, Silas, 110
Benton, Thomas Hart, 178, 199, 204
Bethel Association, 181
Bethel Church (Baptist), 181
Bienville, Jean Baptiste Le Moyne, Sieur de, 13
Bissell, Daniel, 71, 156
Black codes, 47, 77, 175
Blanchette, Louis, 48
Board of land commissioners: establishment by Congress, 95–96; deliberations of, 108–12, 140–42, 168

Boisbriant, Pierre Duqué, Sieur de, 9, 13
Bonaparte, Napoleon, 44–45, 63–65, 68
Boone, Daniel, 130
Boone, Nathan, 130, 131, 149
Boonslick country, 159, 167
Boonville, Missouri, 172
Brackenridge, Henry Marie, 189
Bradbury, John, 189
Breckinridge, John, 67, 79, 87, 111
Breckinridge Bill, 79–80
Browne, Joseph, 103, 123; appointment as secretary, 98; as acting governor, 120–21; removal of, 122
Bruff, James, 73, 77, 91, 93, 99, 104
Burr, Aaron, 117; and Wilkinson, 97–98; in Louisiana, 102–3, 120–21. *See also* Burr conspiracy
Burr conspiracy, 120–21, 123–24
Business activity: in Upper Louisiana, 26, 60–61, 137, 162–64

C

Cadillac, Antoine de La Mothe, 7
Cahokia, Illinois, 4, 12, 31
Camp meetings, 182
Cape Girardeau, district of, 48, 90, 141, 147, 180
Cape Girardeau, Missouri, 57, 171; founding of, 49–50
Capuchins: in Upper Louisiana, 54
Carr, William C., 87, 104–6 *passim*, 110, 111
Carondelet, Francisco Luis Hector, Baron de, 37–38, 39, 42, 43–44, 49
Carroll County, Missouri, 12
Cartabona, Don Silvio Francisco de, 28, 29
Cass, Lewis, 158
Catholicism: in Upper Louisiana, 54–56, 180, 184–85
Cauld, Henry, 176
Cerré, Gabriel, 49
Champlain, Samuel de, 2